CW00525707

JAMES JOYCE AND NATIONALISM

JAMES JOYCE AND NATIONALISM

Emer Nolan

London and New York

First published 1995
by Routledge
11 New Fetter Lane, London EC4P 4EE

Simultaneously published in the USA and Canada
by Routledge
29 West 35th Street, New York, NY 10001

Typeset in Palatino by
EXCEPT*detail* Ltd, Southport

Printed and bound in Great Britain by
T. J. Press (Padstow) Ltd, Padstow, Cornwall

British Library Cataloguing in Publication Data
A catalogue record for this book is available from the British Library

Library of Congress Cataloging in Publication Data
Nolan, Emer,
James Joyce and Nationalism/Emer Nolan.
p. cm.
Includes bibliographical references and index.
1. Joyce, James, 1882–1941 – Political and social views.
2. Politics and literature – Ireland – History – 20th century.
3. Nationalism – Ireland – History – 20th century.
4. Modernism (Literature) – Ireland.
5. Nationalism in literature.
6. Ireland – In literature. I. Title.
PR6019.09Z755 1995
823'.912–dc20 94–8223

ISBN 0–415–10343–6

For
Eileen and Patrick Nolan

CONTENTS

ABBREVIATIONS

CW *The Critical Writings of James Joyce,* edited by Ellsworth Mason and Richard Ellmann (London: Faber & Faber, 1959).

D *Dubliners,* the corrected text with an explanatory note by Robert Scholes (London: Jonathan Cape, 1967).

FW *Finnegans Wake,* third edition (London: Faber & Faber, 1964).

P *A Portrait of the Artist as a Young Man,* the definitive text, corrected from the Dublin Holograph by Chester G. Anderson and edited by Richard Ellmann (London: Jonathan Cape, 1968).

SH *Stephen Hero,* edited with an Introduction by Theodore Spencer. Revised edition with additional material and Foreword by John J. Slocum and Herbert Cahoon (London: Jonathan Cape, 1956).

SL *Selected Letters of James Joyce,* edited by Richard Ellmann (London: Faber & Faber, 1975).

U *Ulysses,* the corrected text, edited by Hans Walter Gabler, *et al.* (London: Bodley Head, 1986).

PREFACE

Few critics of James Joyce can have failed to remark on his 'ambivalence' towards Ireland. Many of them view Joyce's long, voluntary exile and dedication to aesthetic modernism as strangely at odds with his preoccupation with the world of his youth and his compulsive recreation of it in language. The notion of a creative tension between a metropolitan and a native Joyce has consistently been advanced to account for this apparent contradiction in his writings. None the less, critical constructions of the continuum of Joyce's responses to Ireland, from affectionate tolerance to impassioned repudiation, are typically organized around the presumed certainty of his unsympathetic representation of Irish separatist nationalism. This characterizes virtually all accounts of Joyce's politics to date, although such analyses have been produced in a wide range of critical vocabularies, and from a variety of theoretical and ideological perspectives.

It is perhaps unsurprising that Joyce's most influential readers can disclose nothing but polar opposition between Joycean modernism and Irish nationalism. They maintain that his explorations of language, personal identity and history are simply incompatible with the reverence displayed for tradition and community in nationalist ideology. Nationalism, literary critics tend to suggest, in offering a narrow philosophy of racial identity and a mythologized, teleological model of history, can provide only a mirror-image of the imperialism which it may ostensibly oppose. Modernism, at least in the case of Joyce, in opening up writing to the energy and excitement of modernity, introduces a universe of innovation and democratic multiplicity: here, old absolutes and hierarchies are parodied and mocked; venerable, sacred languages – be they of Church, family, historical precedent or nation – laid bare to what Joyce described as the 'sandblast' (*SL*, p. 241) of his destructive stylism. The symbolic violence implied by this conception of writing ultimately yields to an essentially comic vision of the possibility of different languages and cultures peacefully co-exisiting; it has nothing in common with the violent exclusions enforced by nationalism. Thus Joyce is understood to depict an Ireland in which transnational modernity is still struggling to be born. Therefore, the idea of liberation which his work celebrates is unrelated to Irish culture, proceeding from the creative imagination of the emigré artist rather than from the inert realistic substratum of his writing. This received reading of Joyce can make little of the concerns of the marginal, colonized community as they are reflected in his texts, viewing them merely as the content of his experiments with literary form and language, lending colourful but essentially irrelevant local detail for humour or satire.

However, Joyce's native country was not merely belated in respect to the rapidly changing Europe where he chose to spend most of his life. Rather, Ireland underwent an especially abrupt and disastrous accession to modernity – typically the experience of colonized societies – between the middle of the nineteenth century and the revolutionary period of 1916–22. In such conditions, modernization becomes explicitly associated with the culture of the colonial power. Any straightforward embrace or rejection of modernity is difficult for the colonized people, who very often seek to enjoy its benefits, but on their own terms. In early twentieth-century Ireland, a variety of cultural and political movements struggled with the difficulties and ironies of anticolonial nationalism and decolonization. These have been caricatured to such an extent in Joyce criticism that no response other than one of implacable opposition seems plausible from him. For in metropolitan literary theory, nationalism itself is often confused with an attachment to tradition which is pre-modern or anti-modern, in spite of the declarations of historians and sociologists that 'The basic characteristic of the nation and everything connected with it is its modernity'.[1] More precisely, both modernism and nationalism might be defined by their ambivalence towards modernisation, sharing as they do a crucial interest in the issues of cultural change and regeneration, language and popular culture, the realm of the aesthetic and the role of the artist. Nationalism seeks to recreate a sense of traditional community within contemporary mass culture: modernist writing exploits the relentless energy of commercial civilization, but it may also record or lament the progressive abolition of local difference in the modern world. In these terms, Joycean modernism and Irish nationalism can be understood as significantly analogous discourses, and the common perception of them as unrelated and antagonistic begins to break down.

The modernity to which Joyce responds, then, is not transnational or universal, and the major trends in Joyce criticism have occluded the particularity of Irish historical experience as it determines and is reflected in his fiction. His commentators have instead insisted on both reading 'Ireland' through Joyce and interpreting Joyce as 'Irishman'.

The former procedure grants the artist authority to comment on his native culture, while the latter constructs him as passively typical of it – ironically, a judgement itself based on evidence gathered from his own texts, and from what is presumed to be his own portrayal of national character. Each approach has involved critics in a stereotyping discourse about Ireland and the Irish: for many readers, Joyce's work seems to participate in, and therefore legitimate, this kind of discussion. Such critical prejudice necessarily produces distortions, but these are not merely random errors, and they can be elucidated by reference to the historical conditions in which they first arise. Many of Joyce's earliest and most enthusiastic supporters and promoters, for example, were committed to a purely cosmopolitan and internationalist view of modernism. The American liberal tradition in Joyce studies, which now dominates the international James Joyce critical industry, is founded on a belief in the writer's pacifism and tolerant pluralism. Recent accounts of the texts influenced by post-structuralism and French feminist theory have argued that Joyce's writing dismantles those traditional ideologies which render us sexed and civil subjects, among them nationalism. In all of these cases, the latter is considered chiefly in the context of European fascism: such accounts do not acknowledge that nationalisms vary, and are internally divided and disputatious.

Hence this book aims to offer a corrective to pervasive and systematic misreadings of Joyce. I illustrate how these interpretations symptomatize a crucial failure on his critics' part to attend to the full complexity of nationalism in the political culture of modernity. The cliché of Joyce's 'ambivalence' towards Ireland suggests mere confusion or ambiguity: we have overlooked the determinate nature of this response, which in fact corresponds to a dialectic fundamental to both modernism and nationalism. If this has gone unrecognized, it is in part because the dialectical and critical capacity of modernism itself is now being forgotten in the contemporary celebration of the postmodern.[2] Asserting the importance of Irish literary modernism in recovering such a heritage also calls into question the inevitability of an alliance between the post-colonial and the postmodern, so often merely presumed in recent cultural criticism.

Modernism, of course, has enjoyed at best a very cautious welcome in Ireland. However, Ireland's ambivalence towards Joyce is perhaps as important a point of departure for this book as Joyce's ambivalence towards Ireland. The attempt to bring the category of a national literature into alignment with Irish political nationalism has always lagged behind Irish literary achievement. Nationalist critics first confronted the embarrassment of an already existing literature of exceptional distinction produced by writers whom they considered the sons and daughters of a colonial regime. The anti-revivalist polemics of the

'Irish Ireland' movement before independence and the critical orthodoxy which prevailed in the Irish Free State were impotent in the face of the international critical construction of Irish modernism: those glamorous expatriates who are invariably read as sceptical, dissenting individualists, explicitly hostile to the project of building a national literary tradition. Joyce's Irish audience, of course, also extends beyond these intellectuals and writers, encompassing many thousands of Irish people who will never read the texts of this supremely obscure writer, but for whom his name and image have none the less become a significant aspect of cultural identity. The economic importance of tourism in the southern Irish state has perhaps accelerated the commodification of Irish writing and, to the unfailing delight of visiting Joyceans, a large proportion of people have some comment to make about Irish literature or well-known authors: remarks which may well be balanced between pride, resentment, bravado, suspicion and alienation. But the nostalgia industry has by no means succeeded in entirely eradicating an underlying sense of discomfort concerning the virtually unknown contents of Joyce's books. Both Ireland's intense post-colonial self-consciousness, and the nature of the literary texts which are being so used, distinguish this phenomenon clearly from that of, for example, Stratford-upon-Avon, or the local cults which surround the Brontë sisters or Thomas Hardy in England. The attempt to produce an inaccessible, obscene, anti-Catholic and supposedly anti-nationalist modernist author as the repository of a unique sense of Irishness results in the strange fact that Joyce is in many ways both the Irish Shakespeare and, from the point of view of the simple faithful, our Salman Rushdie. The persistent Irish unease with Joyce therefore represents more than the embarrassing residue of a pious and philistine past. It also registers, in a notably unsure way, the existence of an important site of resistance to the canonical or institutionalized James Joyce. It will certainly not be my intention here to imply that a certain reading of Joyce might facilitate the revelation of his true Irishness, or that his works might be handed back to Irish people cleansed of their difficulty and their political complexity. But at the least, it should be asserted that the Irish have by now endured as much sentimentalizing blarney at the hands of Joyceans as they have ever perpetrated on unsuspecting literary tourists and scholars. Such a fate also illustrates the continuing importance of colonialism and its legacies at every stage of the production and reception of Joyce's texts. It is with due regard to this history that we must now return to them.

Many people have contributed to this book. I would like to thank the electors for the Robert Gardiner Memorial Scholarship, Sidney Sussex College, Cambridge, and the Institute of Irish Studies at Queen's University, Belfast, for their financial assistance. I am much indebted to the generosity and insight of those who read and offered criticisms of earlier versions of the manuscript, especially Tim Cribb, Seamus Deane, Declan Kiberd and Adrian Poole, and to Terry Eagleton for his sustaining faith in this project. I am also grateful for the support and advice of Talia Rodgers, my editor at Routledge.

This book was written over a number of years and in several different places, and I would, finally, like to acknowledge the encouragement and kindness of my family, and of many friends in Cambridge, London, Belfast and Dublin during this time. In particular, I must thank Richard Bourke, Nicola Geraghty, Rachel MacRory, Aisling O'Connor, Rachel Potter and Ingrid Scheibler.

INTRODUCTION: MODERNISM AND NATIONALISM

'The more I hear of the political, philosophical, ethical zeal and labours of the brilliant members of Pound's big brass band', declared James Joyce in 1928, 'the more I wonder why I was ever let into it "with my magic flute"'.[1] Joyce may here disavow Pound's enormous ambition, but for this modesty he has been much praised. Indeed, Joyce's canonization as the most congenial of early twentieth-century writers, 'the saving humanist of English language modernism',[2] has taken place largely at Pound's expense. As a young poet, Pound sought to generate an avant-garde which would resist the lethal amnesia of contemporary mass culture. This mission of cultural retrieval and regeneration, he believed, was best served by the boldest literary innovators – through them, an ordered and healthy society might again become possible. But as his radical aesthetics increasingly give way to authoritarian politics, a cautionary tale unfolds. It appeared to critics, especially after the Second World War, that Pound's later writing had become fatally entangled in the very 'national phrases and public emotionalities'[3] which he had earlier identified as inimical to intelligent, responsible art. Pound's final, humiliating incarceration would seem to offer a fitting rebuke to modernist hubris.

Ironically, when Pound first appealed to artists to address the unthinking parochialism of the masses – to satirize, and hence to purge from the body politic, the debased language in which it found expression – his most significant model of such aesthetic 'Katharsis' was the early fiction of James Joyce. So in later decades, it seemed that his Irish protégé had in fact remained truer to Pound's cosmopolitan ideals than the master himself. For Joyce was certainly his match in erudition and craftsmanship, and his vast allusive range suggested an equivalent respect for traditional high culture. Yet he did not mourn for a lost organic order, nor allow himself to be seduced by the charisma of totalitarian authority; instead, his texts could be read as celebrating urban life, happily raiding the resources of modern technology both for subject matter and stylistic or typographical play. Here, then, was a modernism which did not protest against the conditions which made it possible, nor brood anxiously about its own significance and necessity. Admirably well-suited to the university classroom and the international symposium, Joyce's texts were nevertheless fundamentally simple; in him, one could 'rediscover the common decencies' so lacking in Pound, and sometimes in Eliot.[4] Joyce seemed to prove that exciting, experimental art did not necessarily raise difficult political questions, even in the modern age. As Richard Ellmann – whose magisterial 1959 biography did much to create our contemporary estimate of Joyce – writes of his bewildered response to Pound: '[Joyce] was a musician surrounded by preachers and generalisers'.[5]

It is Joyce, then, or a certain reading of him, that has allowed liberal critics to annex at least some portion of modernist literature for their own values; and while he has been much praised, this has not always been for innocent or well-considered reasons. For although many modernist artists depict marginal communities from the viewpoint of exile, their works are frequently seized upon by critics who are confident that such art simply remakes the peripheral in the image of the centre, and in harmony with its interests. An image of Joyce as an Irishman unswayed by patriotism, who not merely refused to participate in a popular nationalist movement in his own country but rebuked and challenged it at every opportunity, thus contributes significantly to our current approval of his ideological maturity. The high value accorded to his art is thus closely involved with orthodox perceptions of its 'universalism'. Partly because of the fates of other kinds of modernism, anti-nationalism becomes the index of Joyce's enlightened acceptance of modern conditions, particularly as these are bound up with the migration of different peoples and the intermingling of their cultures. And if his texts include anything so parochial as a message specifically for his own people, it surely must be the recommendation that they too embrace this modern world, in all its complexity and potential.

But to divide up modernism in this way is falsifying: we may not, in fact, have available to us such a clear distinction between a genuinely universalist art, and an art which betrayed its initially progressive impulses. We cannot rescue a 'good' modernism, and give Joyce's name to it, if its worth is to be calculated simply on the basis of hostility to the non-metropolitan, or irony at its expense. For in the first place, this is to ignore what David Harvey has called 'the complex historical geography of modernism (a tale yet to be fully written or explained)'; many varieties of modernism, as Harvey argues, struggled in vain 'to settle their accounts with parochialism and nationalism'.[6] If we fail to acknowledge this, we risk misrepresenting important tensions even in figures such as Pound and Eliot – and ironically, their early accounts of

Joyce are now used to trivialize such issues in his writing. But although Pound and Eliot, like later Joyceans, may have been convinced, at least at the outset, that Joyce's cosmopolitanism triumphed over his Irishness, they never regarded the question of Ireland in his work as of anything but fundamental significance. When they ceased to trust Joyce's ability to transcend his nationality, they lost respect for his art: for them, unlike later commentators, Irishness is never merely a preliminary wash of sentiment or nostalgia on a modernist canvas. It is misleading to remove Joyce from debates among modernist writers about nationalism and internationalism, for what we then congratulate as his superior wisdom may merely be our own blindness. And such debates, in the field of literary criticism at least, are now generally conducted in the terms of metropolitan modernist theory – this is often, as we shall see, quite at odds with modernist literary practice. Even Pound's politics, for example, involve a complex interplay between international movements and forces, including capitalist modernization itself, and local allegiances and traditions. For modernism, nationalism may be a symptom of cultural degeneracy, or a cure for it – both an aspect of the perceived crisis, and a way of resolving it. Nationalism is not, however, just an unattractive feature of the modern world, which could be transcended in art.

Joyceans, then, read their sacred texts in a spirit of benign multiculturalism, which they imagine to be identical to Joyce's own. They are, in fact, impatient only with Irish culture, simply because Joyce (in their understanding of him) informs them that Irish culture is essentially intolerant. But while their vision of the author may be much brighter and more sanguine than that of his own contemporaries, it also lacks the insight of Pound's pessimism. For although Joyce's admission to Pound's select band depended on the final insignificance of his Irish provenance, Pound is never entirely consistent in this judgement. At times, Joyce's migration signifies a straightforward escape from 'the local stupidity': in leaving Ireland, he discovers the space of modernity ('Joyce has fled to Trieste and into the modern world'), and enters its alternative history ('the one man calling himself Irish who is in any sense part of the decade').[7] If his nationality is a cultural disadvantage, it is one which Joyce has heroically overcome:

> One is so tired of the Irish or 'Celtic' imagination . . . flopping about. Mr Joyce does not flop about. He defines. He is not an institution for the promotion of Irish peasant industries. He accepts an international standard of prose writing and lives up to it.[8]

His continuing, well-nigh obsessive use of Irish material is thus merely incidental. Indeed, Pound commends the global typicality of Dublin as it is represented in Joyce's early fiction:

> Erase the local names and a few specifically local allusions, and a few historic events of the past, and substitute a few different local names, allusions and events, and these stories could be retold of any town.[9]

By what paradoxical logic, however, can the international be figured so successfully by the provincial, when Pound more usually resolutely opposes these to each other? How precisely does the provincial artist cancel or redeem the dreary particularity of Ireland?

Like some other modernist critics after him, Pound may occasionally suggest that, in our reading of Joyce, Ireland's backwardness can simply be discounted. He may also imply (and this is a rather different claim) that Irish society provides a convenient foil for Joyce's ecumenical intelligence. But there is also a sense for Pound in which Joyce's work is actually enhanced by already having contended with the problem of Irishness. In repudiating parochialism, Joyce can be accepted genially into the cultural mainstream; but the warmth of the welcome he receives there also suggests that the mainstream is in dire need of his work, since 'the obstructionist and the provincial are everywhere, and in them alone is the permanent danger to civilisation'.[10] There is a big difference between Pound's brisk confidence in 'an international standard of prose writing', and the depressing generality of those stories which 'could be retold of any town'. That which prevails at the margins also menaces the centre, and if Joyce is so valuable for Pound, it is because his intimacy with provincialism allows him to understand precisely this threat. For Pound, Ireland has a double valence, offering both an image of the periphery and of the centre. Later critics tend to forget this significant dualism.

For if it is true that the increasing cultural homogeneity of modern societies acts to dissolve traditional insularity, it is also true that such societies resemble each other, ironically enough, in refusing to recognise their common destinies. As Wyndham Lewis complains in *Time and Western Man* (1927):

> So while *in reality* people become increasingly one nation (for the fact that they are fanatically nationalist does not prevent them from approximating more and more closely to the neighbours against whom, in their abstract rage, they turn), they *ideologically* grow more aggressively separatist, and conscious of 'nationality'.[11]

Marx predicted that the creation of a new world market by modern industrial production would spell an end to 'national one-sidedness and narrow-mindedness'; the economic activity of the bourgeoisie, now compelled to 'nestle everywhere, settle everywhere, establish connections everywhere', necessarily lending a cosmopolitan character to both production and culture throughout the world.[12] Lewis, on the contrary, claims that industrial society is itself the root cause of virulent identifications, as genuine cultural differences are progressively replaced by adventitious, simulated ones. From this viewpoint, modernity secretes nationalism like 'a patina manufactured for the faking of "antiques"'.[13] For Pound, by contrast, modernization and internationalism may not be inevitably linked; but neither are they, as Lewis would have it, mutual antagonists.

Parochial resistance to cosmopolitanism is characterized by Pound as actively 'obstructing' progress, but it also represents a capitulation to a general bourgeois materialism. For the 'internationalism' Pound denounces is that of modern capitalism, which usurps national economic autonomy and transfers power instead to financiers, creditors and bankers. Its empire of money knows nothing of the traditional cultures in which all languages and all authentic art must be rooted. The 'nationalism' he condemns is that of the philistine middle classes: it is this which Joyce – in Pound's eyes, a disciple of Flaubert – mercilessly subjects to his ironic scrutiny. By contrast, Pound favours an élite 'internationalism' of intellectuals and artists, who might create a better future on the basis of shared cultural resources. But just as in the political theories which he espouses, the nation remains 'the essential carrier of historical development' because of its central role in the organization of economic life,[14] so by the strategic deployment of national images or myths in art, the masses might be encouraged to identify with their own country's interests.

Pound and Eliot, then, agree that Joyce's novels exhibit the immense modern panorama of futility and anarchy by faithfully depicting one nation, exemplary in its dishevelment and degradation.[15] They also hold that Joyce's criticism of Ireland depends on the meta-perspective supplied by his participation in a broader European culture, and Pound in particular is concerned to read Irish nationalism in Joyce as a symptom of local idiocy: 'If more people had read *The Portrait* and certain stories in Mr. Joyce's *Dubliners* there might have been less recent trouble in Ireland. A clear diagnosis is never without its value'.[16] (He refers to the Easter Rebellion of 1916.) There is no necessary implication, however, that such 'universalism' is actually definitive of modernism, or of the progressive work of art. One might indeed infer from Pound that it is proper to prose, an inherently satiric, purgative, 'excremental' form of writing, as distinct from poetry, which he conceives of as imagistic, non-rational and 'phallic'. Certainly, Pound's and Eliot's rejection of one variety of nationalism does not negate all of them, and it is clear enough that their aesthetic internationalism does not flow from any notion of multicultural tolerance or democratic equality. If their poetry appears to be daring, transnational *bricolage*, this does not prevent them from becoming politically embroiled with nationalism, even if neither poet regards his writing solely as its instrument. Hence their respective defences of Italian fascism or English royalism – these are commitments to regional rather than to universal values. Poets like them, in fact, need novelists such as Joyce, for what he destroys, they can recreate in superior forms. In addition, Pound's *inconsistent* reading of the importance of Ireland to Joyce complicates this story. If Joyce's representation of the Irish, with their weakness for patriotic emotion and nationalist politics, can be read as a general critique of modernity, this is because the Irish are seen to share certain negative features with the mass of modern individuals. Ireland can stand in for the 'modern' – understood as *what actually exists* – precisely because Pound abhors so much about the contemporary world. The freedom and order heralded by modern art – that is to say, by the *truly* modern – has yet to come into being: but in the meantime, Pound and his favoured artists are its prophets. Hence the modernity is an incomplete project; and Ireland is highly convenient for this belief, since it encapsulates the worst of the modern, in one sense of that word, by its refusal of a fulfilled modernity.

Despite all his metropolitan insouciance about Ireland's 'troubles', then, Pound's analysis of Joyce's relationship with his native country proves powerfully suggestive. His early view that Joyce repudiates his native culture is now the merest orthodoxy; but we more often ignore Pound's insistent belief that Joyce's critical assessment of the metropolis is *mediated through* his representation of Ireland. Whatever Pound's view of this critique, what matters is his assumption that Joyce's modernism is at loggerheads with modernity, as well as with provincial resistance to it. Those later critics who reject as unwelcome 'preaching' and 'generalizing' what Joyce called Pound's political and ethical 'zeal', are often simply blind to the losses involved in modernization. They are unable to allow that the advent of modernity has tragic as well as emancipatory consequences, either for the citizens of the metropolis, or for the inhabitants of its periphery, where change may be more sudden and violent. Accordingly, they are insensitive to any art which responds to this sense of tragedy, as though only a fascist could dissent from this brave new world. The 'bad' nationalism Pound reads in Joyce, which invokes tradition and community only to mystify petty-bourgeois self-interest, is for him exemplary of the duplicity of the modern; but he retains his faith, even so, in the possibility of a 'good' nationalism, a future in which the traditional and communal values destroyed by bourgeois society will prevail. This is why it is vital for Pound to emphasize that there is no political distinction between Irish and any other European nationalism; a point he is still to be found emphasizing twenty years after the publication of *Ulysses*: 'BUT the main point . . . THAT might have been Brussels, as well as Dublin'.[17]

Irishness, however, remains a potent brew, and Joyce sups with the devil: intoxicated with language and memory, he falls into solipsistic obscurity. By the era of *Work in Progress* (dubbed by Pound 'writings in regress'[18]), the provincialism which he once anatomized so dispassionately threatens to reclaim him. Just before the publication of *Finnegans Wake*, Pound dismisses Joyce: 'Three decades of life have been lived since he began writing, of the last two he has learned almost nothing. Of the dominant and cleaving ideas of the last decade he is nearly unconscious'. American and Irishman may share provincial origins and emigrant status, but the former has also at his disposal a vocabulary of racialized Irishness – these images of dreamy inebriation Pound now employs to mock Joyce's tedious 'flow of conSquishousness'.[19] Pound's wry tolerance of Irish abstraction evokes T.S. Eliot's explanation of W.B.Yeats:

> His remoteness is not an escape from this world, for he is innocent of any world to escape from; his procedure is blameless, but he does not start from where we do . . . . There is something of this crudity, and much of this egoism, about what is called Irish literature.[20]

What we inherit from Pound, then, are several ways of theorizing the relationship between Joyce's writing and the metropolitan avant-garde, but each of them involves an interplay between localism and modernism which should be enough to thwart any attempt to co-opt Joyce as simply an uncritical advocate of change. Among such cheerful co-opters is Michael Long, who writes thus of Leopold Bloom (as spokesman for Joyce): 'He inhabits a world of crowding fragments without feeling, or indulging, the impulse to commanding ordonnance which sent Eliot from London to Little Gidding and Pound from London to *la ville radieuse*'.[21] Joyce, this juggling of place names suggests, never really strayed from London and an equable English reasonableness. Such remarks evince an indifference, typical among contemporary critics, to the non-metropolitan contexts of modernist texts. This is not just critical blindness, however, but a determinate invisibility, which Raymond Williams's account of the genesis of literary modernism helps to explain. The migration of artists from residual or traditional societies, so Williams claims, lent them an enabling estrangement from their new environments; but this was no more than a privileged form of an experience shared by metropolitan intellectuals themselves:

> A new sense of the objectivity of systems, and of this objectivity as something which needed to be penetrated by new forms of analysis, taking nothing as if appeared but looking for deep forms, deep structures, with the eyes of a stranger, came through in field after field: in linguistics, in anthropology, in economics, in sociology, in aesthetics, in psychoanalysis.[22]

Predictably, it is exactly those contemporary forms of analysis – the metropolitan, intellectual counterparts of aesthetic modernism – which are most likely to result in misreadings of the *real* strangers' texts. For our purposes here, this includes many varieties of Marxist and post-structuralist literary criticism – not so much theories *of* modernism, in this regard, as modernist theories themselves. From their vantage point, metropolitan culture becomes synonymous with scepticism and complexity; in its art – and there alone – can the periphery be magically transformed.

True to this doctrine, Derek Attridge and Daniel Ferrer, in their Introduction to the collection *Post-Structuralist Joyce* (1984), regard Dublin and Paris as the opposite poles of Joyce's experience: 'If Dublin was "homeysweet homely", an unfailing source of memories and materials for Joyce's books, it was the "gratifying experiences" of Paris that provided the environment and the audience which those books demanded'.[23] Attridge has repeated this judgement more recently: 'Throughout his career, Dublin remained the other pole of his creative activity, but a Dublin constantly challenged and remade in the light of this internationalist distrust of patriotism and prejudice'.[24] Attridge and Ferrer believe themselves to be conducting a timely polemic against ways of reading Joyce that 'condemn his domesticated ghost to traverse a safe, easy bridge across the Atlantic'. But in the course of claiming that their own critical project, with its zest for recent French critical theory, encounters the same 'fantasies of decadence among the guardians of decency in the English-speaking world . . . a recognisable pattern in regard to French excesses at least since the Revolution of 1789', they neglect the fact that Ireland occupies a very particular and anomalous place in that Anglophone culture. Revolutionary French thought has often influenced the Irish, as the rebels of 1798 might testify; and English definitions of Irish national character are often enough complementary to stereotypes of their other, more powerful neighbours. But Attridge and Ferrer are bent on a familiar condescension:

> let us remember how much of Joyce's peculiar and explosive energy derived from the uncloseable gap between shocking Paris and shockable Dublin . . . . In Ireland, *so far as one can tell*, the intellectual tremors of the 1960s are taking as long to be

> registered as Joyce's own literary earthquake did; Dublin remains a very long way from Paris.[25]

In a similar vein, Marxist critic Franco Moretti asserts in *Signs Taken for Wonders* (1983) that *Ulysses* 'belongs fully to a critical turning point of international bourgeois culture', echoing here Pound's 'whole occident under the domination of capital'.[26] Terry Eagleton elaborates the point:

> Joyce's compliment to Ireland, in inscribing it on the cosmopolitan map, is in this sense distinctly backhanded. The novel . . . deploy[s] the full battery of cosmopolitan modernist techniques to recreate it while suggesting with its every breath just how easily it could have done the same for Bradford or the Bronx.[27]

Once more, only by virtue of his participation in metropolitan culture does Joyce gain access to the realm of the international:

> Joyce, an Irishman (this is the only legitimate domain of the 'genetic' approach) has every reason and every means to probe deeply in the entrails of British society. But if Joyce were an Irish *writer*, comprehensible and containable without any loose threads within Irish culture, he would no longer be Joyce; if the city of *Ulysses* were the real Dublin of the turn of the century, it would not be the literary image *par excellence* of the modern metropolis. Cultural phenomena cannot be explained in the light of their *genesis* (what ever has emerged from the studies that interpreted Joyce on the basis of Ireland?); what counts is their objective *function*.[28]

Joyce's masterwork, then, possesses 'a status which it could not have achieved in the investigation of Ireland's peripheral and backward form of capitalism'; so that the possibility (intermittently acknowledged by Pound) that the 'backward' may offer a privileged perspective on the 'advanced' has now been definitively discarded.

Many recent feminist celebrations of Joyce of a post-structuralist or psychoanalytic bent are similarly marked by such lofty indifference to cultural or political specificity; they are out instead to uncover a 'feminine language' in Joycean modernism which evades 'the male-biased rhetoric of cultural inscription'.[29] Philippe Sollers, for example, explicitly ascribes to Joyce 'the same ambition as Freud' – 'to analyze two thousand years of manwomankind'.[30] The human psyche itself, in this formulation, is a transhistorical, virtually universal entity; and so, for Hélène Cixous, is a subversive 'femininity': '[woman's] libido is cosmic, just as her unconscious is worldwide'.[31] As Suzette Henke has recently proposed: 'A female story dialogically emerges from Joyce's master narrative, appropriates its textual authority, and gradually deconstructs the linguistic codes essential to the logocentric and phallocentric discourse not only of "dear dirty Dublin" but of western patriarchal culture.'[32] By attending to the experiences of Irish women, in short, Joyce illuminates Western patriarchy as a whole – as though the class or colonial factors which shape gender in Ireland were entirely incidental issues.

This insistence on deep structure or 'universalism', however, is not always so evident in much mainstream commentary on the texts; there, the early Pound's sense of Joyce's essentially satiric treatment of the local is greatly softened, and Joyce's Ireland generally treated with amused affection. The belief, more exactly, is that Joyce holds in suspension those ethical or political values on which satire depends, reinvoking them only in his direct discussion of Irish politics. At these points, so the argument runs, a fond indulgence of Irish national character gives way to outrage at the absurd claims of Irish political nationalism, and to a horror of political violence. Joyce the chronicler of vernacular wit and poetry is abruptly countered by Joyce the satiric scourge of native folly and vice. The work of Hugh Kenner (himself an eminent Poundian), from *Dublin's Joyce* (1956) to *A Colder Eye: The Modern Irish Writers* (1983), provides many examples of this oscillation. It is also the exact parallel of Kenner's – and many subsequent Joycean critics' – own response to Ireland. *A Colder Eye*, for instance, offers a wealth of amusing anecdotes about Irish literary culture, a warning, widely quoted among Joyce scholars, about the 'Irish fact' – ('Providence in creating the Irish (finest of deeds) endowed them with craving for occasional emphatic assertions, lacking which the most mellifluous discourse would be as porter poured on the floor') – together with an intriguing explanation of the conflict in contemporary Northern Ireland: 'Recover the mystique of the lost land and the Four Green Fields: your fanatics will make a routine of blowing up babies in their efforts to reclaim the lost fraction of the fourth'.[33] Those who upbraid the Irish for confusing culture and politics seem doomed the repeat the very crime they castigate. Richard Ellmann, for the most part, attributes to Joyce a more gentle, exilic view of Irish nationality: Ireland is 'horrible but unforgettable';[34] Joyce's anger at the failings of its leaders, or their followers, mixed with the regret and disappointment of a patriot. In his later work, Ellmann even disputes orthodox opinions of Joyce's 'apoliticism', pointing out the compatability of the writer's vision of Ireland with that of some nationalists. But the *ne plus ultra* of this revision is the question of physical force: Joyce's unyielding pacifism strictly circumscribes any possible debate about his nationalist 'sympathies'.

Hugh Kenner and Richard Ellmann, both influential and exemplary Joyceans, are thus reluctant to resolve certain tensions between nationalism and modernism which they believe remain unresolved, and yet infinitely fertile, in Joyce's art. But for one early commentator on Joyce – Wyndham Lewis – such contradiction is the starting point, rather than the terminus, of criticism. As we have seen, Lewis argues in *Time and Western Man* that capitalist development and the progress of nationalism are intrinsically linked, whatever the sanguine expectations of Marxists. A world in which people and places are growing more alike becomes obsessed with fetishizing their residual differences, replacing genuine variations by their 'ideological simulacra'. Nationalism, according to Lewis, is a shoddy, wholly *regressive* response to contemporary conditions, but it none the less stands as a response : the question of nationalism cannot be divorced from that of modernity in general. 'Dublin' and 'Paris' – along with all that these names evoke – are not just each others' antitheses. In this, Lewis anticipates a more recent critique of the philosophy and politics of nationalism, for which the creed is a distinctly modern phenomenon, in spite of its own insistence on the antiquity of its claims. Indeed it is this rationalist concern to debunk the mythologies created by nationalists from the community's past, to lay bare their artificiality and fictiveness, which inspires so many scholars and historians of nationalism to oppose it so fiercely as a political ideology. Commentators such as Elie Kedourie and Ernest Gellner are primarily concerned to *expose* the modernity of nationalism, aware that its adherents imagine it to be timeless and 'natural'.[35] And, as Wyndham Lewis insists, if modernity and nationalism are significantly related, this must influence their respective aesthetic expressions. Nationalism and literary modernism, Lewis argues, must also be examined together; indeed for him the conjunction of these in *Ulysses* turns us towards 'one of the fundamental questions of value brought out by [Joyce's] work'.

Lewis begins by describing Stephen Dedalus's exchange with Davin in *A Portrait of the Artist as a Young Man*, during which Stephen, representing the young Joyce, announces his refusal to serve his country:

> So from the start the answer of Joyce to the militant nationalist was plain enough. And he showed himself in that a very shrewd realist indeed, beset as Irishmen have been for so long with every Romantic temptation, always being invited by this interested party or that, to jump back into 'history'. So Joyce is neither of the militant 'patriot type', nor yet a historical romancer. In spite of that he is very 'irish'. He is ready enough, as a literary artist, to stand for Ireland, and has wrapped himself up in a gigantic cocoon of local colour in *Ulysses* . . . .

Although entertaining the most studied contempt for his

> compatriots – individually and in the mass – whom he did not regard at all as exceptionally brilliant and sympathetic creatures (in a green historical costume, with a fairy hovering near), but as average human cattle with an irish accent instead of a scotch or a welsh, it will yet be insisted on that his irishness is an important feature of his talent; and he certainly does exploit his irishness and theirs . . . .
>
> So Englishmen and Frenchmen who are inclined to virulent 'nationalism' or disposed to sentiment where local colour is concerned, will admire Joyce for his alleged identity with what he detached himself from and even repudiated, when it took the militant, Sinn Fein form. And Joyce, like a shrewd sensible man, will no doubt encourage them.[36]

So it seems that this wily provincial is happy to supply a new market with regional flavours, although himself no sentimental Celt or patriot. But outsiders should not take Joyce's false 'history' too seriously; once again, 'Sinn Fein' politics prove the test of his fundamental common sense. It is significant, even so, that no other passage in Lewis's essay credits Joyce with such subtlety – Lewis admits that the notion of Joyce consciously manipulating Irishness will not 'help us to be sure of a very confused issue'. He adds: 'Nor should we be very certain, if we left the matter in that state, of our valuation of Joyce'.

Pound, Eliot and Lewis in fact apply identical criteria in their respective evaluations of Joyce. What this centrally involves is an estimation of how far his practice of literary modernism lends us a critical perspective on modernity. Their conclusions, however, vary. Like Eliot, Lewis notes the importance of a classical principle of order in *Ulysses* (in this case, the unities of space and time) but believes that Joyce, in obsessional fidelity to his theoretical programme, ends up producing 'a barbarous version' of this formula. For Lewis, to use 'locally coloured' or 'irish' materials in charting chaos is to catch water in a sieve: Ireland and the modern world, where Joyce arrives with 'the legendary clatter and bustle of Donnybrook fair'[37] still ringing in his ears, are simply too alike. There can be no relief from the grey tints of a rapidly shrinking world when, as Lewis complains, even a primitive elder dug out of the Aran or Shetland Islands is likely to address the visitor in 'the vernacular of the *Daily Mail*'.[38] Traditional culture, in short, no longer lingers in the margins of our own. So those typically Irish qualities with which Lewis (usually) endows Joyce – introspection, idealism, stupidity – are those of his art as well, in contrast to Lewis's own particularized aesthetic. Joyce offers us in *Ulysses* a 'big variegated heap': 'the decay of a mournful province, with in addition the label of a twenty-year-old vintage, of a "lost time", to recommend it'.[39] He seeks for meaning in interiority and provincialism, rather than in the 'real' world; instead of history, we find a repackaged, privatised past. For Lewis, there is a family resemblance between this version of Bergsonian *dureé* – 'fierce partisanship on behalf of a *time*' – and 'similar partisanship on behalf of a *place*'. The characteristically modernist 'time mind' has much in common with the mentality of nationalism, 'fanatically circumscribing this or that territorial unit with a superstitious exclusiveness'.[40] Lewis spots more shrewdly than Pound that Joyce's Ireland hovers elusively between province and metropolis, past and future, and he attempts to decode this in terms of a larger cultural logic. Despite his racist, colonialist views of Joyce and the Irish, as well as his notably grim vision of cultural modernity, Wyndam Lewis issues a unique and valuable warning that nationalism is 'one of the most obvious critical traps, and at the same time one of the main things requiring a decisive reply, in [Joyce's] work'.[41] It is not hard, reviewing the subsequent critical reception of Joyce, to see how this has been simplified and ignored.

Wyndham Lewis also compares Joyce's deployment of national themes, including himself as national type, with his Irish contemporaries. Lewis writes that the possession of 'personality' has distinguished all the famous Irish literary figures of recent times; and although Joyce, 'steeped in the sadness and the pathetic gentility of the upper shopkeeping classes, slumbering at the bottom of a neglected province', cannot aspire to the glamour of a Wilde, Yeats or Shaw, he is 'by no means without the personal touch'. Joyce's exploitation of his Irishness is not equivalent to Yeats's, but neither for Lewis is Joyce simply an alternative to Yeats in this regard. Rather, 'Joyce and Yeats are the prose and poetry respectively of the Ireland that culminated in the Rebellion' of 1916. For Lewis, Joyce's writing offers not a rebuke to the nationalist revolution, and to the ideologies which inspired its protagonists, but the 'prose' of that rebellion. This is less showy and heroic than its aristocratic counterpart, but a fanciful, anachronistic provincialism underlies both: 'There was an artificial, pseudo-historical air about the Rebellion, as there was inevitably about the movement of "celtic" revival; it seemed to have been forced and vamped up long after its poignant occasion had passed'.[42] Lewis's juxtaposition of Joyce and Yeats in the context of the nationalist ideology of 1916 also remarkably anticipates the concerns of another important Joyce readership: that of contemporary Irish cultural critics. In their writings too, the names of Joyce and Yeats form a familiar couple, but more often as antithetical than, as for Lewis, complementary to each other.

'Let us presume that Ireland is ignorant of Mr Joyce's existence', Pound wrote in 1915, 'and that if any copy of his work reaches that country it will be reviled and put on the index'.[43] But although it is true that an earlier breed of definers of 'Irishness' invited no submissions from James Joyce (as he records in the ninth episode of *Ulysses*), a later generation has granted him, as though by compensation, an extremely prominent position in its debates about cultural nationalism and modernity. At the forefront of this work is a group of writers associated with the journal *The Crane Bag* (Dublin, 1977–85) and the Field Day Theatre Company, founded in Derry in 1980. The history of Joyce's reception in Ireland is full of unexpected twists and reversals, but the Irish admiration for Joyce has always been as complicated as Irish reasons for ignoring or censoring him.[44] Recent Irish criticism has revealed a serious attempt to rethink the significance of the Joycean heritage for present-day cultural politics; but it is has been equally concerned to adapt some of the theoretical discourses we have described here as 'modernist' for an analysis of Ireland's post-colonial situation. The resultant strains and difficulties may often go unremarked, but they reflect back importantly on that theory itself. And although Joyce's Irish readers are apparently at one with other commentators in recovering from his work the idea of an emancipated, post-nationalist modernity, this is not for them a wholly unproblematic notion. It is a point worth emphasizing, since those echoes of the Irish debate which have so far found their way into mainstream Joyce studies have been merely neutralized by its critical and political orthodoxies.

On both sides of the border created in 1922, today's Irish critics find themselves heirs to – or victims of – what James Connolly foresaw as 'the carnival of reaction' if Ireland were partitioned into two sectarian states.[45] They are thus peculiarly well placed to speculate about the continuities between Irish cultural nationalism and the political revolution of 1916–22, and commonly motivated by a profound sense of disillusion at its consequences. 'Nationalism', for the first children of the Irish Free State and the new Republic, signified the official ideology of the post-revolutionary state, designed to distract attention from economic failure and theocratic rule – a trumped-up tale about 'a people coming out of captivity',[46] told by the pusillanimous, middle-class revolutionaries to whom all the benefits of independence accrued. And in the North, the minority Catholic population could only conclude either that the nationalist project had been carelessly abandoned, or its most progressive, Republican elements betrayed. By the late 1960s, however, the southern bourgeoisie had begun to disavow the triumphalist narrative of Irish liberation. Such rhetoric was less important in times of relative prosperity; after the breakdown of the Northern Irish State (1968–72), it was also dangerous – no comradeship could be officially recognized between the founders of the free Republic, and the present-day men and women of violence, with their supposedly bloodthirsty, sectarian creeds. Hence, in contemporary Ireland, a history of nationalist insurrection has been subject to conflicting interpretations, being at different times celebrated, disputed, reclaimed and repudiated. Critics and upholders of the status quo alike, though, have been scornful of nationalism for foregrounding a mythical 'unity' at the expense of social and economic realities. This is a familiar refrain on the political right, which calls on the Irish people to put such fictions behind them, in order to compete more effectively in the international market-place. But perhaps paradoxically, nationalism also remains important for some on the left, who focus on internal injustice and inequality, and argue that the 'unity' of interests created by that free market is equally fictional.

Predictably, the response of intellectuals to these conditions is also complex. Historical studies, for instance, have been dominated for the last twenty years or more by the enterprise of 'revising' Irish nationalism. This has involved a rigorous, sceptical investigation of those notions of invasion, oppression and resistance which were propagated by nationalists, and inculcated as received truth in the new state. In their rare excursions into theoretical reflection, Irish historians have been notably sanguine about their capacity to stand outside nationalist 'ideology', as opposed to the truth of the archive.[47] But it is an obvious irony that their disinterested research has served so well the ideological requirements of both the southern establishment, and of those who defend the union between Great Britain and Northern Ireland. Literary commentators, however, inherit a different legacy of debate. During the 1920s and 1930s, Daniel Corkery, the leading nationalist critic, seemed more concerned with politics than aesthetics in his dismissive treatment of Anglo-Irish literature, which had been largely the creation of the Protestant minority: for Corkery, questions of literary value were apparently less important than legitimating the newly created, confessional state. But many writers and critics, among them the novelist Sean O'Faolain, promoted a countering image of the free-thinking, dissenting artist, and campaigned against cultural provincialism and government censorship.[48] Given the terms of this dispute, it has always seemed obvious to later commentators that, in Ireland, the literary imagination, ideally unconstrained by social or political ends, falls naturally and irresistibly on the side of the 'cosmopolitan' – especially if that is the only word you know for the condition of being free of Irish laws and religion. And with the literary anti-nationalists, we evidently find all the major Irish writers, including James Joyce. His only crime, so far as his successors were concerned, was to complicate their Oedipal struggle with native traditions, by articulating his own so memorably: now every rebellious son of Mother Ireland had to struggle with the ghost of Stephen Dedalus, along with all the other phantoms of the Irish past.

The great exception here, however, is W.B. Yeats. Contemporary critics associate his name, before that of any other artist, with the constrictive legacy of Irish cultural nationalism. This might seem unfair, given Yeats's own alienation from independent Ireland, and his contempt for the Catholic bourgeoisie into whose hands it fell. There seems, at first sight, to be a great distance between his ideal community of virtuous peasants and noble aristocrats, and the 'greasy tills' of Dublin. But the very people whom he excoriated were surprisingly willing to adopt him as their national bard, and they nodded in the direction of his 'culture' by teaching their own children to recite his attacks on their philistinism. The mere concepts of separate identity and destiny, regardless of their particular content, here seemed sufficient to define a national art. Similarly, for Irish literary critics, Yeats now stands for the rhetoric of an exclusively and even racially defined national identity, and for those mythological versions of Irish history which have enjoyed a long and corrupt ascendancy. James Joyce, however, in his absolute refusal of Yeatsian cultural nationalism, provides for many a marvellously convenient name for all the lost opportunities of the revolution. Joyce is then aligned with the positive pole in a host of binary oppositions, between (for example) faith and secularism, provincialism and internationalism, tradition and modernity. Richard Kearney summarizes this conflict:

> In our literature, we . . . discern two opposing tendencies. One led by Yeats sponsored mythology. The other, including Beckett, Flann O'Brien and Joyce, resolved to demythologise the pretensions of the Revival in the name of a thoroughgoing modernism; it endeavoured to liberate literature from parochial preoccupations with identity into the universal concern of language as an endlessly self-creative process.[49]

On first sight such formulations appear to rehearse the opposition between modernism and nationalism which is so familiar from criticism of Joyce. But here the story is not quite so straightforward.

Irish critics have indeed debunked metaphysical definitions of Irish nationality, sceptically interrogating the narrative of national emancipation as it has been taught in independent Ireland. In this, they often seem to suggest that none of the premises of nationalism any longer enjoy validity, and must be jettisoned *tout court*. But neither are they prepared to join that clamour of Irish voices calling simply for more thoroughgoing 'modernization', as a response to current problems. For if such modernity signifies the enlightenment which might transform the repressive Republic, it is often enough couched as a callow recommendation that the Irish should simply forget their troubled past, and concentrate instead on catching up with the rest of Europe and the developed world. The liberal humanist terms in which such prescriptions are often framed do not necessarily engage respect in Ireland, where disinterested liberalism has a somewhat embarrassing history.[50] Moreover, in their adoption of continental theory, Irish critics have looked to European philosophy at precisely the point where its confidence in such Enlightenment rationalism – on which an earlier generation of Irish literary intellectuals depended – is being radically questioned.

Similarly, their accounts of Joyce may seem to consort amicably with recent deconstructive interpretations of the texts, as both sets of readers eagerly extol Joyce's subversion of the false fixities on which any notion of stable identity must rest.[51] But the outcome of debates concerning tradition and modernity in Ireland is rarely the unqualified surrender to sheer heterogeneity which we associate with metropolitan modernism or postmodernism. 'Authenticity', for example, remains an important theme in the work of Richard Kearney and Declan Kiberd, whereas the theorists to which they are occasionally indebted attack the very idea of a self to which one might be true or false. Irish writers have frequently discussed the difficulty of deciding between 'the rival claims'[52] of tradition and modernity, and sought for a perspective (Kearney's improbable suggestion is that of postmodernism itself) which might allow us to mediate between them: in this, of course, they participate in the dilemma of nationalism itself, which typically offers the nation as a potential site for fruitful interchange between the old and the new. Some Irish commentators have gestured to the ancient notion of an Irish 'Fifth Province', a space outside political division and conflict, which might act as a centre for the artistic exploration of Irish history and identity, and perhaps provide new energies for healing and reconciliation. Again, this is a recognizably nationalist notion of the aesthetic, proposing that culture alone might define and unite the putative nation, regardless of its actual disunity or fragmentation.[53] In these ways, contemporary cultural criticism is politically very different from the continental philosophy with which it is sometimes allied. It is no mere assault on what, for example, Phillippe Sollers haughtily refers to as the narcissism of community[54] – indeed, although it takes as the object of its critique the constrictive notions of 'Irishness' propagated by its predecessors, contemporary criticism might be said to constitute a cultural nationalist movement in its own right.

But then how might the Irish articulate a resistance to a common international culture on the basis of modernist styles of thought? Seamus Deane explores this dilemma in his essay, 'Heroic Styles: The Tradition of an Idea'. Deane acknowledges that Joyce's polyglot modernism corresponds to a world in which all particular voices and languages have been rendered equivalent and interchangeable: 'In achieving this in literature, Joyce anticipated the capacity of modern society to integrate almost all antagonistic elements by transforming them into fashions, fads – styles in short'.[55] In this, Deane is alert to some of the political implications of a post-structuralist Joyce; for him, the option of a turn to Joycean styles of thought could never represent a simple or entirely felicitous alternative to Yeats. Rather, 'the polarisation [Joyce and Yeats] identify is an inescapable and understandable feature of the social and political realities we inhabit . . . the highly recognisable world of modern colonialism'. For they both address in their writings 'the mystique of Irishness', that apparently inescapable component of anti-colonial nationalism: Yeats is devoted to the notion of an essential national identity, but Joyce, in rejecting it, instead 'makes a fetish of exile, alienation and dislocation'. So although Joyce opposes a discredited nationalism, he can find no sound or durable alternative to it, and we – like him – are fated to become 'virtuoso metropolitans to the exact degree that we have created an idea of Ireland as provincialism incarnate'.[56] For Joyce, as Deane adds more recently, Irish nationalism is no more than an extension of British and Roman Catholic imperialism.[57]

These conclusions, however, may only follow from a certain tendentious view of modernism itself. The polarism identified here *between* Yeats and Joyce has preoccupied Irish critics, but according to Deane, it is also *internal* to the latter's art – Joyce is himself troubled by the impossibility of reconciling a progressive metropolitanism with 'those vestigial and at the same time authentic qualities which he thinks that nationalism, despite all its distortions, nevertheless enfolds'.[58] That 'ambivalence', which is so fundamental to Joyce criticism, persists. But if Joyce's early work is marked by a tension between these two sets of values, this must gradually diminish; indeed, according to Joycean orthodoxy, nationalist demands in modernist texts may as well be snowballs in hell. Not only are nationalism and modernism 'irreconcilable', but here the very notion of a 'dialogue' between them merely reduces the premodern culture – or the culture undergoing modernization – to the shameful position of 'underdevelopment', and to impotent lament. When political grumbles are forgotten, of course, the cultural treasures of the traditional society can be scattered freely through (say) the Utopian mixture of words and languages we discover in *Finnegans Wake*. The essential point is, though, that once encountered, modernity apparently cannot be effectively challenged, either politically or culturally. Moreover, the art of modernity is capable of absorbing and sublating all protest and resistance.

It is precisely such a view of modernism that leads Marshall Berman to conclude that 'to be fully modern is to be anti-modern . . . it [is] impossible to grasp and embrace the modern world's potential without loathing and fighting against some of its most palpable realities'. The best modern subjects are simultaneously euphoric and depressed, experiencing 'the thrill and dread' of a world where all that was solid melts into air; the typically modernist attitude towards the new order is thus one of irony, rather than criticism or celebration.[59] But if modern culture acknowledges the fear and opposition which it inspires, detailing these responses, on our behalf, like a list of side-effects, surely it can then be all the more confident that they will be tolerated and overcome? One notes that the ironic modern subject none the less co-operates with modernization, if sometimes reluctantly – his or her 'modernism' seems to be fundamentally an adaptive therapy.[60] But, as post-colonial readers, must we accept this critical script, which has been prepared for us in advance by the very system which we may wish to critique? If we renounce a certain metropolitan framework for reading modernism, for example, we may be able to regard the disputes which surround Joyce in a different light. Modernism is not simply *of* or *about* the metropolis, nor addressed solely to its values; we can indeed distinguish between Joyce's representation of imperialism and nationalism, and see how they function in contrasting ways in his texts. For contemporary theory may teach us that to refuse the 'internationalist' perspective is to foreclose cultural perspectives, limiting choice, freedom and human potential, and encouraging dangerous obsessions with national or racial 'essences'. But as Aijaz Ahmad argues, post-colonial theorists have successfully ignored the fact that 'pain of any ethical life is that all fundamental bondings, affiliations, stable political positions, require that one ceases to desire, voraciously, everything that is available in this world' – without such a sense of limit, the ambivalences and the contradictory desires which beset post-colonial writing can never be resolved.[61]

But it is also important to qualify a view of Joyce as straightforwardly anti-nationalist, in order to hinder certain dubious political appropriations of his work. For not all forms of hostility to Irish nationalism are politically alike, as demonstrated by the disagreements between Irish literary critics and Irish historians. Some commentators evidently have difficulty only with a violent nationalism, while others interrogate the meaning of 'peace', 'development' and 'modernity', as well.[62]

G.J. Watson, for example, warns readers that they must interpret *Ulysses* in 'the context of the last fifteen or so bloody years in Ireland . . . where Cathleen Ni Houlihan and Romantic Ireland are alive and well, and functioning on Armalites, Kalashnikovs, and car-bombs'. Such remarks once again demonstrate a remarkable disjuncture between the resonable, moderate tones of Joyce critics, and the staggering presumptiveness of their claims about Irish culture and politics. Watson states:

> The vision of Ireland held by Pearse became canonical in the new Free State; and only comparatively recently has that canonical view been challenged by Irish historians. Joyce with the artist's insight, intuition, and grasp of the forces that were working to make the 'new' Ireland, asks us to consider whether it is 'progress' to found a state on a politics construed as a theology and a history construed as a drama. *Ulysses*, in other words, demolishes the usual view of the inevitable events leading to the present Irish state.[63]

This, at first sight, might seem consonant with what one might call a 'Field Day' view of the failed aspirations of nationalism; but Irish cultural critics do not generally proceed, as Watson does here, to oppose a rational, scientific practice of history to such mystifications – much less one mediated through the historically transcendent genius of the artist. Watson's comments, by contrast, link Joyce with the particular agenda of 'revisionism' in Irish historiography.

Revisionist historians indeed see themselves as having abandoned a tradition of viewing Irish history only through the lens of national struggle. They object to the 'canonical view' of earlier Irish historians as a vulgar narrative, which reduces complex relationships to a battle between the forces of good and evil, with 'all the grey areas erased'.[64] R.F. Foster, for example, opens his recent history of Ireland with the announcement: 'The tradition of writing the "story of Ireland" as a morality tale, invented around the seventeenth century and retained (often with the roles of hero and villain reversed) has been abandoned over the last generation.'[65] Foster's text presents itself as a depoliticized, demythologized history which tells a story too rich and intricate to be subsumed under the headings of colonialism or imperialism – themselves mirages produced by a traditional 'Anglocentric obsession'.[66] James Joyce, too, fled from an oppressive Irish past; his novels, like revisionist histories, apparently demolish simple plots. But even Wyndham Lewis recognizes that Joyce is not, by virtue of all this, simply 'anti-Sinn Fein': with such a conclusion, as Lewis claims, 'We should find ourselves substituting orthodox political reactions to the idea of fanatical "nationalism" . . . for direct reactions to what is in his work a considerable achievement of art'.[67] If the prospect of a 'revisionist Joyce' is to be effectively challenged we must revise our interpretations of his modernism as simply on the side of the 'modern' – lest R.F. Foster, as in Watson's view, should appear a kindred spirit.

But the process of 'substituting orthodox political reactions' which Lewis predicted has gathered momentum in Joyce studies, inspired by a sense of dissatisfaction with earlier opinions of Joyce's profound hostility to all varieties of Irish nationalism, and promoted on the basis of much valuable research contained in Richard Ellmann's *The Consciousness of Joyce* (1977) and Dominic Manganiello's *Joyce's Politics* (1980). These critics' attempt to make sense of what they interpret as Joyce's 'moderate' nationalism avails itself of the fact that there are generally believed to be two traditions in Irish nationalist history: the extremist and radical 'physical force' tradition, and the reasonable, constitutional one. As Joyce, it is felt, cannot be decently aligned with the former tradition, he clearly must find a home with the latter. However, the conjecture and confusion involved in this enterprise is considerable. Manganiello, for example, claims both that Joyce believed that 'nationalism exemplified political delusion in the secular sphere' and that he also 'desired separation from England, but, *although he never stated it*, without alienating the Protestant North'.[68] Manganiello elaborates on Joyce's political position in these terms: 'That Joyce was anti-British did not mean he supported the Irish rebellion. He *must have* thought it absurd, as Conor Cruise O'Brien says now – an inculcation of an extremism that has dyed Irish politics ever since'.[69] Theresa O'Connor adds: 'Linking nationalism with religion, [Conor Cruise] O'Brien argues that both creeds serve to legitimate war and blood-shed because both are rooted in the perverse notion that renewal comes through blood sacrifice. It is precisely this belief that Joyce sets out to decode in *Ulysses*'.[70] But critics' purely speculative coupling of the name of Joyce with that of a revisionist and unionist intellectual should surely be disputed. It is vital that critics should appreciate the variety of emphases in current Irish historiography, before ascribing such apparently inarguable historical wisdom to Joyce in this way.[71]

Moreover, the opposition between moderation and extremism on which both Ellmann and Manganiello rely can be deconstructed. Their habit of reading the issues at stake entirely through the question of violence, for example, leads them both to associate Joyce with the political philosophy of Arthur Griffith, leader of non-violent Sinn Fein in the years before the Rebellion. Manganiello describes Joyce's attraction to Griffith's 'non-violent credo and moderate views', and Ellmann proclaims that '*Ulysses* creates new Irishmen to live in Arthur Griffith's new state'.[72] Griffith may indeed have opposed the use of violence, and therefore may appear 'moderate' – even, indeed, to share what is usually understood to be Joyce's pacifism. But Griffith also held distinctly pro-imperialist views, calling at one time for Ireland to assume an equal role with Britain in the government of an 'Anglo-Hibernian Empire'. Griffith was also notoriously racist and anti-Semitic. His rejection of what his biographer calls 'the liberal-humanitarian ideal of racial equality' stemmed from 'his overreaction against the English and American nativist belief in the Irishman as a white nigger [*sic*]';[73] and his politics were in many regards defined by his rejection of the more libertarian currents of Irish nationalism. Griffith writes:

> The right of the Irish to political independence never was, is not and never can be dependent on the right of the admission of equal rights in all other peoples. It is based on no theory of, and is in nowise dependent on theories of government and doctrines of philanthropy or universalism.[74]

Such statements are deeply at odds with Joyce's sense of himself as the victim and subject of a general British imperialism, and his hostility to racism. For although 'extreme' nationalism, or separatist Republicanism, may be 'immoderate' in relation to violence, but 'as the main conduit for insurrectionary ideas',[75] it was founded on secular principles of universal rights that may make it appear much less narrow and provincial than its alternative.

1

JOYCE AND THE IRISH LITERARY REVIVAL

PREFACE: JOYCE AND YEATS

When James Joyce called on W.B. Yeats in 1902, he found him brooding on his own literary vocation. Yeats advised Joyce that the ugliness of the modern world had come from 'the spread of the towns and their ways of thought'. In cities such as London, he claimed, one no longer finds a 'people', but anonymous crowds. Metropolitan energies may produce a few fully perfected individuals and artists, but these now lack any sense of community or audience. 'The folk life, the country life, is nature with her abundance', Yeats concludes, 'but the art life, the town life, is the spirit which is sterile when it is not married to nature.'[1]

Yeats himself sought to create an advanced art from the materials supplied by popular imagination, and he found Ireland (as he may be recommending to the indifferent Joyce) a congenial place for such experiment. But Joyce, of course, welcomed that modernity which Yeats feared. He did not believe in resuscitating outdated traditions, either to help aspiring artists or to pacify the masses. Instead, his mature work celebrates an ideal of self-creation for all. Even earlier, in *Dubliners* and *A Portrait of the Artist as a Young Man*, his characters are criticized in relation to implicitly cosmopolitan norms – and that includes Stephen Dedalus, his autobiographical counterpart. Art, for Joyce, should be autonomous, above the realm of propaganda and politics: he rejected outright the cultural nationalism of Yeats and the Irish Literary Revival.

It is, however, seriously misleading to consider Joyce's relationship to Irish politics solely in these terms. As a novelist, Joyce worked in that literary mode most closely involved with the culture of the modern nation state: nationalism, in spite of what Yeats may have assumed, is itself one of those contemporary 'ways of thought' about which he complained. Joyce's use of variant forms of the novel in his early work can usefully be read in terms of the broader cultural project of 'narrating the nation', as it has been described by recent theorists.

Moreover, Joyce's implacable opposition to a Yeatsian conception of a common cultural mission for artists, spurned in the name of 'Art', must be counterposed with an examination of the content of their respective writings. In the case of Yeats, this art is distinctly divorced from the social realities signified by nationalist ideology, whereas Joyce, as one of Gramsci's 'organic' intellectuals, is himself a product of an emergent class. The gesture of commitment apparently offered by the work of Yeats, and the corresponding gesture of disengagement offered by Joyce, should be interpreted in the context of the historical and political milieu of the Irish Literary Revival. In particular, Joyce's critique of cultural nationalism and his anticipatory critique of the political revolution which it helped to create were only made possible by the social revolution which had both produced and frustrated his own class. I will argue that his supposed repudiation of the Literary Revival takes its place among competing notions of decolonization current in the Ireland of his time.

NATIONALITY AND LITERATURE: THE CASE OF 'THE DEAD'

Yeats argues in an early essay, 'Nationality and Literature', that any culture's original artists – especially the forgotten authors of ballads and epics – take their inspiration from 'the national character, and the nationistory, and the national circumstances'; in later ages, 'the national imagination' is simply sub-divided and refined, in the more complex artistic forms of drama and finally lyric.[2] His remarks illustrate the elevated position granted to those apparently primitive genres of ballad literature and epic in revivalist aesthetics. The epics at stake here, however, contemporary poets were to recreate from the surviving vestiges of a once glorious Irish tradition. These were to be found, in their written form, in fragmentary and discontinuous manuscripts, and in a still surviving oral tradition of folklore and myth. When rendered into English, and appropriately edited or embellished, this 'revived' Gaelic literature could offer as exotic and exciting an art as any devised by a *fin-de-siècle* London coterie.

Thus an intensified sense of nationhood is the precondition and the consequence of Yeats's art. He shares with the writers of the Irish Literary Revival a dependence upon a reconstructed version of native or folk culture which is both ideological and artistic, and a faith that 'the people' – through an enhanced awareness of their common identity – will ultimately benefit from this aesthetic programme. Such ambitions are signalled by, for example, a letter to potential subscribers to an Irish Literary Theatre, written by Yeats, Lady Augusta Gregory and Edward Martyn in 1897:

> We hope to find in Ireland an uncorrupted and imaginative audience trained to listen by its passion for oratory, and believe that our desire to bring upon the stage the deeper thoughts and emotions of Ireland will ensure for us a tolerant welcome, and that freedom to experiment which is not found in theatres in England, and without which no new movement in art or literature can succeed. We will show that Ireland is not the home of buffoonery or easy sentiment, as it has been represented, but the home of ancient idealism. We are confident of the support of all Irish people, who are weary of misrepresentation, in carrying out a work that is outside all the political questions that divide us.[3]

This innovative art, imbued with the true spirit of Irishness, will not merely create new images of the race, but also correct previous misconstructions of the Irish national character. Simply by assuming cultural authority in this well-meaning way, the revivalists will eliminate colonialist stereotypes from future Irish art.

Standish O'Grady inaugurated the revivalist epic writing tradition with his translations of Gaelic saga material, in particular the cycles of stories which revolved around the great heroes Cuchulain and Finn MacCool; its patrician bias is also explicit in O'Grady's specific concern with the reawakening of the Anglo-Irish Ascendancy to what he considers their historic vocation of national leadership.[4] Hence, George Russell (AE), for example, in an essay entitled 'Nationality and Imperialism', grapples with an important problem for the literary politics of the Revival when he attempts to derive alternative notions of political authority from this epical interpretation of the Irish past. Russell agrees that: 'The idea of the national being emerged at no recognisable point in our history. It is older than any name we know. It is not earth born, but the synthesis of many heroic and beautiful moments, and these it must be remembered are divine in their origin'. But he then proceeds to portray heroes and kings as merely the most perfect avatars of a national genius to which all members of a democratic nation might eventually aspire:

> We can conceive of the national spirit in Ireland as first manifesting itself through individual heroes or kings; and, as the history of famous warriors laid hold on the people, extended its influence through the sentiment engendered in the popular mind until it created therein the germs of a kindred nature.
>
> An aristocracy of lordly and chivalrous heroes is bound in time to create a great democracy by the reflection of their character in the mass, and the idea of the divine right of kings is succeeded by the idea of the divine right of the people.[5]

For, on the one hand, the clear affinity between the themes of literary epic, as explicated by this minority group, and popular nationalist ideology, as it inspired agitation and rebellion, seems evident. As M.M. Bakhtin comments: 'The world of the epic is the national heroic past: it is a world of "beginnings" and "peak times" in the national history, a world of fathers and founders of families, a world of "firsts" and "bests"'.[6] This evokes, for example, Patrick Pearse's sacred histories of Irish nationalism, and his hagiographical accounts of the 'apostolic succession' of its prophets and martyrs. Similarly, identical myths of migration, settlement, foundation, golden age, degeneration and future restoration structure the cultural histories of both W.B. Yeats and of, for example, Eoin MacNeill, co-founder of the Gaelic League, a predominantly Catholic and middle-class organization in both composition and ideology.[7] But in other regards, the noble labour of the Anglo-Irish revivalists had just discovered its most auspicious moment, and just missed it. The Gaelic culture it was faithful to, and occasionally pledged to restore, had been virtually destroyed in the previous two generations since the Famine of the 1840s, although the numbers of native speakers of the Irish language had already begun to fall rapidly by that time. Anglo-Irish culture, which had bred these writers, had, by the beginning of the century, been fatally undermined: economically, by the land settlements agreed with the British authorities, dating from the Land War of the 1880s and culminating in the Wyndham Land Act of 1903; and, politically, by the Liberal Party's commitment to Home Rule for Ireland. As a result of the land reform measures, a radical and rebellious peasantry was transformed into a class of new small landowners. These found themselves for the first time in confident alliance with the growing, but thwarted, urban Catholic middle class. The conflict between this new majority and the Anglo-Irish Literary Revival found its most violent expression in the riots over John Synge's *Playboy of the Western World* in 1907. Some years earlier, a first generation of young university-educated Catholics, and James Joyce's colleagues at University College, Dublin, had also rebuked Yeats in a letter of protest to the national newspapers following the first performance of his play, *The Countess Cathleen*. They accused him in just the same terms that he had employed to denounce earlier representations of the Irish people: 'He [Yeats] represents the Irish peasant as a crooning barbarian crazed with morbid superstition . . . . Is Mr. Yeats prepared to justify this view of our national character . . .? Has Mr. Yeats thoroughly considered the probable effect of presenting this slanderous caricature?'[8] Yeats had pondered the definition of nationhood in these metaphysical terms:

> Is there a nation-wide multiform reverie, every mind passing through a stream of suggestion, and all streams acting and

> reacting upon one another, no matter how distant the minds, how dumb the lips .... Was not a nation, as distinguished from a crowd of chance comers, bound together by this interchange among streams or shadows; that Unity of Image, which I sought in national literature, being but an originating symbol?[9]

The answer history supplied to his question seemed to be a resounding 'no'. He later described the rebels of 1916 as not really of his 'school', and the Gaelic League as 'made timid by a modern popularisation of Catholicism sprung from the aspidistra and not from the root of Jesse'.[10] Confounding Yeats's early hopes, as he had expressed them to Joyce, neither 'town life' nor 'country life', but rather suburbia, had triumphed – a culture which, while lacking either inventiveness or imagination, combined urban materialism with rural complacency.

But what does distinguish a 'nation' from 'a crowd of chance comers'? Perhaps the difficulty Yeats experiences in seeing how a national community is informed by 'a nation-wide multiform reverie' also lies behind George Russell's conception of a democratized epic. For the form of the epic, as Bakhtin argues, is that in which 'beginning', 'first', 'founder', 'ancestor', 'that which occurred before' are valorized temporal categories, corresponding to the 'reverent point of view of a descendant':[11] evidently not at all suitable for a democratic community of modern individuals. Indeed if the novel, for Bakhtin, tends to parody other genres, 'the epic was that genre the novel parodied in its nation-forming role'. Only the novel could be for the contemporary world what the epic had been for antiquity, offering a depiction of a social totality from which citizens might gain a sense of the larger significance of their own lives. Bakhtin seems therefore to oppose *national* epic to modern novel. None the less, he links the emergence of novelistic dialogism to the birth of the modern nation state in two important ways. First, its epoch is that of the common vernacular language in a polyglot world: 'The period of national languages, coexisting and closed and deaf to each other, comes to an end'.[12] The nation becomes self-aware only in relation to others, in external unity: 'This verbal-ideological decentering will only occur when a national language loses its sealed-off and self-sufficient character, when it becomes conscious of itself as only one among other cultures and languages'.[13] Second, the nation is also defined by internal difference and division, in its social stratification and multiplicity of styles. 'Two myths', Bakhtin concludes, 'perish simultaneously: the myth of a language that pretends to be the only language and the myth of a language that presumes to be completely unified'.[14] Therefore the novel is dependent on the conditions of the modern nation state at the same time as it succeeds what Yeats describes as 'the nationistory' as the subject matter, and the temporal co-ordinates, of narrative fiction. Similarly, Benedict Anderson proposes that the experience of temporality in the modern nation state is closely paralleled by that which we uncover in the genre of the novel, which he describes (following Walter Benjamin) as 'homogeneous, empty time'.[15] The solitude in which individual novel – or newspaper – readers lounge is qualified by their sense that these words are being read simultaneously by other individual readers, in a way that overcomes their isolation, in that 'remarkable confidence of community in anonymity which is the hallmark of modern nations'.[16] This secular, time-clocked temporality then *co-exists* with the epic sense of nations, which appear to the individual member to 'loom out of an immemorial past and glide into a limitless future'.[17] Hence Homi Bhabha's insistence that we must attempt to characterize this strange 'double-time of the nation', if we are to understand adequately the potency of nationalism, and its virtually universal contemporary legitimacy.[18]

But critics of Irish literature still occasionally propose that realist fiction is simply the healthy opposite of national myth. John Wilson Foster, for instance, in his *Fictions of the Irish Literary Revival,* argues that the Revivalists significantly failed to contribute to the modern Irish novel. Their 'fictions' were degenerate, mythological ones, and these, Foster claims, are a priori less sustainable in realist novels than in the other kinds of prose narrative – tales, modern epics, translations – which they favoured. 'Realism, objectivity and the proper relation of self and society' constitute the 'excluded middle of the Irish mind', which otherwise oscillates between solipsism, and 'myth and nationality'.[19] Ireland's few courageous realists adopted the cause of sceptical dissent which their Protestant contemporaries, evidently the more suitable candidates for the job, had irresponsibly abandoned. For Foster, this subversive company, anti-nationalist simply by virtue of telling the truth, includes such writers as George Moore and Brinsley MacNamara, and pre-eminently the young James Joyce. Foster considers that 'The Dead' is of particular relevance here, maintaining that in the final paragraphs of that story we witness – for the first time in Irish literature – the birth of a mature, modern individual: a protagonist engaged with cultural memory and national identifications, but not eclipsed by them.

In this way, *Dubliners* might be read as a response to the cultural revivalists who, as strangers to the world of middle-class, urban Ireland, deluded themselves about that 'eloquent and conniving and mean-spirited tribe of [Daniel O'Connell]'.[20] For as F.S.L. Lyons comments, most of the members of the Anglo-Irish literary set could pick and choose their interests and identifications and could therefore 'afford to take an indifferent view of those snares – nationality, language and religion – which Joyce so much feared'. Free-thinking readers may then take delight in Joyce's exposé of popular hypocrisy: in 'After the Race', for example, 'the buried zeal' (*D*, p. 49) of sentimental patriotism moves Jimmy, scion of Irish industry, only when he feels unequal to the wealth and energy of his European friends; in 'Ivy Day in the Committee Room', Henchy, supporter of an election candidate who 'goes in on the Nationalist ticket' (i.e. to join the Irish Parliamentary Party at Westminister), announces that his man is 'in favour of whatever will benefit this country', and proceeds to explain: 'What we want in this country . . . is capital' (*D*, p. 147).

Joyce's unflinching localism, then, subverts the myth-making and the integrative, falsifying vision of cultural nationalism: what he sees steadily, others may now see whole. And so the revivalists' call for a new Irish epic is replaced by, for example, Foster's celebration of a distinctively modern literary genre. But by placing his hopes for Irish cultural adulthood in realist fiction, this critic selects a literary form which is in fact privileged, according to contemporary theorists, in imagining the nation, and focuses on a text – Joyce's *Dubliners* – which is clearly not a fully fledged novel. Moreover, in concentrating on the character Gabriel Conroy, Foster directly challenges familiar readings of 'The Dead'. The concluding paragraphs of this story have generally been read as a rare imaginative surrender on Joyce's part to the emotional appeal of Connemara, Gaelic Ireland or cultural nationalism. It will be my purpose here to explore how such antithetical interpretations of 'The Dead' reveal a great deal about critics' understanding of both nationalism and Joyce. Traditional readings, as I will illustrate, tend to address a revivalist sub-text in the tale; Foster's 'revisionist' account suggests that Joyce has written an allegory of modern selfhood. Both may disclose important features of Joyce's fiction, but in the context of the national 'double-time' discussed above, these readings are in fact complementary to each other in ways which neither can appreciate.

But we must first consider how *Dubliners* as a whole relates to Foster's notion of post-nationalist modernity. When Joyce stated that the title of his collection had 'some meaning', and that he doubted that the same could be said for such words as 'Londoner' or 'Parisian' (*SL*, p. 79), he marked a distinction between his native city and the modern metropolis. Reading these stories, however, we are unsure of whether or not he means this positively – in the style of Yeats, perhaps, who described Ireland as a place where 'the town did not call the tune'.[21] Joyce's comments suggest a *gemeinschaftlich* sense of Dublin life, but no feeling of genuine or restorative community, based on a representation of interpersonal intimacy or obvious authorial affection or empathy, here emerges in any straightforward way. The title does indeed allude to a group of people, and behind that a shared physical space, but the individuals portrayed do not compose a harmonious social whole, in the style of nineteenth-century realism. (The virtual exclusion of the upper and the working classes from the representation serves, paradoxically, both to homogenize and lend a strange sense of isolation to the collectivity it depicts.) Neither are these the richly internalized individuals of classical realism – we are unable to say, for example, whether the same boy or a series of boys provides the protagonists of the early stories. And if all this simply evinces the alienation of modern urban life, then we must also acknowledge that this particular community seems to be specifically mocked for its residual communal values.

In 'Ivy Day in the Committee Room', for example, the characters all know each other well, although they are members of opposed political parties and are supposed to hold very different beliefs, but they are not all that sharply distinguished for the reader. If this is a representation of community, it is a kind of parodied community in which conversation is agreed to be more important than genuine discussion or argument, and a person is criticized only after he has left the room. The electioneers enquire about canvassed individuals by name. They seem surprised when one Grimes announces 'I won't tell anyone what way I'm going to vote' (*D*, p. 137). However, we are told that at the mention of the name of 'Father Burke', the issue again becomes personalized, and Grimes's support for the candidate assured. This is a political style which predates anonymous mass politics, but not necessarily in a positive way. Here, Joyce indeed seems to satirize the Dubliners by implicit contrast with a more modern community of equal, autonomous individuals, rather than register any nostalgia for the kind of face-to-face community which the form of his stories – which retains something of the 'collective hero' of folktale – may seem to evoke.

Joyce uses the literary form of the short story to narrate these truncated biographies. He describes those moments when the lives of Dublin's citizens are disturbed by memory or futile desire, but this society seems incapable of producing individuals who (in Foster's terms) could justify or sustain novelistic treatment. Realist fiction, according to Adorno and Horkheimer, inherits the anti-mythological, enlightenment confidence of Homeric epic and folktale; fairy stories, as Benjamin points out, are 'the earliest arrangement mankind made to shake off the nightmare myth had placed on its chest'.[22] Like the heroes of folktale, Joyce's protagonists struggle against large forces which are only dimly understood, but unlike such heroes, they do not triumph – the stories provide none of the wisdom or counsel of traditional narrative. But Joyce offers no glimpse of an up-to-date free world into which these people could escape. Modernity as such, which 'promises adventure, power, growth, transformation of ourselves and the world'[23] is not ratified; there is here no 'youngest brother who shows us how one's chances increase as the mythical, primitive times are left behind'.[24] Instead, Joyce makes it clear that there is nothing merely superstructural about these characters' provincialism. They are afflicted by fantasies about better places (Buenos Ayres, the Orient, the Wild West, literary London), but because they enjoy no material access to the international realm, they have no real imaginative access to it either. For them, modernity *is* mythological.

Rather than proposing any grand universalist ideals, *Dubliners* illustrates their current impossibility. For Joyce may attack local mores, but he also satirizes the various ways in which Dublin might simply be incorporated into a larger system. This is demonstrated by, for example, his association of Parliamentary nationalism and capitalist development. In these conditions, cosmopolitanism, as a philosophical or existential option, becomes irrelevant. The Frenchman's toast to 'Humanity', in 'After the Race', designed to end the dispute between Jimmy and his English associate, is as meaningless as the young Irishman's patriotism.

Joyce's naturalism addresses a society unfamiliar with a prior realism – the Irish had little experience of Gabriel's bourgeois confidence in 'the solid world itself' (*D*, p. 255). Adorno and Horkheimer may imply that a secure line of development leads from the *Odyssey* to *Middlemarch*, but Joyce's text, by contrast, shows the persistence of pre-realist (folktale) elements in post-realist (naturalistic) forms. This arises, moreover, in the specific context of revivalist Ireland, which had experienced a particularly dramatic transition to modernity in the previous half-century, and where the definition and consolidation of a successionist nation state dominated cultural and political life. The city of *Dubliners* should no longer be critically depicted as a provincial backwater, which simply needs to wake up to the twentieth century. The alternative, however, is not merely to regard it – in Yeatsian style – as the home of a now sadly degenerate 'people', who should try to return to their old ways of life. Rather, by attending to the lived ideology of nationalism, we can observe how Joyce preserves a linkage between modernization and regeneration. This is obscured if we view the book solely in the context of European naturalism, and alternative, symbolic readings of *Dubliners* (as we shall see) merely gesture towards it.

'The Dead' has generally been read as obliging us to revise our interpretations of the stories which precede it. In particular, its readers have felt compelled to reconsider how Joyce's portrayal of Dublin relates to larger constructions of cultural and political 'Irishness'. The undermining of Gabriel Conroy's cosmopolitan pretensions by the revelation of his wife's passion for a dead country boy, and the concluding panoramic vision of Ireland between its eastern and western shores, seem to prove that Joyce is not, after all, immune to revivalist romanticism and primitivism. For many, 'The Dead' seems to provide a 'hinge' between an early and a mature Joyce; Richard Ellmann describes it as Joyce's first 'song of exile' – which may be a cosmopolitan way of saying that it is also his first song of nation.[25] But it has proved more difficult to describe how Joyce produces such a sense of significance and value from this scene of private desolation and loss. Critics generally agree that 'paralysis' cannot generate its own resolution: 'Action has to come from an exterior myth'.[26] In this way, 'The Dead' also seems to be analogous to Joyce's later texts in inviting symbolic decoding, encouraging readers to search for some kind of mythical structure controlling the realist plot. Various suggestions as to the nature of 'The Dead''s sub-text have been relentlessly pursued. Such interpretations have made use of seemingly innocent details, such as the names of the characters, place names and images of light and darkness to elaborate allegories of various kinds, which in turn lend a much greater symbolic resonance to the rest of the story, and to *Dubliners* as a whole.[27] Here we may take John Paul Riquelme's account of the story in his *Teller and Tale in Joyce's Fiction* as exemplary: it is also precisely the kind of reading which John Wilson Foster would be at pains to dispute.

Riquelme claims to find specific echoes of Yeats's Red Hanrahan stories in 'The Dead'. During the course of his adventures, Yeats's hero, the wandering poet and hedge-school master Red Hanrahan, is taken away to the underworld by the fairy women of the Sidhe, and sees in their hands the symbols of the cauldron, the stone, the spear and the sword. Hanrahan is unable to summon the strength and courage to ask their meaning – or even to perceive that these objects are significant – and is informed that, as a result, the fairy Princess Echtege must continue her long slumber. Later in the stories, Red Hanrahan, now lodging in the house of an old crone named Winny Byrne, suddenly notices these same symbolic objects in the common household scene around him, and finally understands their importance. He is embraced by Winny, now transformed into a beautiful young woman, and dies:

> And as he looked at it, the light was shining on the big pot that was hanging from a hook, and on the flat stone where Winny used to bake a cake now and again, and on the long rusty knife she used to be cutting the roots of the heather with, and on the long blackthorn stick he had brought into the house himself . . . . He saw Winny's withered face and her withered arms that were grey like crumbled earth, and weak as he was he shrank back farther towards the wall. And then there came out of the mud-stiffened

> rags arms as white and as shadowy as the foam on a river, and they were put about his body, and a voice he could hear well but that seemed to come from a long way off said to him in a whisper, 'You will go looking for me no more upon the breasts of women'.[28]

Augusta Gregory describes the meaning of these four symbols for Yeats:

> The four jewels, as Willie explained, are universal symbols appearing in debased form on the Tarot, the divining cards of the Egyptians and even on our own playing cards, and foreshadowed the Christian symbolism of the Saint Grail, whose legends Willie loved to trace to Ireland.[29]

Although Yeats is here writing narrative fiction, he does not attend to realist convention. The true meaning of his short stories – like the true meaning of the scene in the underworld – lies in a buried allegory. And Riquelme asserts that the same four symbols, in partially Christianized versions, reappear at the end of 'The Dead', hidden in Joyce's descriptions of the Connemara graveyard with its crooked crosses and headstones, and the spears of its gates.

Richard Ellmann claims that 'mutuality' is the theme of Gabriel's final insight, 'the sense that none has his being alone'.[30] Riquleme, however, asserts that a more specifically national sense of identity or community is at stake in Joyce's text. In arguing this, however, Riquelme presumes that the real meaning of 'The Dead' is entirely divorced from its literal sense. His reading is exemplary. Critics are blind to the fictional representation of nationhood in realist texts, in spite of the fact that theorists of the novel tell us that is precisely where we should expect to find it. Such an interpretation instead places the reader of 'The Dead' in the position of Yeats's hero Red Hanrahan, in need of special wisdom to decipher the mystical codes lurking in everyday reality. And, at the very moment when spiritual illumination changes Winny's humble possessions into symbolic objects (whose meaning, as Gregory confirms, is 'Ireland'), Hanrahan's insight also effects the transformation of the ugly old woman into a lovely maiden. Winny is revealed as a feminine embodiment of the national spirit; a figure for Cathleen Ni Houlihan, the territorial goddess. Gretta Conroy, a woman for whom at least one man has sacrificed himself, is the most 'native' character in 'The Dead'. She too is a fading beauty, and a person of few words; as the story draws to its famous conclusion, she is fast asleep. Is she also a symbol of Ireland or Irishness, like the Princess Echtege or Winny Byrne in Yeats's text? If so, Joyce apparently concurs with the Yeatsian conception of nationalism as the union between an advanced, urban mentality and a passive, feminized tradition which rebukes and educates it: 'The art life, the town life, is the spirit which is sterile when it is not married to nature'.

John Wilson Foster, however, forcefully denies that 'The Dead' can be assimilated to 'the canon of revivalist literature' in this way. Gabriel, rather than surrendering to a cultural tradition which pre-exists him, is for Foster simply a complex individual who grows and changes in response to experience, in a way that no mere Irish 'personality', or creature of Yeats's imagination, could hope to do. The 'journey westwards', towards elemental passion and last things, represents 'a visionary rather than a nationalist or romantic orientation'; Gabriel's voyage is to a place 'beyond cultural myth', and not to be confused with the tourism of cultural nationalists, or the adventures of Yeats's heroes Robartes or Aherne.[31] In this critical account, no overlap whatsoever can be acknowledged between self-created, novelistic identities and traditional or communal identifications.

Foster's reading is convincing so long as we agree that Gabriel, in the final sentences of the text, merely absorbs and sublates the story which belongs to his sleeping wife and her dead lover, incorporating it into his own consciousness. We are familiar, from a long Romantic tradition, with the process by which a strong, central self takes up the experience of another, marginalized subjectivity and lends to it self-consciousness and form. In this, however, it could be argued that Foster's Gabriel provides a parallel to Yeats and cultural nationalism, not their subversion: the people suffer, and the hero-artist takes their suffering on himself and lends it aesthetic shape and significance; the bard transcribes the spontaneous poetry of the folk and hands back to them an heroic epic. Gabriel's dream of the west is thus not very different, in form, from the other fantasies of escape which litter the text – it is simply closer to hand, a more usable myth. For nationalism, perhaps, is an ideological necessity simply because human beings cannot bear too much modernity. National belonging is an enabling illusion for individuals who, in spite of it, live in real social isolation. Foster's stress on Gabriel's emergence as a free individual seriously underestimates the extent to which nationalist ideology is complicit with the formation of such autonomous subjects.

Gabriel's experience, however, is certainly couched in terms of a fading out of identity; his soul 'swoons', and he is described in terms which are themselves stereotypically feminizing. Our reading of the final paragraphs of 'The Dead', then, depends on the extent to which we are willing to admit that Gabriel is losing his 'self-possession', in Ellmann's words. If this occurs, then we are forced to view tradition here as something more than a construct created in order to further individual (masculine) self-realization, as a certain critique of nationalism would allege. This resurgence of tradition, through the figure of the woman and her illicit passion, is destructive of Gabriel's sense of individual self-importance; the story concludes, after all, with a radical challenge to the very idea of personal identity. Gabriel's bourgeois worldliness is overthrown; his comfortable, respectable marriage adulterated. His experience of 'decenteredness' comes from tradition, rather than from his embrace of modernity; or perhaps more accurately, in an Ireland on the very threshold of modernity as represented in Joyce's story, tradition has a very specific force. Mortality – the occasion for Gabriel's reflections on identity is his meditation on death – in itself may be universal, but the particular ways in which it is apprehended here are intimately linked with the cultural situation in which the story is set.

The collectivity which is conventionally read as underlying the story is less Foster's somewhat idealist notion of a 'common humanity' or Ellmann's of 'mutuality', than a specific social grouping, one which embodies the sense of a common cultural fate. In its epical, mystical and symbolical senses, 'nation' has been read as the term that lurks behind this community, and which serves as some source of higher meaning or value. I would suggest that if this significance attaches to Gabriel's vision at the end of 'The Dead', critics have looked for it in the wrong places, or in the wrong register. They have not attended to that 'community in anonymity' which characterizes the modern nation, and the possibility of its fictional representation.

The revelation afforded to Gabriel is mediated by the image of the snow. As Ellmann comments, the snow cannot be death, as it falls alike on the living and the dead. Like an image of the belatedness and retrospective significance that informs the entire story in relation to the collection to which it belongs, the living themselves ultimately appear as merely an ephemeral outcropping of the vast legion of the dead, to whom they cross over, ceaselessly and inexorably. The snow is simply oblivion, the fading out of distinction, identity and meaning which threatens the dead as surely as the living. The snow menaces all, but defines one thing only: 'Yes, the newspapers were right: snow was general all over Ireland' (*D*, p. 255).

Joyce told his brother Stanislaus:

> Do you see that man who has just skipped out of the way of the tram? Consider, if he had been run over, how significant every act of his would at once become. I don't mean for the police inspector. I mean for anybody who knew him. And his thoughts, for anybody that could know them. It is my idea of the significance of trivial things that I want to give the two or three unfortunate wretches who may eventually read me.[32]

As Walter Benjamin observes in 'The Storyteller', the tale rooted in a community, and rich in communicable wisdom, addresses and belongs to a collective to which 'the deepest shock of individual experience, death, constitutes no impediment'.[33] However, by contrast, the novel-reader, banished from the collective life and the counsel of storytelling, attempts to substitute for this the knowledge of mortality which can be gained from fiction, which provides us with 'the warmth which we never draw from our own fate. What draws the reader to the novel is the hope of warming his shivering life with a death he reads about'.[34] Bakhtin claims that it is 'The epic and tragic hero, who by his very nature, must perish'. In comic forms, we find 'heroes of free improvisation and not heroes of tradition, heroes of a life process that is imperishable and forever renewing itself, forever contemporary'.[35] However, history, even contemporary history, does not open up an endless space for the unfolding of events. Every life contains a secret realist plot even in spite of the phenomenological conditions of modernity in which it may be lived. It is mortality which encourages us to perceive temporal relations as significant. And, as Anderson points out, the fear of mortality, the trump-card of traditional religion, is also what nationalism takes up, in order to effect 'a secular transformation of fatality into continuity, contingency into meaning'.[36] It is the magic of nationalism, as of narrative, to transform chance into destiny. Or, as Joyce's contemporary at University College Dublin, Arthur Clery, put the question rather prosaically: 'Who ever yet died for a county? Who would go forth to shed his blood for a county council?'[37] The search for collectivity in anonymity is inspired by the fear of a much greater anonymity: not merely the loss of identity in death, but the loss of the meaning of death, which can only be protected and maintained by a cohesive society. The form of *Dubliners*, then, retains something of the folktale, but with none of its consolations. 'The Dead' dramatizes the spectacular intrusion into this form of a distinctively modern experience of mortality. The superimposition of the two should not surprise us in the light of the strange 'double-time' of nations, which distinguishes the national community from Yeats's 'crowd of chance-comers'. This is Gabriel Conroy's intensely solitary, but yet shared experience. In this, Joyce's writing illustrates as symbolic system (nationhood) what it apparently refuses as ideology (nationalism).[38]

PORTRAIT OF AN AESTHETE

Yeats's embrace of an exotic Orientalism in his Celtic Twilight phase proved very attractive to the young Joyce. Yeats's characters Ahern and Robartes, heroes of *The Tables of the Law* and *The Adoration of the Magi* (1897), provide suitable heretic precursors for the Daedalus of Stephen

Hero, who desires to cast off every social constraint, and to seek for himself another, secret lineage. Stephen enthuses about Yeats's stories:

> Their speeches were like the enigmas of a disdainful Jesus; their morality was infrahuman or superhuman: the ritual they laid such store by was so incoherent and heterogeneous, so strange a mixture of trivialities and sacred practices that it could be recognised as the ritual of men who had received from the hands of high priests, [who had been] anciently guilty of some arrogance of the spirit, a confused and dehumanized tradition, a mysterious ordination . . . . These inhabit a church apart; they lift their thuribles wearily before their deserted altars; they live beyond the region of mortality, having chosen to fulfil the law of their being. (*SH*, p. 183)

Like Yeats himself, Stephen is searching for an alternative and heterodox tradition with which to identify. In typically modernist fashion, Yeats is here engaged on creating through art a tradition to which his own art might then belong; in so far as he employs materials as distant from Joyce's own inherited cultural traditions as they are from his own, the latter is at liberty to respond to and use these in his own writing. There is little trace in Joyce of the specifically Irish or folkloric elements in Yeats's tales: for Yeats, 'Irishness' is an aspect of the identity he desires to create; for Stephen, it is the identity he wishes to escape. In this way Yeats's characters, as they appear in *Stephen Hero*, prefigure for Joyce the great paternal exemplar invoked by *A Portrait of the Artist as a Young Man*; the mythical forebear who summons Stephen both to fidelity, and to absolute originality and individuality:

> His soul had arisen from the grave of boyhood, spurning her graveclothes. Yes! Yes! Yes! He would create proudly out of the freedom and power of his soul, as the great artificer whose name he bore, a living thing, new and soaring and beautiful, impalpable, imperishable. (*P*, p. 154)

This ideal forerunner and begetter represents a 'metafather' who replaces the actual and inadequate paternal figures – Simon Dedalus, priests, teachers and professors – represented in the text. Joyce's 'family romance', his elaboration of an alternative myth of origin, solves what David Lloyd describes as the perennial autobiographical problem of reconciling 'the tension between the desire for self-origination, to produce oneself as if without a father, and the awkward knowledge of indebtedness to what precedes and influences the subject'. For it is an awareness of such indebtedness that this form reveals above any other in its depiction of the evolution of the self in response to external forces.'[39] Lloyd also remarks on the centrality of the autobiographical form in cultural nationalist discourse, which he attributes to their mutual participation in this narrative structure of Freudian family romance. Typically, according to Lloyd, the story of the nationalist hero –who disavows his actual roots – tells of his struggle to discover and identify with 'the spirit of the nation'; as cultural exemplar, or as artist, he then comes to embody this essential spirit, thus prefiguring in himself the national unity which is promised for all.

In its representation of Dedalus's struggle towards a self-authored identity through art, *A Portrait of the Artist* seems to offer a fine example of this form of autobiography. However, in relation to Irish nationalism, Dedalus is engaged on a diametrically opposed family romance, and is indeed devoted to the elaboration of a narrative which distances him from the religious, political and 'national' identifications already established in his biological family. While the content of his quest is in complete contrast to the aspirations of contemporary cultural nationalism – a project which was effectively dominant in the cultural milieu of Joyce's youth – none the less the aestheticist self-creation pursued by Dedalus offers a structural homology to the artistic mission to which it is ostensibly opposed. In his resolutely individualistic self-fashioning, Dedalus ironically re-enacts the self-making and self-discovery of the nationalist cultural project. Here I will pursue the implications of this in the light of the re-emergence of the concept of 'the conscience of the race' at the conclusion of Joyce's text.

As critics of *A Portrait of the Artist as a Young Man* have often observed, Stephen's aspiration towards a fully autonomous and self-created identity is nowhere securely achieved in that text. Instead, Dedalus is presented as a subject forever in process, and the projected moment of his ultimate self-fulfilment in art is postponed beyond the limit of the narrative. Maud Ellmann indeed proposes that *A Portrait of the Artist* illustrates the impossibility of any such programme, and instead 'presents a Stephen Dedalus who is dismembering, not developing but devolving, not achieving an identity but dissolving into a nameless scar'.[40] She here addresses the inevitable erosion of any transcendental perspective by the experience of the biological body, and of the materiality of language. In the perpetual contagion between word and flesh, body and language which *A Portrait of the Artist* enacts, the individual is finally revealed not as a pure, self-identical entity but the site of endless libidinal flux and interchange. The omnipotent, secluded artist can hold everything except his own body in aesthetic stasis: he is powerless, as it were, to stop his fingernails sprouting. As Ellmann implies, there can be no pure disembodied realm of art when, in psychoanalytic terms, the aesthetic signifies for Dedalus merely an aspect of an 'economy of hoarding', or the place where he stores 'the transcendentalized retentions of epiphany'.[41] 'Literature' is what is kept back, *detained*, as Stephen puts it, from 'the tradition of the marketplace' (*P*, p. 192) and 'the chaos of unremembered writing' (*SH*, p. 82).

We must add to this account, however, that the bodily experience of this adolescent and unstable organism is inescapably social and political as well. The regulation of the body is at the centre of the system of religious morality that Stephen seeks to challenge, but his own body denies to him the position of detached, rational and scientific observer which he needs in order to attack religious orthodoxy.[42] In this text, therefore, to attend in post-structuralist fashion to the dismantling of the stable, centered subject is paradoxically also to observe the protagonist yielding to already ideologically charged claims of inheritance and blood-relation on the individual organism. Individuality collapses, that is to say, into an already established collective and historical tradition. When Joyce's friend, the nationalist Tom Kettle, writes in 1912 – 'Your very physical body is not your own. It consists of an initial legacy from your ancestors, and a daily plagiarism from the earth'[43] – he merely testifies to the irrelevance of liberal individualism to the society from which he comes. The respective analyses of Lloyd and Maud Ellmann, I would propose, can be read as significantly complicating, in a number of ways, a conventional reading of Stephen Dedalus' desire to leap out of a stagnating provincialism into a liberating, post-nationalist modernity. In the first place, the text produces a highly complex notion of 'tradition'. It is both the dreary biological backdrop against which Stephen's individuality must be displayed, in the context of his immediate familial and social environment, and it is a tool borrowed from a cultural movement devoted to transforming that environment. To the extent that Catholic Irish nationalism is at odds with a more consistently secularizing and individualist nationalism, it seems to figure for Stephen as the undifferentiated background into which his subjectivity threatens to disappear. The irony in which he is caught is that his attempts to submit this context to a liberalizing critique reflect the ambitions of the Anglo-Irish cultural nationalism from which he is otherwise estranged. At the least, I consider that Dedalus's commitment to 'escape', 'flight' or exile should not be appropriated too quickly for a familiar depoliticized individualism; and in the Irish context the alternative to such individualism is not only the libidinally decentered subject, but (as with Gabriel Conroy) the subject decentered into the broader collectivity of political tradition.

Chief among the religious strictures to which Stephen is subjected is the demand for sexual continence. It is also, as he confides to his friend MacCann, the one to which he is most notoriously unequal (*SH*, p. 56). Stephen's oscillations between self-loss and self-containment are played out in the intimacy of the brothel or the confessional; in this sense at least Stephen is, in spite of what his friend Davin tells him, a terrible man who is *never* alone (*P*, p. 206). Stephen wishes to subvert these constraints on sexuality by the exercise of reason. He challenges MacCann's right to legislate for 'normal human natures': does MacCann have the right to call himself 'normal' if he has no need for sexual contact with women? If MacCann is 'normal', then is it normal to be tone-deaf and short-sighted? This line of self-defence is in perfect accord with Stephen's general belief in the importance of bringing scientific rationality to bear on all aspects of human life, in harmony with the principles of the 'modern method':

> The modern spirit is vivisective. Vivisection itself is the most modern process one can conceive. The ancient spirit accepted phenomena with a bad grace. The ancient method investigated the law with the lantern of justice, morality with the lantern of revelation, art with the lantern of tradition. But all these lanterns have magical properties: they transform and disfigure. The modern method examines its territory by the light of day. (*SH*, p. 190)

Stephen's blithe deconstruction of 'normality' runs aground when it comes to aesthetic discussion. In *A Portrait of the Artist*, when his theory of the static nature of aesthetic experience is refuted by Lynch's writing his name on the backside of the Venus of Praxiteles, Stephen is obliged to qualify his pronouncements with the proviso that he is speaking only of 'normal natures'. He tells Lynch that he profoundly disdains the association his friend makes between sex and art; he dislikes arguments which assert that, for example, men perceive women's bodies as attractive because of the necessity for the propagation of the species. Such arguments, he alleges, lead 'to eugenics rather than to esthetic' (*P*, p. 213). However, to his discomfort, some of his own arguments begin to lead him also in that same worrying direction. The political and the ethical questions which Stephen faces, when couched in the terms of scientific materialism, become inflected by a grosser materialism of blood and genetics. In this we can recognise a modernism not merely of rationalist demystification, but one which has truck with ideas of biological determinism and even of race-consciousness which would elsewhere appear to be quite foreign to Joyce's fiction.

In *A Portrait of the Artist*, MacCann's accuses Dedalus, after a dispute about the signing of a petition for universal peace: 'I believe you're a good fellow but you have yet to learn the dignity of altruism and the responsibility of the human individual' (p. 203). However, this charge is first made in *Stephen Hero* in the characteristically *fin-de-siècle* context of a discussion of heredity and degeneration. There, MacCann claims that sexual licence is 'a sin against the future', and to the Ibsenite Stephen's horror produces this moral from *Ghosts*. Stephen retorts that MacCann treats the play as if it were a scientific document: but he has already made clear his own aspiration that art should approach to precisely this condition. Dedalus announces his artistic mission to the President of his College as 'an examination of corruption' (*SH*, p. 96). The living subject of Stephen's investigation of corruption, of his 'vivisection', is his own body, whose physical waywardness and instability taunt his pubescent pride and fastidiousness. Corruption in the examining subject himself upsets the objectivity of the project: 'It shocked him to find in the outer world a trace of what he had deemed till then a brutish and individual malady of his own mind'(*P*, p. 93). Moreover, the very individuality and discreteness of his body is vulnerable to scientific consideration. 'Do you believe in heredity?', his fellow students enquire, using his own sceptical rationalist beliefs against him. They continually assert that Stephen is held to his native traditions not by some easily refuted and spurned mystical tie, but by genetic inheritance; as his mother tells him, 'None of your people, neither your father's or mine, have a drop of anything but Catholic blood in their veins' (*SH*, p. 139). In his uncomfortable awareness of this, Stephen is challenged:

> Living in an age which professes to have discovered evolution, can you be fatuous enough to think that simply by being wrong-headed you can recreate entirely your mind and temper or can clear your blood of what you may call the Catholic infection? (*SH*, p. 211)

To his dismay, scientific rationality begins to confirm the claims not of modern enlightenment, but those of tradition itself. Stephen accepts this quasi-materialist imagery to the extent of fearing, in the Catholic Eucharist, 'the *chemical* reaction which would be set up in my soul by a false homage to a symbol behind which are massed twenty centuries of authority and veneration' (*P*, p. 247, my emphasis).

Stephen seems to associate his bodily insecurity primarily with his mother's physical weakness and insubstantiality. As his sister bleeds to death through her navel – never having separated herself from her mother successfully or established an independent identity – Mrs Dedalus pleads with her undergraduate son: 'Do you know anything about the body?' (*SH*, p. 168): she looks to the scientist to help her to supplement her own inadequate maternal instincts. His sister's death coincides with Stephen's darkest reflections on his life and art:

> He laid a finger on every falsehood it contained: [an] egoism which proceeded bravely before men to be frighted by the least challenge of the conscience, freedom which would dress the world anew in [the] vestments and usages begotten of enslavement, mastery of

an art understood by few which owed its very delicacy to a physical decrepitude, itself the brand and sign of vulgar ardours. (*SH*, p. 167)

Here, acknowledgement of oppression and of the demand for responsibility, together with the blatant exhibition of the mechanism by means of which these conditions are transcended in art, coincide with the artist's sense of the insufficiency of the body's own inherited constitution. Stephen continuously stresses that the demands of the patriots on him are physical: threats to his time, energy, strength, and, ultimately, in the person of Old Gummy Granny of *Ulysses* Chapter 15, his survival; he is asked to become the living vessel of tradition. This awareness of tradition and the vocabulary of race which it involves is illustrated as Stephen gazes from the street at members of the Ascendancy at ease in their Kildare Street club:

> The name of the hotel, a colourless polished wood, and its colourless quiet front stung him like a glance of polite disdain. He stared angrily back at the softly-lit drawing-room of the hotel in which he imagined the sleek lives of the patricians of Ireland housed in calm. They thought of army commissions and land agents: peasants greeted them along the roads in the country: they knew the names of certain French dishes and gave orders to jarvies in highpitched provincial voices which pierced through their skintight accents.
>
> How could he hit their conscience or how cast his shadow over the imaginations of their daughter, before their squires begat upon them, that they might breed a race less ignoble than their own? And under the deepened dusk he felt the thoughts and desires of the race to which he belonged flitting like bats, across the dark country lanes, under trees by the edges of streams and near the poolmottled bogs. A woman had waited in the doorway as Davin had passed by at night and, offering him a cup of milk, had all but wooed him to her bed; for Davin had the mild eyes of one who could be secret. But him no woman's eyes had wooed. (*P*, p. 242)

Here, the sense of physical or material inheritance and that of *moral* responsibility blend into each other. It is of course the latter which Dedalus ultimately embraces in his ambition to create 'the conscience of the race', but here we see his earlier apprehension of the link between his individual existence and 'the race to which he belonged'. The Joyce who is too often identified simply as an apologist for spiritual transcendence reveals in these passages, and elsewhere in his work, a quasi-materialist consciousness of kinship, race and inheritance.

'Borrowed styles are no good' was Joyce's apparently unlikely advice to a young Irish writer in the 1930s, 'You must write what's in your blood and not what is in your brain'.[44]

Joyce's representation of Stephen's development in this precise cultural context also lends to the Dublin of *A Portrait of the Artist* a very different atmosphere from that which pervades *Dubliners*. In place of urban anonymity, one encounters here a world of intense, claustrophobic intimacy resonant with the clamour of a variety of social styles and voices. As Bakhtin points out, this is the kind of social environment which is so essential to the form of the *Bildungsroman*:

> The importance of struggling with another's discourse, its influence in the history of an individual's coming to ideological consciousness is enormous . . . . The process is made more complex by the fact that a variety of alien voices enter into the struggle for influence in the individual's consciousness (just as they struggle with one another in surrounding social reality).[45]

Bakhtin, as we have seen, suggests that the modern nation is the privileged site of such discursive interplay and *heteroglossia*. Elie Kedourie attacks nationalism for its very valorisation of social conflict and self-determination in this way. It is always, he argues, productive of strife to take autonomy as the highest moral and political good, as it is never 'a condition achieved here and now, once and for all, it is rather to be struggled for ceaselessly, perhaps never to be attained or permanently secured'.[46] *A Portrait of the Artist*'s depiction of Dedalus's supposed rejection of the ideology of cultural nationalism, then, remains complicit, to this extent, with the terms of nation-building. However disgusted Stephen is with 'the compact body of Irish revivalists' (*SH*, p. 43) in his college, he is never entirely disengaged; he is alienated rather than isolated. He is afforded the opportunity to define and redefine his artistic credo in the face of the Church's own 'ambassadors' (*SH*, p. 210–11); he is sought out for personal interview by the President of the College, and his views are notorious among his peers. Stephen is present at the opening of the Irish Literary Theatre and witnesses the furore over Yeats's *The Countess Cathleen*; later, during the *Playboy* controversy, Joyce confessed his disappointment at missing the excitement of the riots to his brother Stanislaus: 'I feel like a man in a house who hears a row in the street and voices he knows shouting but can't get out to see what the hell is going on'.[47] This is a neat reversal of the image Joyce later employs to describe Shem the Penman's writerly withdrawal and domestic seclusion – 'kuskykorked . . . up tight in his inkbattle house' (*FW*, p. 176) – sheltering from all the wars. Stephen's intimacy with the emergent forces in Irish society is suggested by the fact that one Hughes (apparently Joyce's fictional name for Patrick

Pearse, whose Irish classes he attended) stands up to refute the artist after he delivers his paper on 'Drama and Life' to the College Literary and Historical Society. Ireland's renegade artist may be roundly denounced by its future revolutionary leader, but he is for all that, addressed and acknowledged by him. Hughes proclaims:

> Mr. Daedalus was himself a renegade from the Nationalist ranks: he professed cosmopolitism. But a man that was of all countries was of no country – you must have a nation before you could have art. Mr. Daedalus might do as he pleased, kneel at the shrine of Art (with a capital A), and rave about obscure authors. In spite of [his] any hypocritical use of the name of a great doctor of the Church Ireland would be on her guard against the insidious theory that art can be separated from morality. If they were to have an art let it be moral art, art that elevated, above all, national art. (*SH*, p. 108)[48]

In this society, Stephen's refusal of political commitment in art becomes the subject of general comment and controversy. His assertion of artistic autonomy is assailed and defended, continually thematized and understood as politically charged from the outset. This gesture therefore carries a resonance and an importance here that it could not have sustained in an equivalent English social situation. Even the question of exile is publicly discussed, with the opinions of the author's mother duly canvassed and reported. This distinguishes Stephen (and Joyce's) decision to leave Ireland from that of a long tradition of Irish expatriate writers: here it is consistently foregrounded as the *content* of the writing, and not just as its context.

Joyce, then, professes aestheticism, but does not write aestheticist literature. Rather, he writes not so much as, but *about* an aesthete. In Bakhtin's terms, the language of aestheticism does not function so much as a primary means of representation but as the *object* of representation, parodied and stylized, as is the fate of all discourses when they are incorporated into the novel form:

> Thus when an aesthete undertakes to write a novel, his aestheticism is not revealed in the novel's formal construction, but exclusively in the fact that in the novel there is represented a speaking person who happens to be an ideologue for aestheticism, who exposes convictions that are then subjected in the novel to contest.[49]

The Ireland Joyce knew, it should be emphasised, lacked virtually any tradition of bourgeois, liberal or individualistic dissent. Such calls for a common, disinterested cultural programme as have been issued in

Ireland arise consistently from within the Protestant community, which historically has been viewed by the great majority of people as the ally and beneficiary of a repressive colonial administration. They have tended to arise, moreover, as a cultural solution to that community's religious and political isolation, and at times when it was faced with new political threats from majority movements. Joyce's apparent taking up of the cause of disinterestedness, along with that of the autonomy of the artist, from within the Catholic community, must thus be distinguished from both an Anglo-Irish and an English liberalism. It comes, that is to say, from a society in which such questions as whether Jesus was the only man who ever had pure auburn hair or who was exactly six feet tall (*SH*, p. 139) are a topic of serious discussion – a far cry, indeed, from literary London and Coole Park. This distinction ought also to be signalled by Stephen's evident discomfort with English liberalism itself. As he reluctantly tells the well-meaning Englishman, Haines, in *Ulysses*: 'You behold in me, Stephen said, with grim displeasure, a horrible example of free thought' (*U*, p. 17). In a culture lacking a dominant liberal tradition, Stephen experiences his own agnosticism as a painful anomaly.

When we view *A Portrait of the Artist* in this context, the conventional wisdom that regards Stephen as an individual who manages to 'escape from ideology'[50] becomes even more difficult to sustain. The English liberal Haines in *Ulysses* advises him helpfully: 'After all, I should think you are able to free yourself. You are your own master, it seems to me'. Stephen knows all too well, as *A Portrait of the Artist* as a whole demonstrates at a formal level, that such a belief in the possibility of individual liberation is always already ideological. H.G. Wells's review of *A Portrait of the Artist*, in which he praises the book for the 'convincing revelation it makes of the great limitations of a great mass of Irishmen', surely owes its trenchancy to Wells's fear that the English reader might otherwise be deceived or confused by what appears to be a liberalistic dimension in Stephen Dedalus's thought. Wells sees fit to warn:

> everyone in this Dublin story, every human being, accepts as a matter of course, as a thing in nature like the sky and the sea, that the English are to be hated. There is no discrimination in that hatred, there is no gleam of recognition that a considerable number of Englishmen have displayed a very earnest disposition to put matters right with Ireland, there is an absolute absence of any idea of a discussed settlement, any notion of helping the slow-witted Englishman in his three-cornered puzzle between North and South. It is just hate, a cant cultivated to the pitch of monomania, an ungenerous, violent direction of the mind . . . these bright-green young people across the Channel are

something quite different to the liberal English in training and education, and absolutely set against helping them.[51]

The specific political detail of Wells's interpretation is all the more extraordinary in view of the fact that 'England' is scarcely mentioned in Joyce's novel. The very possibility of such contemporary accounts of the book renders it all the more surprising that Art – 'with a capital A'– as a place beyond ideology, the vision of an arena of perfect disinterestedness, individuality and freedom, is still advanced as the political message of *A Portrait of the Artist*. Dominic Manganiello, for example, provides a contemporary restatement of this position:

> the emancipation made possible through literature transcended those notions of freedom embraced by nationalists and socialists . . . . Enthusiasms must be tempered in the crucible of art, and must be judged in perspective . . . . Although Ireland's political hopes were buried with Parnell, Stephen's mission of ennobling his country holds a new promise of freedom, since the artist asserts that the individual is more important than institutions such as Church and State.[52]

Nevertheless, Manganiello's general case in *Joyce's Politics* does address an important paradox in Joyce's aesthetics: the absolute rejection of a didactic function for art, together with the retention of a confidence in the salutary effect of representative art. The latter provides a place where the people of Ireland might apprehend a negative image of themselves in Joyce's 'nicely polished looking glass', and an ultimately positive one in the artist's image of 'the uncreated conscience of the race'. Paradoxically, Joyce's commitment to European naturalism continually pushes him back into the petty-bourgeois milieu of his youth. Naturalistic fidelity to a degraded reality and aestheticism become strange allies in his early fiction, in which paralytic banality is relieved only by the fineness of its depiction in language. The petty-bourgeois social group at the centre of such Irish naturalism, however, is also one which will make the political revolution itself, which can scarcely, for example, be asserted of the characters of Arnold Bennett. It is, therefore, as Manganiello correctly identifies, around the question of the representation of the Irish people that Joyce's project again appears to betray an affinity with Yeats's. Here, as I propose to discuss in the final section of this chapter, Joyce again demonstrates a kinship with cultural nationalism, if this term is appreciated as encompassing a much more varied and complex set of propositions than the notion that – as, for example, Manganiello proposes – Irish patriots held that it was much better to die in Ireland, for Ireland, than live anywhere else.[53] When David Cairns and Shaun Richards, in a similar vein, conclude of

Joyce's *Dubliners* – 'The reality, however, was that Joyce was holding to the principle of liberation of self and nation through loyalty to individual truth rather than in obeisance to short-term nationalist shibboleths'[54] – it should be remembered that, even in Ireland in the first decade of the century, nationalism and 'short-term shibboleths' are not synonymous. Recent attempts to interpret Joyce as a kind of elevated, more sophisticated form of Irish nationalist neglect the fact that nationalism tends anyway to see itself as a sophisticated cultural movement. In its Romantic, European guise, it is an ideology devoted to self-creation and self-expression, education and art – a lonely project, in advance of the creation of the ideal national community, in a projected future and a collective freedom.

'THE BATTLE OF TWO CIVILIZATIONS': JOYCE AND DECOLONIZATION

The dispute between W.B. Yeats and the students of Dublin's University College over *The Countess Cathleen* in 1902 prefigured the violent clashes over John Synge's *The Playboy of the Western World* five years later. Nothing less than Yeats's whole conception of cultural nationalism, of his role as national poet and the proper nature of an Irish National Theatre, were at stake in these controversies. His antagonists were predominantly adherents of an emerging, largely Catholic and self-styled 'Gaelic' nationalism, the kind of people who made up the membership of the Gaelic League and the Gaelic Athletic Association. D.P. Moran, editor of *The Leader* newspaper and one of the best-known propagandists for an exclusively Catholic Irish identity, dubbed this clash between the 'true' Irish and the Anglo-Irish 'The Battle of Two Civilizations' in a 1900 essay, and subsequently in his book *The Philosophy of Irish Ireland* (1905). The historian F.S.L. Lyons borrows this term for the title of his chapter concerning the period of the Irish Literary Revival in *Ireland Since the Famine* (1971), which in turn provides the basis for his well-known *Culture and Anarchy in Ireland* (1982). Lyons's suggestive and influential conception of revivalist Ireland has tended to dominate those accounts of Joyce which attempt to contextualise his work historically. The readings of his texts which emerge on this basis tend to grasp Joyce as offering a contemptuous, even-handed rejection of both Celtic Revivalism and 'Irish Ireland' – as calling down a plague on both houses. This apparent symmetry of response is, I would argue, spurious: Celtic Revivalism and 'Irish Ireland' were not in fact equivalent phenomena; and the latter in particular has been travestied and misunderstood by commentators in ways which obscure the nature of Joyce's relationship with it.

Lyons's narrative charts the gradual 'disenchantment' of those among the Anglo-Irish Ascendancy who had decided to throw in their lot with their fellow Irish people, and the tragic destruction of their misguided but noble dream of 'a fusion of cultures'. The revivalists – so the argument runs – elaborated a conveniently cross-denominational 'Celtic' stereotype of the Irish; the propagandists of the Catholic majority proposed an equivalently specious and pernicious 'Gaelic' one, rejecting in arrogantly sectarian spirit any contribution to the national movement by those who did not satisfy their narrowly conceived definitions of Irishness. According to Lyons, the failure of the Irish Irelanders was that 'they could admit no resting place between the rejection of the English culture and the restoration of the Gaelic culture'. In this schema, the early Yeats is revealed as the moderating voice in cultural debate, 'trying to hold a middle position between the anonymity of cosmopolitanism and the parochialism of Irish Ireland'.[55] Lyons curiously couples Joyce with Edward Dowden, professor of English at Trinity College, Dublin, as 'cosmopolitans', refusing equally the calls of 'Anglo-Ireland' and 'Irish Ireland'. That Ireland's foremost native novelist should be bracketed with an Ascendancy literary scholar notorious for his almost complete indifference to Irish culture is an irony which symptomatizes a fundamental flaw in Lyons's case. Joyce's relative silence on this major ideological struggle, together with his apparent seduction by Ascendancy charisma in the sphere of politics, as evinced by his 'bad case of arrested Parnellism' (Lyons), has led to such judgements as Dominic Manganiello's : 'For Joyce, the battle of the two civilisations was, in effect, pointless'.[56] But Joyce cannot be as unproblematically enlisted for an aloof, enlightened cosmopolitanism as Manganiello would believe: his rejection of Revivalism is a characteristic gesture of the world of native Catholic nationalism – the world within which he was brought up. It can be argued that his effective exclusion of Anglo-Irish culture from his fiction indeed parallels its exclusion by nativist nationalism.

Let us consider Joyce's depiction of the Irish people in the light of this Gaelic or 'nativist' cultural nationalism, as represented by Moran. Edward Said describes nativism as the 'insufficient and yet absolutely crucial first step' in any anti-imperialist politics. This must be followed, he claims, by a further 'liberationist' moment, for the full promise of national liberation to be realized.[57] It is easy perhaps to grasp Joyce's later work as in many regards *prematurely* liberationist, displaying the equality and interchangeability of all languages and cultures irrespective of the relations of power or domination which may currently obtain between them. However, in Joyce's early fiction we can also see the traces of a 'nativist' position. This, as I demonstrate, proves partially to resist the contemporary critique of cultural nationalist ideology provided by David Lloyd, especially in his essay 'Writing in the Shit: Nationalism and the Colonial Subject' (1988).

The debates between Yeats and the public he had sought so ardently primarily concerned the question of the proper, or just, representation of the Irish people. For its author, *The Countess Cathleen* offered a creative image of rural Ireland, and revealed a deep spiritual truth about Irish aristocratic valour. However, for a significant sector of Irish Catholic opinion, it represented an unacceptable slur, and a grotesque caricature of a peasantry for whom in fact religion was never secondary to material survival. From the point of view of these protesters, to present a 'true' image of the Irish was necessarily to present a pleasing or flattering one. Only this could provide a corrective to the slanderous stereotypes which were the stock-in-trade of Anglo-Irish stage comedy and political satire. Yeats wrote in 1909 that he believed that these insulting versions of Irish national character had already been challenged and refuted by the writers of the Young Ireland movement sixty years earlier, in their propagation of 'a mass of obvious images' to inspire national life. He and his colleagues, as he remarks in disappointed retrospection, had endeavoured to do similar work, but in 'a more profound and therefore more enduring way'. However, by the time of Synge's appearance on the scene, Yeats's group had realized that they must

> renounce the deliberate creation of a kind of Holy City in the imagination and express the individual. The Irish people were not educated enough to accept images more profound, more true to human nature, than the schoolboy thoughts of Young Ireland. You can only create a model of a race to inspire the action of that race as a whole, apart from exceptional individuals, when you and it share the same simple moral understanding of life. Milton and Shakespeare inspire the active life of England, but they do it through exceptional individuals. Having no understanding of life that we can teach to others, we must not seek to create a school.[58]

The nature of the supposed alliance between flattery and anti-colonialism, of which Yeats and Synge are often conceived as victims, is articulated by George Bernard Shaw, writing of the *Playboy* crisis:

> The Clan-na-Gael [American Fenians] . . . suddenly struck out the brilliant idea that to satirize the follies of humanity is to insult the Irish nation, because the Irish nation is, in fact, the human race, and has no follies, and stands there pure and beautiful and saintly to be eternally oppressed by England and collected for by the Clan.[59]

This implies that the 'nativist' cultural nationalist movement is merely one of self-flattery, and that to dispense with what Roy Foster describes as 'the compelling Manichean logic' of traditional nationalist myth is automatically to cast doubt on the very reality of the colonial experience.[60] It is this series of false assumptions which I hope to interrogate with reference to the Catholic/Gaelic position.

Joyce proclaimed to his prospective publisher in 1906 his belief that with the stories of *Dubliners* he had taken 'the first step towards the spiritual liberation of my country'. However, he also wrote later to his brother Stanislaus:

> The Dublin papers will object to my stories as to a caricature of Dublin life. Do you think there is any truth in this? At times the spirit directing my pen seems to me so plainly mischievous that I am almost prepared to let the Dublin critics have their way (*SL*, p. 70).

Joyce, like Yeats, is accused of 'caricature': indeed he anticipates or possibly even courts such charges. However, his representation, unlike Yeats's, is calculated to offend, is *knowingly* iconoclastic and irreverent. Madden accuses Stephen Dedalus: 'No West-Briton could speak worse of his countrymen. You are simply giving vent to old stale libels – the drunken Irishman, the baboon-faced Irishman that we see in *Punch*' (*SH*, p. 69).[61] This signals Joyce's awareness of the argument that to fail in praise of the Irish was simply to restate hoary English stereotypes. Joyce commented also to his brother on the 'unnecessarily harsh' picture he had given of Dublin, but added a reminder of 'how useless these reflections are': even if he were to rewrite *Dubliners* entirely, he would still find 'the Holy Ghost sitting in the ink-bottle and the perverse devil of my literary conscience sitting on the hump of my pen' (*SL*, p. 110). It is *conscience* which produces distortion; the evangelical spirit which draws him towards blasphemy: his remarks are animated by a sense of both guilt and responsibility and a polemical urgency which Yeats's lack.

However, Joyce's unflattering portrait of Dublin life in itself in no sense attests to his anti-nationalism. The alternative cultural nationalist movement was not simply devoted to pious self-congratulation. Even D.P. Moran railed against the Yeatsian project not as unflattering, but as artificial, or historically and culturally unfounded. Moran's entire polemical campaign was directed *towards* the excoriation of the Irish, and in his writings he continuously bemoans the absence from Ireland of any tradition of any 'literature of national self-criticism'.[62] He claims that its place instead is filled by the nationalist politicians, who habituate their electorate to flattery, windy oratory and empty invective, and collude in the propagation of myth and the 'hysterical artificial stimulation of racial hatred'.[63] The broad democratic popular base of the national movement, the Catholic Irish nation, he considered guilty of tolerating and supporting such cant. Moran saw clearly the danger inherent in offending the Irish self-image at the moment of their attempt to confront English rule in Ireland directly, but persisted in spite of it: 'If this view in any way soothes the conscience of the English for their own country's cruel injustice in Ireland I cannot help it'.[64] It is particularly ironic for Moran that he is himself best remembered as a puerile name-caller and bigot, and as such has been interpreted as providing material for Joyce's portrait of the citizen in *Ulysses*'s twelfth chapter.[65] In fact, his own satiric portrait of the corrupt Irish nationalist in *The Philosophy of Irish Ireland* closely resembles Joyce's representation of the hypocritical rhetoric of the Cyclops:

> Was it not Fergus O'Connor, of Chartist fame, something of a giant in physique, who told a gaping English mob that only for famines every Irishman would be as fine a specimen as he? And you will meet men every day who will ask you how in the world could Ireland be prosperous considering that England stole our woollen industry from us some hundreds of years ago.[66]

In the light of this, we can appreciate the existence of elements in Joyce's selective, homogenizing and unflattering portrait of the Irish which align it with a nativist rather than a Yeatsian kind of cultural politics.

'Traditional' cultural nationalists are charged in *The Philosophy of Irish Ireland* with having produced a false notion of Irish culture as the basis of their work. Moran writes of the Revival:

> A certain number of Irish literary men have 'made a market' – just as stock-jobbers do in another commodity – in a certain vague thing, which is indistinctly known as 'the Celtic note' in English literature, and they earn their fame and livelihood by supplying the demand which they have honourably and with much advertising created. We make no secret of the reason why we have dropped our language, have shut out our past, and cultivate Anglo-Saxon ways. We have done them all in the light of day, brutally, frankly – for a living. But an intelligent people is asked to believe that the manufacture of the before mentioned 'Celtic note' is a grand symbol of an Irish intellectual awakening. This, it appears to me, is one of the most glaring frauds the credulous Irish people ever swallowed.[67]

In this they collude with political nationalists, from Henry Grattan to Parnell, who fought for Irish political autonomy while lacking an informed sense of the full cultural meaning of Irish nationality. The Irish political movement had entered into alliance with disaffected colonists and Ascendancy values, and sought for independence only within English terms. In short, it had in Moran's view functioned as an agent of 'Anglicization'. Clearly, the latter term here stands as a byword for 'modernization'. As the student of nationalism may observe, Moran has identified the central irony which characterizes the relation between any nationalist movement and modernity. He calls for Ireland to embrace modernization, and is then confronted by the problem of articulating an 'essentially Gaelic' way of promoting industrialization or running factories. We can, however, see the sturdy Gael as more equal to such a role than the dewy-eyed Celt, and so at the least concede that Moran's myth was more thoroughly *modernizing* than Celticism.

For Joyce's commentators, however, 'Catholic', popular or 'nativist' nationalism signifies above all exclusiveness and sectarian or racial prejudice. The citizen's attempt to deny Bloom's 'Irishness' is consistently regarded as the exemplary dramatization of Joyce's hostility to nationalism. (If Joyce is primarily concerned with a denunciation of Catholic Gaelic nationalism in his representation of Bloom, then it might be argued that a sympathetic representation of an English person or an Irish Protestant in 'Cyclops' would have been a more apposite rebuke to the discriminations usually enforced by that ideology. Indeed *Ulysses*'s allegorical incarnation of Englishness and Irish Protestantism in the figures of Haines and Deasy respectively must surely raise problems for any account of Joyce's liberal broadmindedness.) However, if we consider – to take a contemporary example – Ulster Unionists' opposition to Irish nationalism, we may note that it is based not on the threat of exclusion, but rather of what is believed by Irish Protestants to be a blind and misconceived inclusiveness. David Lloyd, indeed, argues that Irish cultural nationalism is primarily concerned with the sublation of diversity and difference. He argues that nationalist ideology invariably tells of an original, unreflective wholeness of the people, which has now fallen into disunity. Nationalism seeks to transcend this condition in the eventual achievement of a restored and self-conscious unity. Its specific project in Ireland since the nineteenth century has been 'the forging of a sense of Irish identity that would transcend historically determined cultural and political differences and form the reconciliatory centre of national unity'.[68]

Oliver MacDonagh appears to concur with Lloyd's judgement in his identification of the overcoming of difference as a central tenet of Irish nationalism. However, he also asserts that this is not in fact historically necessary to its claims at all. The emphasis on transcending sectarian division – what the United Irish Movement proclaimed in the eighteenth-century as the substitution of 'the common name of Irishman in place of the denominations of Catholic, Protestant and Dissenter' – springs from the fact that definitions of Irishness have always been the preserve of classes who by any other criteria but their own would be excluded:

> Both the radical and the moderate wings of Irish nationalism, each overwhelmingly Catholic in composition from 1800 on, accepted the image of the Irish nation as adumbrated first by the liberal wing of the Anglo-Irish Ascendancy, and then developed in an inclusive, supra-sectarian direction by the dissenting and bourgeois 'left' among Irish protestants. This meant blind assumptions that Ireland was one and indivisible politically, and that religion was a false divider of Irishmen, used as such by British governments intent on maintaining control of the island.[69]

In the light of Lloyd's argument, Moran may still be viewed as advancing a call for an inter-*class* alliance against British rule, but the sense in which nationalism can still be criticized as the creation of a premature unity and the pursuit of a family romance with what Lloyd describes as 'putative forefathers' is significantly qualified. Lloyd registers no distinction between an Ascendancy and a nativist position: in the latter case, there is no question of some conscious choice to identify with popular experience. It is in this context that Moran articulates a deep scepticism concerning the dominant cultural nationalist conception of a 'composite' vision of Irish nationality:

> No one wants to fall out with Davis's comprehensive idea of the Irish people as a composite race drawn from various sources, and professing any creed they like, nor would an attempt to take up racial prejudices be tolerated by anyone. We are proud of Grattan, Flood, Tone, Emmett and all the rest who worked for an independent Ireland, even though they had no conception of an Irish nation; but it is necessary that they be put in their place, and that place is not on the top as the only beacon lights to succeeding generations.[70]

David Lloyd, in 'Writing in the Shit: Nationalism and the Colonial Subject' considers Daniel Corkery's *Synge and Anglo-Irish Literature* (1931) as exemplary of the project of cultural nationalism in Ireland. In this book Corkery offers a sceptical assessment of the literary revival just nine years after the foundation of the Irish Free State – a revision which is often read as a kind of respectably academic reformulation of Moran's cultural prejudices. Especially notorious is Corkery's call for a literature which will fulfil his threefold definition of 'Irishness', in its closeness to the themes and preoccupations of: 1) the religious consciousness of the people; 2) Irish nationalism; 3) the land.[71] Lloyd states:

> The proper function of the Irish writer would accordingly be to

> *represent* the people, in every sense of that word. If at one level, this involves the demand to depict Irish people and their ways, it is intrinsic to Corkery's argument that proper depiction is a function of the representativeness of the writer as Irish. In a sense of the word quite strictly analogous to its usage in democratic political theory, the writer is the people's representative.
>
> Accordingly, the concept of representation here involves an implicit narrative of development: by representing in himself the common identity of Irish people, by 'canalizing some share of Irish consciousness so that that consciousness would better know itself' (Corkery, p. 6) the writer produces the national and subjective unity which is as yet only a latent potential.[72]

Lloyd thus conflates a nativist cultural nationalism with a Yeatsian aesthetic. He achieves this by displacing the question of representation entirely into that of the *medium* of representation, namely, the Irish language, suggesting the fundamental incoherence of proposing a properly 'Irish' art while evading the problem of the extinction of the native language. However, while it is true that on this question Catholic Irish nationalists are engaged as surely on 'family romance' as members of the Protestant Ascendancy, their larger engagement with nationalism is not merely reducible to this. A Yeatsian 'representativeness' of the artist is distinct from Corkery's idea of 'representation', which in fact amounts merely to a renewed demand for *realism*, which was at no stage Yeats's concern. 'Representation', for the Anglo-Irish nationalist tradition, signifies the attempt to wrest political leadership of the people as well as an aesthetic project; the nativist nationalists are simply struggling to represent *themselves*, free of the dilemmas of patronage, bad faith and 'negative identification'[73] which afflict the more enlightened wing of their colonial rulers. It is not that Joyce himself is any sense absolved from such dilemmas; it is rather that he negotiates them from within a consciousness of the stereotyping of colonialism, and of the dangerously thin line between that stereotyping and his own literary enterprise.

2

ULYSSES, NARRATIVE AND HISTORY

The naive or mythical view of Irish history is important for readers of Joyce, since he uses it throughout *Ulysses* and *Finnegans Wake*. The fact that it is endlessly interesting to most Irishmen and infinitely tedious to most Englishmen can be a serious obstacle to the understanding of Joyce's major works.

Matthew Hodgart, *James Joyce: A Student's Guide*[1].

PREFACE: STORIES AND STYLES

Towards the end of Chapter 15 of *Ulysses* ('Circe') Major Tweedy, father of Molly Bloom, and member of the Royal Dublin Fusiliers, who 'rose from the ranks' (*U*, p. 46) of the British army, confronts the citizen, dropsical Irish nationalist: '*(Major Tweedy and the Citizen exhibit to each other medals, decorations, trophies of war, wounds. Both salute with fierce hostility)*' (*U*, p. 487). '*Massed bands*', further stage directions tell us, '*blare* Garryowen *and* God Save the King'. Garryowen is the name of the citizen's dog in Chapter 12 ('Cyclops') and of a place in Limerick. It is also the title of an Irish drinking song. Don Gifford and Robert J. Seidman gloss this reference with a quotation from its refrain:

> Instead of Spa we'll drink brown ale,
> And pay the reckoning on the nail,
> No man for debt shall go to gaol,
> From Garryowen in glory.[2]

'God Save the King' is the title of the National Anthem of Great Britain. Verse and chorus (although annotation may be judged unnecessary) are:

> God save our gracious king,
> Long live our noble king,
> God save the king.
> Send him victorious,
> Happy and glorious,
> Long to reign over us,
> God save the king.

This short exchange illustrates certain features of narrative and style typical of *Ulysses* as a whole. Perhaps the first thing to note of the confrontation between the Major and the citizen is that it comes to nothing. The fight which Cissy Caffrey, Cunty Kate and Biddy the Clap eagerly anticipate does not materialize. In their disappointment, the prostitutes stand for any reader of *Ulysses* who has not yet abandoned his or her expectation of narrative progression. Second, the two songs are evidently to be understood as playing simultaneously, the one utterance melting indifferently into the other. The styles of language associated with them are here merely suggested by the citation of their titles. The songs are not quoted, nor subjected to the comic exaggeration or distortion which might amount to parody. But in their literal indistinguishability they serve to demonstrate what is implicit elsewhere: in *Ulysses* it is usually impossible to say whether parody elevates or ridicules any particular style, as each blends with the next in the frenzy of textual play.

In this small way, therefore, the absence of evident plots and of any ethical notion of style in *Ulysses* are already obvious. However, this passage has not been chosen at random, but because of its specific content. The lines which describe the Major and the citizen indicate antagonism but suggest symmetry. Their salute is a sign of recognition as well as of respect to mutually exclusive and supposedly opposing loyalties. They are both ridiculous; however, if either of them looks funnier it must be the citizen, for at least Tweedy really is a military man. The Irish nationalist merely mirrors the uniform and gestures of the soldier although he is hardly able to stagger from his bar stool to the door of the pub, as we have already seen in Chapter 12. The encounter here stages and defuses a scene of possible aggression. And if the passage reveals the secret equivalence of British soldier and Irish nationalist, such a process of levelling might also be understood as being at work in the juxtaposition of the British National Anthem and the Irish drinking song. The confrontation between the two figures can thus serve to illustrate the critical case that this practice of writing erodes the grounds on which we could evaluate or seek to choose between the ideologies for which the pair stand, British imperialism and Irish nationalism respectively. My reading of the text, however, is devoted to challenging this conclusion. Here, I examine how such a view of *Ulysses*'s 'anti-nationalism' is associated with a certain interpretation of Joyce's abandonment of narrative or plot in the text; in the following chapter, I explore these issues by considering Joyce's representation of nationalism in relation to questions of style.

Simply by dint of its realism – the material the text supplies for a diagnosis of the economic and political malaise of the group of lower middle-class men who constitute its primary focus, its descriptions of their proneness to alcoholism, violence and debt (as indeed the words of

'Garryowen' suggest) and of the bleak lives of their dependants, especially the Dedalus family – *Ulysses* powerfully suggests Joyce's hostility to British colonial rule in Ireland. But for many commentators, this does not amount to nationalism: indeed, as we have seen, according to some of Joyce's more recent critics – hostile alike to what Tweedy and the citizen stand for – it in fact adds up to something a great deal more radical and valuable, exposing the contradictions and weaknesses inherent in the nationalist project from the start. Colin MacCabe, for example, remarks that Joyce's life before 1914 lent the writer the opportunity to observe the three great movements of twentieth-century history (anti-colonialism, communism and fascism) constitute themselves around the three great themes of nineteenth-century history, (democracy, socialism and nationalism).[3] This formulation admits of *no* alliance between nationalism and anti-colonialism: it is not surprising, then, that in its opposition to nationalism, MacCabe reads *Ulysses* as adumbrating an alternative form of anti-colonial politics. Seamus Deane argues that the modernist Joyce, in severing the traditional affiliations between narrative and history, opens up a vision of apparently endless possibility at the level of language while incorporating into his writing the terrible burden of Irish historical experience by displaying the failures of nationalist imaginings at the level of content.[4] Joyce's departure from novelistic convention attests to his historical consciousness, exposing the collusion between literary form and a drastically impoverished version of history. Resistance to narrative continuity is thus itself an oblique political act. Similarly, for Colin MacCabe, Joyce's liberation of narrative fiction from the categories of character and plot signals his 'more and more desperate attempt to deconstruct those forms of identification which had allowed the national revolution to mean the very opposite of a liberation for Ireland . . . such a nationalism confers identity and belief where we would find desire and knowledge'.[5] It is as though, from this critical viewpoint, Joyce is wise before the revolutionary event precisely because he is writing after it, prefiguring in (say) the sterile mirror-image of soldier and citizen what he takes to be the deadlocked outcome of the Free State itself.

Because the topic of narrative in *Ulysses* is inevitably linked with oral performance and storytelling, it is closely associated with the question of style. In the next chapter, therefore, my emphasis will be on the way in which such questions of narrative and style converge around the problem of Joyce's aesthetic exploitation of what he calls in *A Portrait of the Artist* 'the sacred eloquence of Dublin' (*P*, p. 200). This in turn raises the spectre of 'Irish style', and the cliché of the quaint but hopelessly impractical Irish talker, in the light of what Declan Kiberd describes as modern Irish writers' 'dignified assertions of a people's right to be colourless'.[6] But the relationship between style and parody is also complex. In general, parody involves a deliberate disjunction of style and content to comic effect: high style to low content, or an elevated content to low style, or both, as in the case of 'Garryowen' and 'God Save the King'. I want to examine the consequences of the adaptation of a low style to a low content, particularly through themes and languages of violence. Joyce significantly emphasizes the violence of his stylistic parodies in a 1919 letter to Harriet Shaw Weaver:

> The word *scorching* . . . has a peculiar significance for my superstitious mind not so much because of any quality or merit in the writing itself as for the fact that the progress of the book is in fact like the progress of some sandblast. As soon as I mention or include any person in it I hear of his or her death or departure or misfortune: and each successive episode, dealing with some province of artistic culture (rhetoric or music or dialectic) leaves behind it a burnt up field. (*SL*, p. 241)

But Joyce's hatred of violence is consistently read by, for example, Hugh Kenner, Richard Ellmann and Dominic Manganiello as the very cornerstone of his politics: these accounts of his pacifism, at least as it is articulated by *Ulysses*, need qualification. To this end, in the next chapter, I consider the linguistic styles linked to Irish nationalism – in both its elevated versions which predominate in Chapter 7 ('Aeolus') and the demotic rhetoric which characterizes Chapter 12 – in order to suggest how the language of, say, 'Garryowen' differs in both the way it is deployed and in its political significance from the kind of language associated with 'God Save the King'.

I am concerned firstly, however, to examine the category of narrative as it is deployed by Joyce's post-structuralist commentators. In particular, I will pay attention to the ways in which such a sense of narrative intersects with a certain sense of history – a history which is insistently foregrounded in those early episodes which best exemplify the 'stream of consciousness' of Stephen Dedalus and Leopold Bloom respectively. In these early chapters of *Ulysses*, complex and contradictory associations between 'history' and 'narrative' emerge. Recent celebrations of the novel's apparent deconstruction of plot would seem implicitly to characterize narrative in highly traditional ways: the point of my own reading, however, is to extend the category of narrative to include just the kind of very short story that the confrontation of Tweedy and the citizen typifies. *Ulysses* is not, to be sure, a continuous linear story; but it is composed of a multiplicity of such stories, a knot of superimposed, complementary narratives in which the individual actors often appear to be dispensable while the underlying narrative paradigms persist. These micro-events, by force of their repetition and variation, can indeed be read as constituting a set of ironically and conflictively interrelating narratives, such that no one of these textual events can be taken in isolation. To view the confrontation between citizen and soldier as complete in itself is likely to involve a somewhat different judgement on political nationalism from a reading which re-inserts that encounter into the narrational complex of the text as a whole. Similarly the apparently private consciousnesses of the three central characters, Dedalus, Leopold and Molly Bloom look different when seen as implicated in the collective stories of the community.

Let us consider these questions in the light of parts of Chapter 15 ('Circe'), and Joyce's introduction to the novel, Chapter 1 ('Telemachus'). Here, certain strategies employed by Stephen Dedalus at the level of literary content in his negotiations with Dublin on 'Bloomsday' can be read as corresponding to major formal strategies of Joyce's in *Ulysses*. In his encounter with the British soldier Private Carr, Stephen behaves 'anti-narrationally', refusing to play the role allotted to him by the colonial power, but in doing so simply succeeds in becoming the victim of its violence. A modernist refusal of narrative and emancipation from colonial power, may not, in short, be as unproblematically conjoined as some contemporary critics assume.

Like the prostitutes, Private Carr is a notably vulgar reader of Joycean narrative, struggling to interpret Stephen's enigmatic utterances. Stephen knows that he is being understood as anti-British – 'Green rag to a bull' (*U*, p. 483) as he confides to Bloom – but makes no attempt either to placate or confront the soldier. Carr threatens violence: 'I'll wring the neck of any fucker says a word against my bleeding fucking king' (*U*, p. 488). Stephen evidently wants to continue the argument with the soldier because 'He provokes my intelligence' (*U*, p. 484), even though the intellectual potential of this dialogue seems from the outset to be pretty limited. Ultimately, in his attempt to meet violence with brilliance, Stephen is knocked to the ground, to be hauled away by a few cronies of his father, kowtowing to the civil authorities at the same time as they try to extract him from their clutches. Stephen disdains the simple narrative of aggression proposed by the soldier, and suffers for it: modernist fiction may refuse plot in order to deny the reader's 'pleasure' but open up 'desire' (MacCabe *James Joyce and the Revolution of the Word*, p. 156), but here, at least, pain is the result.

But if Dedalus eschews the vulgarity of plot, he is elsewhere politically constrained to resist that freewheeling modernistic parody which might appear to be its alternative. That parody, as practised by Buck Mulligan, represents for Stephen a fundamental indifference to (and hence complicity with) colonial domination, for all its superficial subversiveness. Just as Stephen deliberately talks over the head of the soldier, so Mulligan chats patronisingly to Haines about the milkwoman in Chapter 1. Mulligan glosses for Haines the woman's pious exclamation: 'The islanders . . . speak frequently of the collector of prepuces' (*U*, p. 12). This might be read as a parody of Haines, as Mulligan exploits the comically technical language of anthropological research. He makes fun of Haines, as much as or indeed perhaps more than of the woman, but of course Haines is not mocked in the same way because he can understand the joke. The woman, who unlike the soldier is powerless, makes no response. Mulligan treats Haines, who is the local representative of imperial England – 'His old fellow made his tin selling jalap to Zulus or some bloody swindle or other' (*U*, p. 6) – in the same indifferent comic manner as he treats everything else. Stephen, in his insistence to Mulligan on the moral seriousness of his behaviour towards his dying mother, and in his refusal to banter with Haines, appears to believe that certain issues should be protected from Mulligan's rationalist demystifications and vacuous parodies. Mulligan, according to Stephen, plays the role of 'A jester at the court of his master, indulged and disesteemed, winning a clement master's praise. Why had they chosen all that part?' (*U*, p. 21). He has become another gifted Irishman who plays to the British audience. His mockery of the Irish is entirely consistent with the fact that he himself embodies a certain stereotype of the linguistically gifted Irishman. Stephen's ultimate charge against Mulligan, however, is not that of 'mocker' but 'Usurper' (*U*, p. 19). I would suggest that what Mulligan, Ireland's 'gay betrayer', has *usurped* is precisely Dedalus's self-appointed role as Ireland's very serious betrayer. It is Stephen's reluctance to scoff at what he opposes that leads Mulligan, in turn, to accuse him of simply inverting, rather than dismantling, traditional pieties: 'Because you have the cursed jesuit strain in you, only it's injected the wrong way.' (*U*, p. 7).

It is often noted that *Ulysses*'s parodic strategies are paralleled by Mulligan's, though as Colin MacCabe argues, with perhaps suspicious vehemence, we must 'ruthlessly distinguish' between these two modes of parody, the one radically challenging the positions of author and reader, unsettling and unlimited in its effects, the other straightforward, comic and didactic.[7] This emphatic distinction – odd for a post-structuralist to enforce – can be questioned: character and novel do indeed share certain strategies, one of which is simple repetition. This is evinced by their attitude, for example, towards sacred ritual. Mulligan claims that he can joke about death because he sees so much of it, and the majesty of the single death is consequently eroded:'You saw only your mother die. I see them pop off every day in the Mater and Richmond and cut up into tripes in the dissectingroom' (*U*, p. 7). This prefigures Bloom's demystifying reflections at Paddy Dignam's funeral:

> He must be fed up with that job, shaking that thing over all the corpses they trot up here. Every mortal day a fresh batch: middleaged men, old women, children, women dead in childbirth, men with beards, baldheaded business men, consumptive girls with little sparrows' breasts . . . . Says that over everybody. Tiresome kind of a job. But he has to say something. (*U*, p. 86)

Mulligan's spoof electric-powered transubstantiation also parallels Bloom's scandalously irreverent musing on the Eucharist:

> For this, O dearly beloved, is the genuine christine: body and soul and blood and ouns. Slow music, please. Shut your eyes, gents. One moment. A little trouble about those white corpuscles . . . . That will do nicely. Switch off the current, will you? (*U*, p. 3)

> Shut your eyes and open your mouth. What? *Corpus*: body. Corpse . . . . Rum idea: eating bits of a corpse. (*U*, p. 66)

The former, of course, proceeds from the blasphemous delight of the lapsed Catholic, the latter from the observations of the non-Catholic. However, this registers a distinction between insider and outsider which *Ulysses* as a whole, as 'the type of all anti-auratic texts, a mechanical recycling of a sacred document',[8] is unable to preserve, as it passes all that was holy through the processes of modern, mechanical reproduction and repetition, levelling the distinction between sacred and profane, high and low. Through Stephen, the novel recognizes the political limitations of parodic practice, while engaging in precisely such practices on its own part. Indeed as such parody becomes less constrained and more general, it can be seen as becoming less dangerous and less critical, rather than (as MacCabe claims) more so. In the complete absence of a possibly 'normative' speaking voice, the practice of modernist parody gives way to one of postmodern pastiche. As Jameson comments:

> Pastiche is, like parody, the imitation of a speaker or unique style, the wearing of a stylistic mask, speech in a dead language: but it is a neutral practice of such mimicry, without the satiric impulse, without laughter, without the still latent feeling that there exists something *normal* compared to which what is being imitated is rather comic.[9]

The scene with Mulligan, Haines and Stephen, then, dramatizes a Joycean dilemma: how to process the styles of Irishness, the verbal habits of the 'islanders', from the point of view not only of a 'sympathetic alien' (as Stephen describes himself in *Stephen Hero* and as Haines represents here), nor simply from the standpoint of a disdainful native (Mulligan), but from the position of an engaged but critical insider. But it is a question of who will receive this discourse as well as produce it: the milkwoman, the 'Poor old Woman', stands as the representative of an uncomprehending Irish audience and Haines for a readily available metropolitan readership. This dilemma is understood as colonial from the outset.

SIREN CALLS

A consideration of Chapter 11 ('Sirens') demonstrates how the limited sense in which I use the term 'narrative' can call into question certain powerful readings of *Ulysses*. Here I engage in particular with Colin MacCabe's remarks about the episode in *James Joyce and the Revolution of the Word*, which offer a useful illustration of how deconstructive criticism deals with the specific historical and political questions raised by Joyce's text. MacCabe's account has been followed by several other post-structuralist accounts of the episode, but these in general lack its specific address to the issue of Irish nationalism.[10]

MacCabe's reading concurs with traditional accounts of Chapter 11 in its valorization of the solitary Leopold Bloom, who refuses the consolations and pleasures enjoyed by the drunken, sentimental, patriotic crooners in the Ormond Bar, the tipplers who both pander to and are teased by the barmaids. Bloom as writer – he here composes his reply to Martha's flirtatious letter – contributes to MacCabe's interrogation of the opposition between writing and the voice in this episode. Bloom, MacCabe argues, defers the gratification of sexual desire by composing a letter to a correspondent that he will never meet. Thus – unlike his companions – he acknowledges the materiality of the signifier rather than the imaginary unity of conversation or sex. His use of a script that is not habitual to him and his adoption of a pseudonym demonstrate that he apprehends the arbitrary nature of linguistic codes and the ultimate fictiveness of his own identity. Bloom's demolition of musical illusion – brought about by his demystifying understanding of the anatomy of the human vocal organs and of the mathematical basis of harmony – also shows him to be a good modern subject, suspicious and self-divided, wary of violating the alterity of other subjects by imagining himself to be in 'fictional' communion with them. In this way, MacCabe maintains that Bloom eschews the 'full unified identity offered by nationalism',[11] that imaginary collectivity in which the drinkers bathe, and effects a deconstruction of origin which 'has definite political effects as it demonstrates a contradiction between writing and nationalism'. In short, Bloom disavows the pleasures of drink, song and what MacCabe refers to as 'the easy moralism of political commitment'.[12]

The chapter as a whole takes the form of a composition or

performance – inaugurated by the command 'Begin!' and concluding with '*Done*' – of the scattered linguistic fragments which comprise the opening pages. The theme of music is introduced by Miss Douce's humming and becomes more formal and public when the drinkers begin to play the piano and arrange a series of impromptu performances among themselves. This gradually acquires patriotic overtones as they persuade Ben Dollard to sing the traditional ballad, 'The Croppy Boy'. The theme of nationalism is made explicit by the final quotation from Robert Emmet's apocryphal 'Speech from the Dock'. The last words of the nationalist hero before his execution in 1803 are reputed to have been: 'When my country takes her place among the nations of the earth, then and not till then let my epitaph be written. I have done'.

Emmet's words are both quoted and put to work in this episode. The concluding word of his speech – 'Done' – ends this piece of writing as well. This parallels the way in which Bloom, although deliberately separating himself from the group and their activities, remains dependent on the temporal structures they provide, even in the organisation of the private experiences of his own body. For Bloom, however, these structures are divorced from the demands of performance and the risk of failure. When Simon Dedalus sings, he produces the *illusion* of 'endlessnessnessness' (*U*, p. 227), of drowning in song. However, as performer, he – together with his audience – is concentrating: 'it leaped serene, speeding, sustained, to come, don't spin it out too long long breath he breath long life' (*U*, p. 226). By contrast, Bloom secretly manipulates the rubber band which he has removed from his package of writing paper, while he is thinking of the melody he imagines Blazes Boylan and his wife Molly to be sharing: 'Love's old sweet *sonnez la* gold. Bloom wound a skein round four forkfingers, stretched it, relaxed, and wound it round his troubled double, fourfold, in octave, gyved them fast' (*U*, p. 225). He fidgets rhythmically, in silent and private imitation of Simon's song, while meditating on the play of desire in narrative and its inevitable closures. His rubber band is also an erotic fetish (it echoes the barmaid's elastic garter), and his game with it mimes the intensification and release of tension in sexual activity. Bloom, however, pulls his plaything too hard, and it gives way:

> Thou lost one. All songs on that theme. Yet more Bloom stretched his string. Cruel it seems. Let people get fond of each other: lure them on. Then tear asunder. Death. Explos. Knock on the head . . . . Are you not happy in your? Twang. It snapped. (*U*, p. 228)

So Bloom does not simply stand aloof from the desires and gratifications which he observes around him; rather, what the drinkers experience collectively, he experiences on his own. He literally goes through the motions associated with sex, song and story, but does not *perform* them with others. We are even informed that Bloom chooses to write his letter in the hotel bar because 'Quills in the post office chewed and twisted' (*U*, p. 228). The instruments of writing themselves are marked by the oral frustrations which, for MacCabe, hold the drinkers in their grip: the two activities do not belong to entirely different economies.

The drinkers' post-structuralist critics note how, as they listen to the music together, the members of Simon Dedalus's audience appear not merely to be imaginatively fused, but almost literally and, as MacCabe argues, necessarily *paralysed*.[13] Bloom is not paralysed, apparently, for ultimately he is able to leave the bar. However, the sensuous apprehension of the music which the drinkers enjoy – 'Brain tipped, cheek touched with flame, they listened feeling that flow endearing flow over skin limbs human heart soul spine' (*U*, p. 225) – is closely paralleled elsewhere in the text by descriptions of Leopold Bloom's own physical experience of anxiety. This occurs, for example, when he reflects on his wife's imminent adultery and the impending loss of his daughter's virginity: 'A soft qualm, regret, flowed down his backbone, increasing. Will happen, yes. Prevent. Useless: can't move. Girl's sweet light lips. Will happen too. He felt the flowing qualm spread over him. Useless to move now' (*U*, p. 55). Here, Bloom translates regret into paralysed resignation quite as effectively as his tipsy fellow citizens.

Bloom's isolation is also read as enabling him to criticize the emotional involvement of the drinkers in the sad story of the doomed Irish croppy. The audience know in advance what the tragic fate of the rebel will be; they luxuriate in this confirmation of narrative expectation, and in the sense of resignation which it induces: 'A yeoman captain. They know it all by heart. The thrill they itch for. Yeoman cap . . . . Very sad thing. But had to be' (*U*, p. 234–5). But, by the same token, it should also be observed that Bloom himself enjoys the most vulgarly teleological experience represented in *Ulysses*, during which the trajectory of his desire coincides exactly with that of Gerty MacDowell, reader of trashy romantic fiction, as well as with a large crowd of onlookers on Sandymount Strand which is watching the fireworks:

> And then a rocket sprang and bang shot blind blank and O! then the Roman candle burst and it was like a sigh of O! and everyone cried O! O! in raptures and it gushed out in a stream of rain gold hair threads and they shed and ah! they were all greeny dewy stars falling with golden, O so lovely, O soft, sweet, soft! (*U*, p. 300)

If the drinkers are charged with a kind of mental group masturbation, then Bloom is hailed by critics as a 'hero of sexual modernity'[14] for a more furtive version of the real thing.

Colin MacCabe, of course, ultimately wants to produce Bloom as a better *revolutionary subject* than the men he leaves behind in the Ormond bar. But it is by no means obvious to all like-minded critics that these nationalists partake of that antiquated, autonomous subjecthood which MacCabe rejects, and which he must now attack not just on grounds of its paralysing effects but because of its masculinist *violence*. For Derek Attridge at least, the collectivity which the drinkers establish is one of subversive, erotic freeplay: the 'imaginary unity' of the whole represents the destruction of the equally imaginary self-containment of its constitutent parts, namely, the individual bodies. Their abolition of the lonely, monadic self is then progressive and liberating: only 'a sexually repressive morality insists on the wholeness and singleness of body and mind or soul'.[15] The drinkers are fluid and diffuse, possessing little individuality or interiority: they would seem well suited to a modern art that 'posits a future-oriented creation of meaning, in a more democratic inter-subjective mode, among the equal voices of writer, reader and character . . . all together in one discursive communion'.[16]

But this is a possibility which, for political reasons, MacCabe must dismiss. Rather, at that moment of fusion when Bloom submits to the pleasure of the music (Siopold! *U*, p. 227), he is momentarily false to himself as a split subject and surrenders 'to the effacement of the signifier'.[17] It seems anomalous that Bloom's one experience of such 'inter-subjective communion' and loss of individuality should be represented – by a post-structuralist – as a moment of tragic failure and inauthenticity. As Patrick MacGee adds sympathetically: 'The dialectic of desire, the need for recognition, can tempt even the wariest and most disenchanted wanderer'.[18] For MacCabe's reading oscillates between condemning inaction and condemning that forcefulness – associated here with nationalist commitment – which might appear its antithesis: in spite of all the poetic liquescence and *jouissance* of 'Sirens', the desires rampant in the Ormond bar are conventional, penetrative and male. Bloom is attracted by the women as strongly as the other men, but he does not express a desire to penetrate them sexually, to violate the hymen. Rather he desires to write something on this symbolic parchment, or at least, to make the woman respond to or recognize him: 'Blank face. Virgin should say: or fingered only. Write something on it: page . . . . Say something. Make her hear (*U*, p. 234).

Patrick MacGee explains:

> Bloom's temptation is that he wants to say something, to make the siren hear and recognise him. He resists this temptation by writing a song without words, with a pen that makes invisible

> marks. Self and other are shown to be . . . manipulated by the same intersubjective ventriloquism through which the subject of a discourse grounds his desire in the desire of another.[19]

Bloom accepts the gulf between himself and the woman. He thus communicates with no one, in case that should involve him in scandalously positing a desire on their part to communicate with him. Thus Bloom has been lauded not just for his mobility, but for his principled objections to doing anything. The men may indeed be sexist, but the sublimation of their erotic wishes in narrative and especially in the political story of the ballad impel the episode. They stand between Blazes Boylan and Bloom, between immediate genital gratification and its perpetual postponement. Bloom can respond to sexual difference and otherness only by fleeing them. MacCabe is then caught between attacking 'individuality' and congratulating the individual who has escaped from it. He preserves all the traditional terms of Bloom's enlightened superiority to his fellow citizens, merely updating the vocabulary in which it finds expression. He has thereby missed an opportunity to investigate how nationalist ideology might engage forms of subjectivity other than this caricature of a necessarily quietist, autonomous self; in any case, we can dispute MacCabe's presumption that Bloom – more than any of the other Dubliners – departs from this paradigm.

In his conclusion to *James Joyce and the Revolution of the Word,* Colin MacCabe argues that the treatment of nationalism in Joyce's fiction is especially significant in the context of certain failures of socialism in the early twentieth century. He refers in particular to the rush by Social Democratic parties to support national and imperial interests in the First World War, and to the inability of the Second International

> to confront and analyse those elements of politics that are not simply reducible to a rational conflict of interests. For in politics it is not simply interests but imaginary identities which are at stake . . . . The displacement of those identifications involves more than is provided by a rational discourse about interests or by the offer to replace country and faith by international brotherhood.[20]

Nonetheless, to have understood the operations of these irrational ideologies would have been to take a step towards emancipation: 'in the absence of a theory of these practices [i.e. the repressive identifications typical of nationalism] there was no possibility of systematically elaborating appropriate strategies in different situations'.[21] For MacCabe, Joyce's treatment of such imaginary identifications in Chapter 11 lends itself to a psychoanalytic and deconstructive reading, which in turn is clearly offered by MacCabe as a contribution to such a theory of nationalism. Neither these identifications, nor the methods of reading appropriate to their examination, operate in what might traditionally be understood as 'rational' ways. Nevertheless, MacCabe seeks to recoup their insights, in the last analysis, for the interests of rational politics: they cannot be displaced by a *merely* rationalistic discourse, he states, but they *ought* to be combatted by a more subtle understanding of their operations. This suggests that it would be both possible and desirable to dismantle them. MacCabe also repeatedly allies a Brechtian practice of 'insisting on the materiality of the vehicle',[22] in order to replace empathy by creative and transformative political practice, with a more recognizably Derridean stress on the materiality of language and on the arbitrary relationship between the differential processes of signification and the external world which it may seek to represent.

What MacCabe fails to emphasize, however, is that the Brechtian account of representation is unembarrassed in its claim to substitute a rational account of relations of power and material interests for ideological mystification. In this light, and in direct opposition to MacCabe's position, we could propose that the imaginary identifications of Irish nationalism in early twentieth-century Ireland may indeed *appear* to be entirely delusory *until* they are properly examined in the overall context of social relations at that time. In that context, anti-imperialist nationalism encompasses rational and progressive elements which may indeed find expression and meaning in identifications that carry other dubious ideological implications. Any emancipatory politics, as MacCabe points out, must address itself to these, and Marxism should indeed have learnt much from its historical failure to understand nationalism; but such identifications need not be understood wholly negatively. Indeed, no group is likely to engage in collective political practice in the absence of some sense of common identity. MacCabe's account of the importance of psychic reality in politics reveals itself here to be reliant on a simplistic notion of psychoanalysis, if it proposes that merely by understanding such identifications we can eliminate them from social life. MacCabe's attempt to produce Bloom as a subject already liberated from them – in the form of narrative relations among the drinkers – in Chapter 11 could be read as implying that the anti-nationalist Bloom enjoys a more developed understanding of the rational self-interest of the Irish people than do his fellows. But MacCabe's stirring call for systematic political strategies find as little specific grounding in Bloom as it apparently does in the depiction of the drinkers and singers.

'Emmet, and nationalism, wish to fix meanings and abolish writing' MacCabe concludes.[23] He states that Mr Bloom at the end of Chapter 11 'considers' Emmet's words. Although Bloom is described as seeing 'a gallant pictured hero' in Lionel Marks's window, the further remark 'Seabloom, greaseabloom viewed last words' (*U*, p. 238) certainly leaves open the possibility that Bloom actually *reads* these words, this unwriterly injunction, perhaps as a caption to the portrait. Emmet's words are usually regarded with great reverence in Ireland; 'the most memorable words ever uttered by an Irish man', according to Patrick Pearse.[24] Utterly unimpressed as Bloom may be, his fart is hardly issued in a spirit of carefree vulgar indifference. He is careful to release it discreetly, waiting until there is no-one behind him and he is safely covered by the noise of a passing tram. His fart is controlled and restrained, like Simon Dedalus' song and unlike Bloom's own earlier game with the elastic band: 'Tram Kran Kran Kran. Good oppor. Coming. Krandlkrankran. I'm sure it's the burgund. Yes. One, two' (*U*, p. 239). Bloom's eye uses the linear organization of Emmet's sentence to organize the retention and release of air from his bowels, precisely as he earlier employed the morning newspaper while on the toilet:

> Quietly he read, restraining himself, the first column, and yielding but resisting, began the second. Midway, his last resistance yielding, he allowed his bowels to ease themselves quietly as he read, reading still patiently, that slight constipation of yesterday quite gone. (*U*, p. 56)

'He allowed his bowels': nothing could be more distant from (say) Attridge's celebration of the loss of bodily unity and control. One may also be tempted to respond to MacCabe's comments on 'The Speech from the Dock' with an alternative articulation of its message. Emmet's last speech does not 'forbid writing', but rather it postpones it. His statement asserts that it would not yet be possible to write out the meaning of his death in the cause of the liberation of Ireland. A free Ireland alone could attest to the meaning of that action: the articulation of its significance could not precede the achievement of that liberation on a material level. It implies that writing about nationalism is by necessity deformed in contemporary conditions. The freedom to write, claimed by, for example, MacCabe for Bloom, is therefore premature. Neither is it achieved at the level of content: Bloom's letter, appropriately enough for a message produced by 'a pen that makes invisible marks' (Patrick MacGee) – clearly a state of the art instrument for New Men worried about the violence of inscription – does not actually get written or sent during the course of 'Sirens'.

THE NIGHTMARES OF HISTORY

In 'Tradition and the Individual Talent', T.S. Eliot recommends as appropriate for the creative writer a sense of history which

> involves the perception not only of the pastness of the past, but also of its presence; the historical sense compels a man to write not merely with his own generation in his bones, but with a feeling that the whole of the literature of Europe from Homer and within it the whole of the literature of his own country has a simultaneous existence and composes a simultaneous order.[25]

In Eliot's formulation, modernism is grasped as the effort to overcome cultural fragmentation and discontinuity, to remember the past and make it meaningful for the present. Joycean modernism, by contrast, is more usually understood as an attempt to escape from the past into a truly contemporary moment, by means of a wilful Nietzschean forgetting of history, a repudiation of the legacy of dead generations. As Joyce writes in an essay on James Clarence Mangan:

> No doubt they are only men of letters who insist on the succession of the ages, and history or the denial of reality, for they are two names for one thing, may be said to be that which deceives the whole world. (*CW*, p. 81)

The description of Stephen Dedalus's experiences as a teacher of history, and his forced endurance of the anecdotal ramblings of his employer Mr Deasy in Chapter 2 of *Ulysses*, are very often read as illustrating the need to break out of historical consciousness. As Stephen tells Deasy: 'History is the nightmare from which I am trying to awake' (*U*, p. 28). E.L. Epstein's judgement on the episode is exemplary: '"History" is the "art" of the "Nestor" chapter; Joyce's concern is to make it seem a false art, "the denial of reality".'[26] Therefore, the historical records which the boys are expected to memorize and which Stephen is charged with examining, and the boring and inaccurate tales of Deasy, who embodies – for Epstein – 'Irish historical memory' stand for: 'history in its most trivial aspects, as an academic subject based on the falsifying memory of the past, an avaricious gathering in of trifles, entirely missing the essence of the life of man through purblind probings into non-essentials'.[27]

In contrast, the artist Stephen appreciates 'the true static or hypostatic way to apprehend history'. He views history as 'visionary and graspable only by timeless moments of vision'; and this insight is conveyed principally through his characteristic mental act of 'hypostatisation of a process into an image . . . in a style that robs the expression of these timeless moments of the natural kinesis of language'.[28] This, in turn, can stand as an image of Joyce's anti-narrational practice of writing in general. History, as narrative, imposes crippling restrictions on the potential of language, just as the vulgarity of brute fact ousts historical possibility: 'Had Pyrrhus not fallen by a beldam's hand in Argos or Julius Caesar not been knifed to death. They are not to be thought away. Time has branded them and fettered they are lodged in the room of the infinite possibilities they have ousted' (*U*, p. 21). However, what cannot be *thought* away may, as Seamus Deane implies, be *written* away, once fiction has broken its hampering alliance with history, which is maintained through narrative. In its project to encompass and give expression to all the infinite, lost possibilities of language and history, therefore, it could also be argued that Joyce's writing abolishes history by destroying the *pastness* of the past. In 'Tradition and the Individual Talent', Eliot seems to suggest that the distance between the contemporary and the historical is obvious, and that it takes cultivation and imagination to appreciate tradition as a living force: in Ireland, as in Joyce's work, the reverse seems to be the case. In a situation of continuous political change and uncertainty, the effects of a violent history remain palpable. Joyce writes in his essay 'Ireland, Isle of Saints and Sages' of the 'long memory of the Irish citizen':

> He does not forget the sack of Drogheda and Waterford, nor the bands of men and women hunted down in the furthermost islands by the Puritan, who said that they would go 'into the ocean or into hell', nor the false oath that the English swore on the broken stone of Limerick. How could he forget? Can the back of the slave forget the rod? (*CW*, p. 168)

However, a colonized people does not suffer only from physical coercion. As Frantz Fanon describes: 'colonialism is not satisfied with holding a people in its grip and emptying the native's brain of all form and content. By a kind of perverted logic, it turns to the past of the oppressed people, and distorts, disfigures and destroys it'.[29] Paradoxically, then, Joyce's comments also provide a hint of exactly how 'the back of a slave' may forget the rod, when the head of the slave is emptied in this way: 'It is not hard to understand why the Irish citizen mingles the names of Cromwell and Satan when he curses', he remarks. In his head, the colonized subject has confounded an historical ill with an eternal and transcendent principle of evil. History is lent the force of myth, and the individual appears powerless, controlled by unseen forces forever beyond his or her agency. Decentered subjects, and the disavowal of linear narrative in the writing of ex-colonial modernists such as Joyce, signify something other than mere textual effects.[30]

T.S. Eliot's account presumes also the material availability of the documents of the cultural past. In Chapter 2 of *Ulysses*, however, Irish nationalism has more in common with an unofficial, popular and oral history than it does with an authoritative, institutionalized canonical history. The children are not obliged to recite or mechanically learn *Irish* history. The episode, in its dramatization both of the question of the physical survival of historical evidence, and of the power relations which impede Stephen in his dialogue with Deasy, mimes the production of this subversive, unwritten history as well as interrogating the authority of the existing historical record. In as much as Stephen's mental history tends towards anti-narratological modes, the episode also suggests sound historical and materialist reasons for this. Moreover, as I will demonstrate, by no means all of Stephen's reflections have the character of a static counterpoint to an external narrative. Commentators such as E.L. Epstein fall into the trap of failing to distinguish between a purely idealist conception of history and that attempt at a materialist history which, given that it must proceed in the absence of material evidence and in the interstices of a canonical history, can easily be mistaken for such an idealist mode.

This is illustrated by one of Stephen's first exchanges with Deasy:

> – You think me an old fogey and an old tory, his thoughtful voice said. I saw three generations since O'Connell's time. I remember the famine in '46. Do you know that the orange lodges agitated for repeal of the union twenty years before O'Connell did or before the prelates of your communion denounced him as a demagogue? You fenians forget some things.
>
> Glorious, pious, and immortal memory. The lodge of Diamond in Armagh the splendid behung with corpses of papishes. Hoarse, masked and armed, the planters' covenant. The black north and true blue Bible. Croppies lie down. (*U*, p. 26)

The series of phrases which comprises Stephen's unvoiced response to Deasy's defence of the political credentials of the Orange Order appears to take an anti-narratological form: Deasy's sentences are replaced by Stephen's scattered words and phrases. However, it also provides the context or sets the scene for Deasy's narrative: it serves to set Deasy's claim against the historical fact of the killing of Catholics in Ulster in the eighteenth century. Stephen, if anything, seems to protest against the violence which is occluded by Deasy's narrative account of history, rather than deem historical fact uninteresting or irrelevant. Deasy's history is, as commentators have pointed out, mostly incorrect, but this knowledge, as it is provided either by Stephen, or by external commentary, is clearly important in our interpretation of the episode.[31] Joseph A. Buttigieg, in his consideration of Joyce as Nietzschean artist, points out that such a figure does not 'entertain any illusions about the driving force which compels one to stand in opposition to history: it is will to power, and has nothing to do with "truth" and "justice"'. As Nietzsche states in *The Use and Abuse of History* :

> Man must bring the past to the bar of judgement, interrogate it remorselessly, and finally condemn it . . . . It is not justice that sits in judgement here, nor mercy that proclaims the verdict, but only life, the dim driving force that desires – itself.[32]

It is therefore significant that Stephen has recourse to all of these considerations during the course of 'Nestor'. He questions the children about Pyrrhus:

> – I forget the place, sir. 279 B.C.
> – Asculum, Stephen said, glancing at the name and date in the gorescarred book.
> – Yes, sir. And he said: *Another victory like that and we are done for.*
> That phrase the world had remembered. A dull ease of the mind. From a hill above a corpsestrewn plain a general speaking to his officers, leaned on his spear. Any general to any officers. They lend ear. (*U*, p. 20)

At one level, this seems to furnish a good example of Epstein's 'hypostatisation of a process into an image'. The repetition of 'any' suggests a bored dismissal of the significance of particular detail. However, in another sense, Stephen is *insisting* on detail, especially that of 'the corpsestrewn plain'. Again, it is the fact of bloodshed that anecdotal histories continuously gloss over: the syntax of universalization is employed because it is a general truth which is being elided.

Throughout the episode, the idea of a passage from 'kinesis' to 'stasis' is also contradicted by Stephen's attempt to lend to scenes and objects now silent and at rest a narrative of their production or history. He considers the Arabic numerals, with which the child struggles, in the context of their culture of origin:

> Across the page the symbols moved in grave morrice, in the mummery of their letters, wearing quaint caps of squares and cubes. Give hands, traverse, bow to partner: so: imps of fancy of the Moors. Gone too from the world, Averroes and Moses Maimonides, dark men in mien and movement, flashing in their mocking mirrors the obscure soul of the world, a darkness shining in brightness which brightness could not comprehend. (*U*, p. 23)

The elegant paintings of racehorses in Deasy's study also bely his memory of the dirt and noise of the racetrack: 'Where Cranly led me to get rich quick, hunting his winners among the mudsplashed brakes, amid the brawl of bookies on their pitches and reek of the canteen, over the motley slush' (*U*, p. 27). Stephen releases pictures and symbols from representations which occlude their real nature. In defiance of Deasy's anti-Semitism he remembers the Jewish people of Paris, recognizing in them the long memories and secret history of the suffering:

> On the steps of the Paris stock exchange the goldskinned men quoting prices on their gemmed fingers. Gabble of geese. They swarmed loud, uncouth, about the temple, their heads thickplotting under maladroit silk hats. Not theirs: these clothes, this speech, these gestures. Their full slow eyes belied the words, the gestures eager and unoffending, but knew the rancours massed about them and knew the zeal was vain . . . . Their eyes knew their years of wandering and, patient, knew the dishonours of their flesh. (*U*, p. 28)

As the shouts from the hockey pitch merge with the imagined sights and sounds of the battlefield, Stephen meditates: 'Time shocked rebounds, shock by shock. Jousts, slush and uproar of battles, the frozen deathspew of the slain, a shout of spearspikes baited with men's bloodied guts' (*U*, p. 27). This is a 'denarrativized' image, but also one which arrests time in order to disclose a significant parallel between two disparate phenomena. In this, Stephen acts in harmony with Walter Benjamin's description of a materialist history, one which alternatively narrativizes and then resists the onward flow of chronological time, in a significant constellation of disparate events:

> Universal history has no theoretical armature. Its method is additive; it musters a mass of data to fill the homogeneous, empty time. Materialistic historiography, on the other hand, is based on a constructive principle. Thinking involves not just a flow of thoughts, but their arrest as well. Where thinking suddenly stops in a configuration pregnant with tensions, it gives that configuration a shock, by which it crystallizes into a monad.[33]

Stephen's literalization or narrativization of the image of the 'nightmare' of history – 'What if that nightmare gave you a back kick?' (*U*, p. 28) – is typical of his strategies throughout the episode. 'All human history moves towards one great goal, the manifestation of God', Deasy announces to Stephen. To this he responds: 'That is God . . . . A shout in the street'. However, Stephen's remark does not denote a random, quotidian and contemporary reality, to which he intends to devote his art in the place of 'History'. Rather, in context, it has a precise referent: it is the shout of the winning hockey team. Official history, he asserts, is merely the uproar of the victorious.

These principles also govern Stephen's reflections in Chapter 3 ('Proteus'). During this episode he wanders along Sandymount Strand, where the city of Dublin meets the sea with a fraying of its edges and a display of its refuse: 'Heavy of the past' (*U*, p. 37). Here, he ponders, all things might yield up their stories to him, if it were not for the fact of their decay and loss of definition through time: 'These heavy sands are language tide and wind have silted here' (*U*, p. 37). Instead, he imagines the various scenes of invasion and violence which the place has witnessed. He believes himself to be involved in the history of his ancestors not merely imaginatively, but, as we have seen in *A Portrait of the Artist*, quasi-materially, by means of his blood-inheritance: 'Then from the starving cagework city a horde of jerkined dwarfs, my people, with flayers' knives, running, scaling, hacking in green blubbery whalemeat. Famine, plague and slaughters. Their blood is in me, their lusts my waves' (*U*, p. 38). He also recalls a more recent memory of hunger, when in a frenzy of impatience he fantasized about murdering an obstructive official in Paris:

> Forget: a dispossessed. With mother's money order, eight shillings, the banging door of the post office slammed in your face by the usher. Hunger toothache. *Encore deux minutes*. Look clock. Must get. *Fermé*. Hired dog! Shoot him to bloody bits with a bang shotgun, bits man spattered walls all brass buttons. (*U*, p. 35)

But in this case the violence committed was imagined, so the dismembered man can be reassembled: 'Bits all khrrrrklak in place clack back. Not hurt? O, that's all right. Shake hands'.

Such an association between symbolic and physical violence, however, is foregrounded in Chapter 9 ('Scylla and Charybidis'). Here, the possibility of the aesthetic transcendence of the violence of history is specifically thematized and interrogated at the level of content. An implicit comparison is drawn between Stephen Dedalus and Shakespeare, in an investigation of the historical conditions which facilitate such a transcendence.

In Chapter 9, the absurd Mr Best, safe in his library cell, is free to dwell on all the lost possibilities of history: 'Here he ponders things that were not: what Caesar would have lived to do had he believed the soothsayer: what might have been: possibilities of the possible as possible: things not known: what name Achilles bore when he lived among women' (*U*, p. 159).

In this episode, Stephen relentlessly and aggressively challenges this fantasy of freedom, as he interrupts the gentlemany literary discussion which proceeds in the National Library under the benign adjudication of the Quaker librarian. When he has finished, the latter even-handedly offers the discussion over to Stephen's rival Mulligan:

> – Yes, indeed, the quaker librarian said. A most instructive

> discussion. Mr Mulligan, I'll be bound, has his theory too of the play and of Shakespeare. All sides of life should be represented.
> He smiled on all sides equally. (*U*, p. 162–3)

Stephen is conscious, as he delivers his theory concerning *Hamlet* and Shakespeare's biography, of this lecture as performance, as a forceful disruption of the habitual chat of this group of interlocutors who, as Mr Best reveals, do not really 'care a button about who is killed or is guilty' (*U*, p. 159). Stephen attempts to draw them into his plot: 'begging with a swift glance their hearing . . . Make them accomplices (*U*, p. 154) . . . . They list. And in the porches of their ears I pour (*U*, p. 161). Colin MacCabe notes not merely this aggression, but that Stephen is fixed in 'a posture of aggression'.[34] Dedalus must disavow the style he adopts here, MacCabe argues, if he is to become a Joycean artist, as:

> It is by repressing his desire to speak a truth so final that it will freeze speaker and audience in their place that Stephen can prepare the way for a writing which will promote amicability in the multitudinous possibilities that it opens up.[35]

However, it must also be noted that Stephen is speaking in a community which already considers itself to have established such a friendly, liberal interchange of ideas. His highly reductive reading of Shakespeare's text as simply continuous with the jingoism of Kipling, and nineteenth-century British imperialism in general –

> Not for nothing was he a butcher's son, wielding the sledded poleaxe and spitting in his palms. Nine lives are taken off for his father's one. Our Father who art in purgatory. Khaki Hamlets don't hesitate to shoot. The bloodboltered shambles in act five is a forecast of the concentration camp sung by Mr Swinburne. (*U*, p. 154)

– is interesting only as a response to the extraordinarily idealistic notions of art which are current in this circle. As Joyce's AE (George Russell) comments: 'Art has to reveal to us ideas, formless spiritual essences. The supreme question about a work of art is out of how deep a life does it spring' (*U*, p. 152). The introduction of Russell is not, of course, accidental. Many of the leading figures of the Irish Literary Revival – Hyde, Gregory, Synge, George Moore, James Stephens, Yeats – are mentioned, and John Eglinton (Magee) participates in the discussion. The interplay between tolerance and aggression is already given a precise cultural context in this episode, which is that of the Revival and its relation to the English literary tradition. What Mulligan recommends to Stephen as 'the Yeats touch' (*U*, p. 178) is specifically rejected by him. Such a diplomatic tolerance overlooks the violence on which the literary tradition, which the revivalists aspire to emulate, is founded, and induces passivity. Joyce quotes ironically from a play by AE:

> *What of all the will to do?*
> *It has vanished long ago* . . . (*U*, p. 169)

They also, of course, neglect to mention Stephen as the possible creator of a figure to set beside 'the Saxon Shakespeare's Hamlet':

> Our national epic has yet to be written, Dr Sigerson says. Moore is the man for it. A knight of the rueful countenance here in Dublin. With a saffron kilt? O'Neill Russell? O yes, he must speak the grand old tongue. And his Dulcinea? James Stephens is doing some clever sketches. We are becoming important, it seems. (*U*, p. 158)

Stephen's colleagues lovingly accept a Romantic account of Hamlet's loss of 'the will to do', which the librarian introduces by a reference to Goethe's description in *Wilhelm Meister's Apprenticeship*: 'A hesitating soul taking arms against a sea of troubles, torn by conflicting doubts, as one sees in real life . . . . The beautiful ineffectual dreamer who comes to grief against hard facts' (*U*, p. 151).[36] As Gifford and Seidman point out, Matthew Arnold also borrows Goethe's description of the 'beautiful and ineffectual dreamer' for his portrait of Shelley as 'a beautiful and ineffectual angel', fluttering his wings helplessly against the cruel world.[37] Its citation here, then, involves a subtle reference to the critic who so famously defined the Celtic temperament, in its perpetual revolt against fact and its hopeless sentimentalism, definitions which proved so ideologically productive for Yeats and the Revival.[38] This vision of the dreamer artist, Hamlet as Celt, is assailed by Stephen, even in his accumulation of such apparently innocuous details as the house Shakespeare owned in Ireland yard (*U*, p. 167) and that 'he drew a salary equal to that of the lord chancellor of Ireland' (*U*, p. 165).

Mark Schechner describes the nature of Stephen's attraction to the figure of Shakespeare:

> It is a tale of two Shakespeares: one a middle-class actor and playwright whose plays bear the imprint of family intrigue, and the other a metaphysical deity who is transcendent, autonomous, fatherly and yet bisexual . . . . Stephen has constructed a dialectic of creativity that transforms Shakespeare *immanent* (in and of the family) into Shakespeare *transcendent* (a family unto himself) . . . . Stephen, it seems, aspires not to the condition of real doing but to the Shakespearean condition of symbolic doing. His con-

> scious identification is not with the man of action but with the master of symbolic creation.[39]

Stephen appreciates not merely the discontinuity between these two things, but also their interplay. Life and art appear, if anything, too close for comfort, rather than art representing the complete transformation and reworking of the former: 'His life was rich. His art, more than the art of feudalism as Walt Whitman called it, is the art of surfeit' (*U*, p. 165).

Stratford and London are the places associated, in Stephen's account of Shakespeare, with wounding and its compensation respectively. He illustrates the distance between these two English towns by a comparison between the two cities he himself knows best:

> What is a ghost? . . . . One who has faded into impalpability through death, through absence, through change of manners. Elizabethan London lay as far from Stratford as corrupt Paris lies from virgin Dublin. Who is the ghost from *limbo patrum*, returning to the world that has forgotten him? (*U*, p. 154)

The returning ghost is a figure representing the mature Joyce as much as the young Stephen, who is already in possession of a few Parisian airs, thanks to his brief flight. However, Shakepeare's passage between these two poles of this creative life is easy. His experience is quite unlike that of a modern exile:

> He carried a memory in his pocket as he trudged to Romeville whistling *The Girl I left behind Me*. (*U*, p. 156–7)

> He returns after a life of absence to that spot of earth where he was born, where he has always been, man and boy, a silent witness and there, his journey of life ended, he plants his mulberrytree in the earth. Then dies. (*U*, p. 175)

Shakespeare succeeded in compensating in art for his seduction and betrayal by his wife because he 'found in the world without as actual what was in his world within as possible' (*U*, p. 175). But this was a matter of historical good luck – 'All events brought grist to his mill' (*U*, p. 168) – and enterprise. Stephen charges:

> rich country gentleman . . . a capitalist shareholder, a bill promoter, a tithefarmer (*U*, p. 167). The son of a maltjobber and moneylender he was himself a cornjobber and moneylender, with ten tods of corn hoarded in the famine riots . . . . Shylock chimes with the jewbaiting that followed the hanging and quartering of the queen's leech Lopez, his jew's heart being plucked forth while the sheeny was yet alive: *Hamlet* and *Macbeth* with the coming to

> the throne of a Scotch philosophaster with a turn for witch-roasting. The lost armada is his jeer in *Love's Labour Lost*. His pageants, the histories, sail fullbellied on a tide of Mafeking enthusiasm . . . . The *Sea Venture* comes home from Bermudas and the play Renan admired is written with Patsy Caliban, our American cousin (p. 168) If you like the epilogue look long on it: prosperous Prospero, the good man rewarded, Lizzie, grandpa's lump of love, and nuncle Richie, the bad man taken off by poetic justice to the place where the bad niggers go. (p. 175)

Shakespeare is accused, at the least, of benefiting from the spoils of Elizabethan imperial adventuring and the spirit of English nationalism, pandering to anti-Semitism and the persecution of women, failing to help the starving, and even more precisely, complicity in the colonial authority represented by Prospero in *The Tempest* over 'Patsy Caliban', the name combining that of the Irishman as imbecile and that of colonized savage. This, Stephen alleges, is also the play admired so greatly by Ernest Renan, the critic from whom Arnold largely derived his neo-colonial Celticism. These are the preconditions for Shakespeare's art. By contrast Stephen, in their absence, is doomed never to 'find in the world without as actual what was in the world within as possible'.

None the less, as Schechner observes, the example of Shakespeare as an artistic precursor who succeeded absolutely in aesthetic self-creation persists. The playwright 'was and felt himself the father of all his race, the father of his own grandfather, the father of his unborn grandson, who by the same token, never was born, for nature, as Mr Magee understands her, abhors perfection' (*U*, p. 171). Dedalus, in his struggle to wake up from his historical nightmare, needs and desires such an exemplar. Stephen's apparently triumphant articulation of this ambition occurs also in this episode:

> – As we, or mother Dana, weave and unweave our bodies, Stephen said, from day to day, their molecules shuttled to and fro, so does the artist weave and unweave his image. And as the mole on my right breast is where it was when I was born, though all my body has been woven of new stuff time after time, so through the ghost of the unquiet father the image of the unliving son looks forth. In the intense instant of imagination, when the mind, Shelley says, is a fading coal, that which I was is and that which I am and that which in possibility I may come to be. So in the future, the sister of the past, I may see myself as I sit here now, but by reflection from that which then I shall be. (*U*, p. 159–60)

But here this promise of autonomous self-creation is based on an analogy with the perpetual recreation of the human body by nature, through time. As mother Dana (an ancient Irish goddess) weaves and unweaves the body, she grants to the self continuity in history. However, as physical recreation, or material subsistence, is necessarily exhaustible and finite, the body, as in Yeats's image of the 'dying animal', more conventionally stands as the very antithesis of art. The realm of the aesthetic, in contrast to the world of nature, offers the prospect of a leap out of history, an escape from mortality. In his description of transcendence, Stephen has recourse to the most precarious, organic and maternal of guarantees. An equivalent disjunction is apparent in the second analogy he draws. The poet achieves his triumphant conquest over the tyranny of history in 'the intense instant of imagination'. However, rather than this being presented as a victory for the self-fathering artist, it is the precise moment both of his capture by the ghosts of the past, his 'unquiet fathers', and the moment of his death, as 'unliving son'. The moment of escape is the same as the moment of surrender to the maternal principle of life and death, and to the father's demand for death in life. The effort to escape history and abolish narrative in a vision of supra-historical dialogue and interconnection finally succumbs to a recognition of the most final and inarguable narrative closure of all.

THE LIVING DEAD

Many critics have remarked that in *Ulysses* Joyce presents us with an image of a city in which not much happens or is likely to happen, apparently oblivious to the fact that 'these same streets were to become the scene of fierce revolution within little more than a decade'.[40] Such judgements as Franco Moretti's that 'the status of history in *Ulysses* is intrinsically rather low'[41] are more usually founded on those episodes which centrally feature Leopold Bloom, rather than on the speculations of Stephen Dedalus. In particular, such readings tend to focus on Chapter 8 ('Lestrygonians') and on the image there of Bloom as a version of the modernist *flâneur*, an advertising agent moving through the streets of Dublin, a desacralized and endlessly distracting urban space. Stephen, even if only as intellectual, remains in contact with different and historically prior conceptions of space. This divergence is dramatised by their contrasting meditations on repetition and simultaneity. For Stephen, repetition can still evoke communion and sacredness. In Chapter 3, for example, he reflects on the fact that at any given time several celebrations of the Mass are likely to be proceeding in churches very close to each other:

> And at the same instant perhaps a priest round the corner is

> elevating it. Dringdring! And two streets off another locking it into a pyx. Dringadring! And in a ladychapel another taking housel all to his own cheek. Dringdring! Down, up, forward, back. Dan Occam thought of that, invincible doctor . . . . Bringing his host down and kneeling he heard twine with his second bell the first bell in the transept (he is lifting his) and, rising, heard (now I am lifting) their two bells (he is kneeling) twang in diphthong. (*U*, p. 33–4)

What Stephen apprehends as ritual, Bloom wearily perceives as meaningless proliferation: 'Funerals all over the world everywhere every minute. Shovelling them under by the cartload doublequick. Thousands every hour. Too many in the world' (*U*, p. 83).

In Chapter 7 ('Aeolus') repetition and apparently infinite production come dramatically to the fore at the level of content. The processes of modern industry and printing, which constantly threaten the observer with the possibility of endless repetition – 'Now if he got paralysed there and no-one knew how to stop them they'd clank on and on the same, print it over and over and up and back' (*U*, p. 98) are depicted through the medium of a language which also displays the first spectacular evidence of the syntactical and typographical experiments which eventually come to predominate in *Ulysses* as a whole: 'Grossbooted draymen rolled barrels dullthudding out of Prince's stores and bumped them up on the brewery float. On the brewery float bumped dullthudding barrels rolled by grossbooted draymen out of Prince's stores' (*U*, p. 96). It is significant to note that mechanical reproduction enters the text simultaneously at the levels of content and language. However, either mechanical or organic images can be employed to describe the perpetual circulation of the various elements of urban life – trams, sacks of letters, barrels of Guinness, people – and Bloom uses both during his reflections in Chapter 8: 'And we stuffing food in one hole and out behind: food, chyle, blood, dung, earth, food: have to feed it like stoking an engine' (*U*, p. 144). Bloom's vision of repetition within a closed system, in which nothing can substantially change, achieves its most pessimistic formulation in his conclusive summary of life in the city:

> Things go on same, day after day: squads of police marching out, back: trams in, out. Those two loonies mooching about. Dignam carted off. Mina Purefoy swollen belly on a bed groaning to have a child tugged out of her. One born every second somewhere. Other dying every second . . . . Cityful passing away, other cityful coming, passing away too: other coming on, passing on. (*U*, pp. 134–5)

Bloom's remarks can persuasively be read as also offering themselves as a resumé of *Ulysses* as a whole. As Daniel Moshenberg comments: 'Thus, though much happens, not much changes or is changed. Even the few changes of the human population that do occur have a kind of equalising content; one birth, one death, the accounts of humankind remain balanced'.[42] It is, however, this conclusion which I seek here to challenge. Although Joyce's text does significantly register the advent of mechanical reproduction in the modern city, this is largely mediated through the consciousness of a figure (Bloom) who compulsively generalizes his own specific condition to a pervasive mechanization of social experience as such.

Homer's Lestrygonians are cannibals, but they are represented here for Bloom simply by carnivores, and indeed eaters of all kind. He observes a great deal of food and consumption in this episode simply because he is so hungry: 'The heavy noonreek tickled the top of Mr Bloom's gullet (*U*, p. 129) .... Pungent mockturtle oxtail mulligatawny. I'm hungry too (*U*, p. 130) .... Hope they have liver and bacon today' (*U*, p. 135). It is his own appetite, then, which inspires this appalling vision of endless gluttony and savagery. Bloom, however, decides not to gratify his carnivorous desires at lunchtime. He is so sickened by the sight of the lunchtime diners in Burton's restaurant that he retires to the pub for a quiet sandwich instead:

> Smells of men. Spaton sawdust, sweetish warmish cigarette smoke, reek of plug, spilt beer, men's beery piss, the stale of ferment.
>
> His gorge rose.
>
> Couldn't eat a morsel here. Fellow sharpening knife and fork to eat all before him, old chap picking his tootles. Slight spasm, full, chewing the cud .... Scoffing up stewgravy with sopping sippets of bread. Lick it off the plate, man! Get out of this. (*U*, p. 139)

'Eat or be eaten. Kill! Kill!': this is Bloom's judgement on the spectacle of this greed. Earlier in the day, during the 'Hades' episode, Bloom announced his philosophy of 'Let the dead bury the dead', and affirmed vitality in the midst of morbid depression: 'In the midst of death we are in life. Both ends meet. Tantalising for the poor dead. Smell of grilled beefsteaks to the starving' (*U*, p. 89). The earlier episode appeared to conclude with Bloom's embrace of human fellowship and closeness: 'Plenty to see and hear and feel yet. Feel live warm beings near you. Let them sleep in their maggoty beds. They are not going to get me this innings. Warm beds: warm, fullblooded life' (*U*, p. 94). However, in the face of actually existing human community and warm human bodies, this robust common man proves unable to imagine, for example, communal eating outside an economy of greed and selfishness:

> Suppose that communal kitchen years to come perhaps . . . . Devour contents in the street . . . . All for number one. Children fighting for the scrapings of the pot. Want a souppot big as the Phoenix Park. Harpooning flitches and hindquarters out of it. Hate people all around you. (*U*, pp. 139–40)[43]

He represents the citizens of Dublin both as savagely appetitive and, because of the circularity and ultimate futility of the 'peristaltic' processes in which they are engaged, materially insubstantial and ghostly. In short, whereas in 'Hades' he speculated that the dead are jealous of and taunted by the the living, he here presents the living as ghosts, and charges the hungry with gluttony: 'Hot fresh blood they prescribe for decline. Blood always needed. Lick it up smoking hot, thick sugary. Famished ghosts' (*U*, p. 140).

Significant dissonances begin to emerge in the representation of Bloom. He appears in *Ulysses* both as life-affirming *homme moyen sensuel*, contentedly fleshy and lustful, and as extraordinarily squeamish and reserved in his negotiations with actual human bodies. This contradiction enables us to call into question the picture he paints of the citizens of Dublin, in which they appear as versions of Pound's 'impotent, impetuous dead', perpetually demanding their libation of blood, but never managing to escape from the monotonous, infernal round of life in death. In 'Lestrygonians' Bloom views the human body as a consumption-machine. At an earlier point in the text this carries comic and demystifying implications in its refusal of sombre religiosity, but seems here increasingly the mark of an alienated vision. Society presents itself to him merely as a panorama of blood-lust and natural appetite: the modern world is grasped as a post-historical era, inhabited only by living dead, whose very possession of human instincts is horrifying.

This ghostliness is symbolized and given a precise political context by Bloom's sighting of John Howard Parnell, the great man's brother, a less vivid version of the lost leader: 'Image of him. Haunting face . . . . Look at the woebegone walk of him. Eaten a bad egg. Poached eyes on ghost' (*U*, p. 135). Parnell, as we have seen in 'Hades', had quickly become the focus of the Messianic hopes of his disappointed supporters. As the mourners pay their respects at the grave of 'The Chief' in Glasnevin, Mr Power reports: '– Some say he is not in that grave at all. That the coffin was filled with stones. That one day he will come again' (*U*, p. 93). In Bloom's remembered or quoted version of Simon Dedalus's Parnellism, it appears as an even more futile Utopianism – a hope not just that Parnell never really died, but that he might be resurrected: Simon Dedalus said when they put him [i.e. David Sheehy] in parliament that Parnell would come back from the grave and lead him out of the House of Commons by the hand' (*U*, p. 135). So these ghostly citizens await a suitably phantasmal deliverance. The episode is scattered with promises of 'great times coming' (*U*, p. 134), although these are merely quotations. The prospect of better times is degraded to the level of an advertising jingle: 'Elijah is coming. Dr John Alexander Dowie restorer of the church in Zion is coming. Is coming! Is coming!! Is coming!!!' (*U*, p. 124). Even when such expressions of Utopian longing do not reach Bloom in this degraded form, it is consistently the medium into which he translates them. In the newspaper office, for example, Bloom notes the resemblance between the backwards letters manipulated by the typesetter and the Hebrew script he remembers his father reading at Passover. At first glance, this might seem an act of discerning a meaningful history within the alienated modern language of the machine. He recalls the chant:

> All that long business about that brought us out of the land of Egypt and into the house of bondage *alleluia* . . . . And the angel of death kills the butcher and he kills the ox and the dog kills the cat. Sounds a bit silly until you come to look into it well. Justice it means but it's everyone killing everyone else. That's what life is after all. (*U*, p. 101)

Gifford and Seidman gloss this as a rendition of the cumulative chants of the *Chad Gadya*, which includes the lines:

> And the Holy One, blessed is He, came and killed the Angel of Death that slew the slaughterer and slaughtered the ox that drank the water that quenched the fire that burned the stick that beat the dog that bit the cat that ate the kid that father bought for two zizium. One kid, one kid.[44]

They also refer to one account of the traditional interpretation of this chant:

> The history of successive empires that devastate and swallow one another (Egypt, Assyria, Babylon, Persia, etc.) The kid, bottom-most and most injured of all is, of course, the people of Israel. The killing of the Angel of Death marks the day when the kingdom of the Almighty will be established on earth; then, too, Israel will live in perfect redemption in the promised land.[45]

Everything preys on and devours that which is smaller than itself, the prayer declares, but the most vulnerable and long-suffering of all will finally be elevated and redeemed. Bloom, however, interprets this merely as a description of the *lex talonis*, the law of 'an eye for an eye', or as he puts it 'everyone killing everyone else'. He negates the promise of liberation by his significant verbal slip, his repetition of 'bondage'.

To the extent, then, that Bloom's flawed and homogenizing historical memory eradicates from the history of the Jewish people the promise of a better future, it also proves insensitive to the similar messianic hopes of the Irish in the aftermath of Parnell. In this, Joyce is attentive to the loss of aura or charisma in both the modern world in general, and early twentieth-century Ireland in particular; but the fact that this secularisation is largely registered through Bloom highlights its source in a particular history, and dramatises its links with that uncritical acceptance of the discourse of modernity which he represents.

3

'TALKING ABOUT INJUSTICE'[1]

Parody, satire and invective in *Ulysses*

PREFACE: LANGUAGE AND COMMUNITY

Raymond Williams observes the paradox that Joyce's discovery in *Ulysses* of 'an ordinary language, heard more clearly than anywhere in the realist novel before it', co-exists with Joyce's apparent rejection of the possibility of any actually existing society providing an image of authentic community. In Williams's view, any community represented in the text is instead dismissed by Joyce as 'ephemeral, superficial, or at best contingent and secondary'. *Ulysses*, Williams argues, is the story of three forms of consciousness, Molly, Stephen and Bloom, who are related to each other most fully only at an abstract and symbolic level: 'no longer a place and time, for all the anxious dating of that day in Dublin'. He concludes that, for Joyce, the 'only knowable community is in the need, the desire, of the racing and separated forms of consciousness'.[2] But when Joyce comments that *Ulysses* is about the last great *talkers*, he may not be referring to Bloom or Stephen. The principle of linguistic extravagance in performance is not embodied primarily by the central figures, and the 'ordinary language' represented in the text is not primarily or exclusively the property of its heroes.

Williams's point of departure in his discussion of *Ulysses* is the moment early in the morning when Bloom greets Larry O'Rourke outside his pub. Bloom plans to exchange a few remarks with his neighbour: 'Stop and say a word: about the funeral perhaps. Sad thing about poor Dignam, Mr O'Rourke' (*U*, p. 47). By contrast, as Williams describes, 'what he actually says when he reaches O'Rourke is flat and external'. However, he does not mention that Bloom's planned conversational opening is itself banal compared to the memory of Simon Dedalus's imitation of O'Rourke, which briefly flashes through Bloom's mind: 'Simon Dedalus takes him off to a tee with his eyes screwed up. Do you know what I'm going to tell you? What's that, Mr O'Rourke? Do you know what? The Russians, they'd only be an eight o'clock breakfast for the Japanese'. Dedalus's response to O'Rourke is, in its parody of the man's speaking style, somewhat hostile: Bloom's civil greeting is friendly but much less vivid. Dedalus makes fun of the publican by imitating his manner of speech, for, we presume, the amusement of a later audience which included Bloom. This small detail, then, does indeed evoke a notion of community, one which is bound together in acquaintance and even in intimacy, but not, invariably, affection. In the Dublin of *Ulysses*, everyone is vulnerable to the imitations of Simon Dedalus, to the circulation of jokes at their expense, just as in *Ulysses* all styles are vulnerable to Joyce's imitative facility and stylistic 'sandblasting'. Simon Dedalus's small performance, a manifestation of a kind of community which Williams does not address, is in this sense a story about style.

This disjunction between Bloom's speech and the speech of the citizens of Dublin in general is central to Hugh Kenner's argument in *Dublin's Joyce*. Here, Kenner asserts: 'Since the eighteenth century it has been a city of the dead, a person set down in Dublin might reflect'.[3] Kenner presumes, in short, that the sole golden age of community glimpsed in Joyce's novel is the world of Dublin in the heyday of Ascendancy culture, when the great men of the independent Irish Parliament (abolished by the Act of Union in 1800) were responsible for the production of a public language of unsurpassed eloquence and power. This is the epoch which is indeed invoked so nostalgically by the modern-day lawyers and journalists who converse in the offices of the *Freeman's Journal* in Chapter 7 of *Ulysses*:

> Where have you a man now at the bar like those fellows, like Whiteside, like Isaac Butt, like silvertongued O'Hagan . . . . Grattan and Flood wrote for this very paper, the editor cried in his face. Irish volunteers. Where are you now? Established 1763. Dr Lucas. Who have you now like John Philpot Curran? Psha! (*U*, pp. 113–14)

For Kenner, the interesting features of the Dublin speech audible in *Ulysses* – and on the streets of Dublin today, so he implausibly suggests – are merely fossilised remnants of the glories of this past age, suggestive reminders of an extraordinary culture which are now hopelessly anachronistic and disabling. Bloom, whose head, as Kenner observes, is stuffed with jargon and clichés, none the less represents 'the voice of the future' in a wholly positive way.

In this chapter, however, I hope further to distinguish between the language of the people in the newspaper office – a group which formed the natural constituency of the Irish Parliamentary Party in the wake of the Parnell split, and the inheritors of the constitutional tradition in Irish nationalism – and other features of demotic speech in *Ulysses*, as they are displayed particularly by the nationalists who attack Leopold

Bloom in Barney Kiernan's pub. Chapter 12 ('Cyclops') is central to this argument because it is there that Bloom's speech is in most blatant contrast to that of his fellow citizens. There, those features of the language of the community – relentless inquisitiveness, energetic parody and invective – which are in evidence throughout, are most pronounced. They are also given explicit political overtones. 'Politics' is described as the 'Art' of the episode in Joyce's schemata, and the portrayal of the citizen is based on the figure of Michael Cusack, founder of the Gaelic Athletic Association and member of the Irish Republican Brotherhood. The latter underground organization was heir to the Fenian tradition of militant, separatist Irish nationalism, and secretly plotted the Rebellion of 1916. Clearly, there is some continuity between the world of the *Freeman's Journal* – the paper which the citizen calls contemptuously by its popular name 'The old woman of Prince's Street' and further attacks as 'the subsidised organ' (*U*, p. 245) – and the world of Barney Kiernan's pub. Several individuals apart from Bloom feature in both episodes, including J.J. O'Molloy and Ned Lambert. However, I consider that critics of 'Cyclops' have repeatedly neglected the central importance of the citizen's rejection of the politics of the newspaper room, in its allegiance to what he calls 'the pledgebound party on the floor of the House'. The drinkers in Kiernan's pub, in their discussion of related political issues are usually understood, in Hugh Kenner's words, as 'vulgarising'[4] these themes: I hope to demonstrate that they can also be interpreted as *radicalizing* them. On the basis of a re-examination of this episode we can attend to Joyce's dramatization of ideas of 'dialogue', argument and community which are both central to any account of the public world depicted in *Ulysses*, and clearly important to the text's account of Irish nationalism. It may remain difficult to abstract, in Williams's terms, an image of a knowable human community from the novel, but in the light of my reading we may at least be in a position to interrogate more fully what is at stake if it is allowed that Bloom represents 'the voice of the future', in specific opposition to an actually existing community, and also to describe those elements in the representation of the present which point towards the possibility of the future creation of such an authentic community. Otherwise this lingers merely in the form of a nostalgic memory of a past which is forever lost, or else, as Joyce writes of Bloom's meditations in 'Ithaca', an unattainable Utopia, 'there being no known method from the known to the unknown' (*U*, p. 575).

Fredric Jameson describes how the gossip and rumour of the community in *Ulysses*'s Dublin provides the 'close oral daily history' by means of which that community defines itself and the dimensions of the city are maintained within humane limits: for him too, the kind of community at stake is by definition both intimate and positive.[5]

But it is also arguable that by its very nature gossip is aggressive as well as bonding, its promise being to tell its audience something about another person which they would not reveal themselves. Rumour may be scurrilous in content, but gossip always is. One of the first acts of gossip represented in *Ulysses* illustrates this fact, as Nosey Flynn reports to Davy Byrne that Bloom is a member of the Freemasons:

> – He's in the craft, he said.
> – Do you tell me so? Davy Byrne said.
> – Very much so, Nosey Flynn said. Ancient free and accepted order. He's an excellent brother. Light, life and love, by God. They give him a leg up. I was told that by a – well, I won't say who. (*U*, p. 145)

We also glimpse the conventions which govern the circulation of gossip in Chapter 6. On the way to Paddy Dignam's funeral, Bloom begins to retell the story of Reuben J. Dodd and his son, but manages by his poor style of narration to hopelessly confuse Simon Dedalus, the only member of the audience who does not know what happened. Eventually Martin Cunningham aggressively intervenes to silence Bloom, and takes over the storytelling. His success is a matter of style and vocabulary as well as narrative coherence, as we can see by comparing Bloom's introduction to the story with Cunningham's:

> – That's an awfully good one that's going the rounds about Reuben J. and the son . . . .
> – There was a girl in the case, Mr Bloom began, and he determined to send him to the Isle of Man out of harm's way but when they were both . . . .
> Martin Cunningham thwarted his speech rudely.
> – Reuben J. and the son were piking it down by the quay next the river on their way to the Isle of Man boat and the young chiseller suddenly got loose and over the wall with him into the Liffey. (*U*, p. 78)

Cunningham's local inflections and his colloquial vocabulary and turns of phrase distinguish him clearly from Bloom. In spite of his 'rudeness' to Bloom here, the positive side of his conversational prowess is also revealed when the talk turns to suicide and he intervenes to protect Bloom's feelings, knowing him to be the son of a man who killed himself. In fact, in spite of his initial offence to Bloom, the latter describes Cunningham a moment later as having 'Always a good word to say'. Shari Benstock glosses this exchange in the funeral car with an account of how this anecdotal, performative style of conversation contrasts with our usual understanding of social talk and gossip:

> Although narrative art shares with everyday speech this impetus to thrust the speaker into the social community, to count himself present by drawing attention to himself and differentiating himself from the group, storytelling is distinguished from the give-and-take of conversation by its endeavour to halt dialectic and impose monologue . . . . Against the capricious drift of conversation, the teller's voice compels his audience to be silent, presumably allowing intrusion upon the established frame of the narrative only when its suits his purposes . . . it intrudes upon the social context and strives towards completion against the ever-present knowledge that at any moment it may be interrupted, distracted, silenced, or in some way prevented from continuing.[6]

This style of social interaction is also evident in the course of the conversation in the newspaper office, in Lenehan's repeated attempts to tell his riddle about *The Rose of Castille* and in Bloom's ineffectual attempts to win the attention of the editor to discuss his advertisement. It is particularly apparent in the tolerance displayed by all the men for Professor MacHugh's long formal speeches on history and law, culture and language. Even Stephen is moved to blush, 'his blood wooed by grace of language and expression' (*U*, p. 115). In his enjoyment of this rapt audience, MacHugh is understood to belong to a long oratorical tradition in Irish culture and politics. He is compared by Stephen to Daniel O'Connell, of whom Stephen reflects: 'Hosts at Mullaghmast and Tara of the kings. Miles of ears of porches. The tribune's words, howled and scattered to the four winds. A people sheltered within his voice' (*U*, p. 118). O'Connell's campaign for Catholic Emancipation in the early nineteenth century is often cited as the first significant mass political mobilisation of the Irish peasantry in a recognisably 'nationalist' movement. Like so much of Irish history, as Stephen has recognised early in the text, this campaign, which preceded the age of mass literacy in Ireland, left little material record or written evidence: 'Dead noise. Akasic records of all that ever anywhere wherever was'. It points to the limitations of a purely oratorical politics in the modern world. Ironically, MacHugh adopts this high public style in order to deliver a warning to the Irish people to *overcome* their obsession with language, and in particular the powerful rhetoric of Empire: 'We mustn't be led away by words, by sounds of words. We think of Rome, imperial, imperious, imperative' (*U*, p. 108). The Irish, MacHugh seems to say, must reject oratorical splendour, just as Moses, as reported here in a speech by John Taylor on the revival of the Irish language which MacHugh repeats, closed his ears to the eloquence of his Egyptian masters who asked:

> *Why will you jews not accept our culture, our religion and our language? . . . .*

> *You have no cities nor no wealth: our cities are hives of humanity and our galleys, trireme and quadrireme, laden with all manner of merchandise furrow the waters of the known globe. You have but emerged from primitive conditions: we have a literature, a priesthood, an agelong history and a polity.* (*U*, p. 117)

However, in spite of this caution, MacHugh actually depicts the Irish as continuously prone to being led astray by words. It is a stereotypically Irish failing evinced even by his own extreme sensitivity to language, and which is also associated with his recognizably Celticist stress on the spirituality and the nobility of the Irish race in contrast to the philistinism of the English. This is an opposition equivalent to that between the doomed ethereal glory of Greek civilization and the militaristic Roman one which replaced it, a tragic history encapsulated for MacHugh in a comparison between the words *Kyrios* and *Domine*:

> Success for us is the death of the intellect and of the imagination. We were never loyal to the successful . . . . I speak the tongue of a race the acme of whose mentality is the maxim: time is money. Material domination. *Domine*! Lord! Where is the spirituality? Lord Jesus? Lord Salisbury? A sofa in a west end club . . . . We are liege subjects of the catholic chivalry of Europe that foundered at Trafalgar and of the empire of the spirit, not an *imperium*, that went under with the Athenian fleets at Aegospotami. (*U*, p. 110)

The price of this indomitable spiritual superiority in the real world of politics is, of course, perpetual defeat. Failure indeed only serves to demonstrate the eternal bravery and otherworldliness of the Celtic people, of whom Ernest Renan, Matthew Arnold and, in this episode, Mr O'Madden Burke say: 'They went forth to battle, but they always fell' (*U*, p. 110).

There appears, then, to be a contradiction at the heart of the political culture represented in this episode. On the one hand, it is characterized by a tremendous respect for 'high language', and for the rhetorical tradition of the past. However, in their daily lives these individuals speak a vernacular style of English which has no place for such artificial eloquence. This latter style is here exemplified by Simon Dedalus's remarks. His parodic and comic voice is entirely impatient with elevated public discourse, and scorns its pretensions.

The men begin by discussing a speech by Dan Dawson which has been reproduced in the daily paper. They mock the banality of its repetition of the sentimentalizing clichés of Celtic Revivalism in its most debased or popular form. To Dawson's pseudo-poetic words – *'some purling rill as it babbles on its way . . . played on by the glorious sunlight or 'neath the shadow cast o'er its pensive bosom by the overarching leafage of the giants of the forest'* – Simon Dedalus responds bluntly: '*The pensive bosom and overarsing leafage.* O boys! O boys! . . . . Shite and onions!' (*U*, p. 102). But this demotic vulgarity is undercut by the general reverence for political rhetoric, which is not at all so clearly distinguished from this second-hand 'blarney' as these scoffers seem to imagine. As Bloom comments privately: 'All very fine to jeer at it now in cold print but it goes down like hot cakes that stuff' (*U*, p. 104). These men, as their precarious situation among the clanking printing-presses suggests, are stranded in print culture. They are out of their natural linguistic medium, their very high-sounding words perpetually interrupted by the comic parodies which take the form of contemporary newspaper headlines. As they deal in 'Innuendo of home rule' (*U*, p. 99) like Bloom's advertisement, they are comfortable on, to paraphrase what the narrator recommends to the citizen in Chapter 12, the 'parliamentary side of their arses' (*U*, p. 280). In this environment, the kind of language represented by Simon Dedalus can make no political impact.

Chapter 12, however, even more blatantly juxtaposes colloquial invective and parody with the styles of modern journalism and advertising, as the former are reproduced and parodied in the chapter's numerous and lengthy interpolations. As David Hayman points out, the styles of the parodies which punctuate the meeting between Bloom and the citizen in Chapter 12 are very largely nineteenth-century adaptations of earlier styles, often typical, as Kenner observes, of a kind of Celtic revivalist 'translatorese', especially as those stilted and artificial styles 'tend towards newsprint'.[7] I will attempt to examine both the citizen's rhetoric and his politics in the precise historical context of modern print culture and in its relation to modern cultural nationalism. In contrast to the kind of language typical of Chapter 7 – a version of a familiar notion of Irish eloquence or 'blarney', language well-nigh defined by its divorce from the realm of action – the 'troglodytic'[8] citizen has generally been read as the embodiment of another equally potent Irish stereotype. This is the image of the Irish person as terrorist rather than as poet. These two can be understood, however, as different sides of the same coin: the practically incompetent Celt resorts either to mysticism or to random, meaningless violence. I want to suggest, however, how Joyce's text exploits and is indeed indebted to the kinds of linguistic operations associated with nationalist rhetoric in this chapter.

We have already glimpsed the general skill in invective and parody which characterizes the Dubliners of *Ulysses*. In Chapter 7 we begin to see also, at the level of content, an even more precise analogue of the formal technique of 'Cyclops', that of the mock-heroic translation of information from a modern idiom to a stylized archaic style. The occasion for this kind of degraded archaism is talk about alcohol. Both euphemism and vulgarity testify, of course, to the importance of the pub in this society:

> – Gentlemen, Stephen said. As the next motion on the agenda paper may I suggest the house do now adjourn? . . . .
> – 'Tis the hour, methinks, when the winejug, metaphorically speaking, is most grateful in Ye ancient hostelry . . . .
> – To which particular boosingshed . . .? My casting vote is: Mooney's! (*U*, p. 118)
> – I quaffed the nectarbowl with him this very day. (*U*, p. 216)

By the time we reach Barney Kiernan's pub, we find that the barman has virtually to translate a whole series of code words in order to decipher an order:

> – Hear, hear to that, says John Wyse. What will you have?
> – An imperial yeomanry, says Lenehan, to celebrate the occasion.
> – Half one, Terry, says John Wyse, and a hands up. Terry! Are you asleep?
> – Yes, sir, says Terry. Small whiskey and a bottle of Allsop. Right, sir. (*U*, p. 269)

However, most readings of the Cyclops chapter agree that the citizen is specifically *condemned* for this kind of verbal skill in parody and especially invective, which, it is argued, perfectly demonstrate the cynicism and xenophobia of his brand of Irish nationalism. Instances of particularly savage – and amusing – invective abound:

> – To hell with the bloody brutal Sassenachs and their *patois* (*U*, p. 266).
> – The curse of a goodfornothing God light sideways on the bloody thicklugged sons of whores' gets! No music and no art and no literature worthy of the name. Any civilisation they have they stole from us. Toungetied sons of bastards' ghosts (*U*, p. 266–7).
> – The French! says the citizen. Set of dancing masters! Do you know what it is? They were never worth a roasted fart to Ireland. Aren't they trying to make an entente cordial now at Tay Pay's dinnerparty with perfidious Albion?. . .
> – And as for the Prooshians and the Hanoverians, said Joe, haven't we had enough of those sausageeating bastards on the throne from George the elector down to the German lad and the flatulent old bitch that's dead? (*U*, p. 271)

Indeed it has been asserted traditionally that this portrayal of the citizen is virtually the only instance of straightforward satire in the book, the single place in which the general 'moral neutrality'[9] of Joyce's work is flagrantly abandoned. However, in our consideration of

Chapter 12, I believe that we must put into question not just the verbal activities of the community as they are represented, but also the politics of the means by which Joyce represents them. What is at stake is an aggressive practice of parody and invective at a second, or formal, level.

A mimetic relation seems to obtain between Joyce's gossip about Dublin and the Dubliners' gossip among themselves. R.M. Adams, for example, concludes a long and detailed investigation into the factual background of *Ulysses* by suggesting how the book is the longest and most complicated piece of gossip in the world: 'Loaded with ambivalences of arrogance and loathing, it is an intricate and unstable balance of creative and destructive instincts'.[10] Adams records all the scandalous details of friends' lives of which Joyce made liberal use, and the old family and personal grudges against acquaintances in the city that he paid off by scurrilous presentations of them in his book, in an 'increasingly bold imposition of raw Dublin materials'. The anxiety expressed by Joyce in his letter to Harriet Shaw Weaver in 1919 concerning the destructiveness of his stylism and his discomfort over the injuries apparently endured by people named in his text was, we can safely conclude on the basis of Adams's information, successfully overcome. Vivian Mercier, moreover, pinpoints Joyce's skill in invective and lampoon as that place in his work where he appears most closely in touch with Gaelic traditions, especially in his strangely anachronistic faith in the magical power of words to hurt – a faith which ran strongly through the native Irish poetic tradition and was manifested in the prevailing belief in the efficacy of satire or the poetic curse.[11] In this sense, Joyce is behaving just like an ancient Irish bard when he sends copies of his satirical poem 'Gas from a Burner' to all the individuals he pillories in the poem. It is not, we might suggest, because Joyce is so distant from Dublin that he feels able to slander its citizens, but because he is so intimate with them and their linguistic conventions. I want to examine, therefore, the extent to which received ideas of satire are appropriate in the context of the citizen if Joyce can be read as using as his means of attack verbal techniques derived from the community itself. Does Joyce *satirize* the invective of the citizen, which is a kind of exaggerated version of the community's compulsive gossip, in order to side with the ungossipy Bloom, or does his implication in the same community's language make impossible the critical distance which the conventional reading implies? However we may assess Hugh Kenner's account of the relationship between Chapter 12 and Joyce's view of the 1916 rebellion –

> When the biscuit-tin, by heroic amplification, renders North Central Dublin a mass of ruins we are to remember what patriotic idealism could claim to have accomplished by Easter 1916. Thanks

> to a knot of hotheads with no prospect whatever of accomplishing what they proposed, Dublin had been the first European capital to undergo the bombardment of modern warfare, and James Joyce had little use for the oratory that fuelled hotheadedness.[12]

surely we must at least concede that Joyce had indeed a great deal of *use* for this kind of language.

The contextualization of the rhetoric of Chapter 12 also complicates a reading of the episode as validating Bloom in some relatively unqualified way. Many critics have pointed to the absolute centrality of this interpretation of 'Cyclops' in any overall interpretation of Joyce. Delmore Schwartz's remarks are exemplary:

> Joyce's sympathy for and concentration on the common man (who is a Jew and a target of anti-semitism), upon ordinary life and the speech of the people is the center of his work, and he is certainly neither indifferent nor hostile to the tradition of democratic liberalism.[13]

Lionel Trilling comments:

> By 1907 his socialism had evaporated, leaving as its only trace the sweet disposition of Leopold Bloom's mind to imagine the possibility of rational and benevolent social behaviour and the brotherhood of man. This however, is a residue of some importance in the history of literature: it makes *Ulysses* unique among modern classics for its sympathy with progressive social ideas.[14]

Moreover, Chapter 12 read as 'a deliberate rejection of violence and especially the violence of nationalist Ireland'[15] also appeals strongly to a post-structuralist thematics of dialogue and flux, represented here by Colin MacCabe:

> It is within this perspective that we can read the whole joyous activity of the Cyclops sequence, an activity that generates in turn endlessly different ways of signifying the world but refuses to judge between them . . . . What is opposed to the violence of the Citizen (based as it is on a fixed representation of the world) and the verbal violence of the Nameless One (also founded in a fixity of meaning) is the joyful entering into the various ways of signifying the world and self.[16]

This dialogical principle is, according to this reading, both embodied by Bloom and demonstrated in the parodic interpolations. Bloom, like the text, never 'subordinates one discourse to another in a hierarchy of representational forms', as Patrick McGee puts it.[17] Ironically, this opens the way for a positive reading of Bloom by critics who would not otherwise necessarily attach much importance to the substance of his remarks: he does, after all, express sentiments such as that love is the 'meaning' of life, which are hardly strikingly Derridean in form. A critic such as Richard Ellmann is, however, quite happy to agree with Bloom, but he must therefore proceed to distinguish between the kind of parody to which the nationalists are subjected and the parody of Bloom himself. After all, Bloom's interventions are taken up and sported with by the insistent parodic voice of the interpolations as much as those of anyone else; but for Ellmann the 'positive' side of 'Cyclops' must be divorced from this kind of savage parody. This point is so crucial in Ellmann's overall understanding of Joyce that he deals with it even in his short preface to the Gabler edition of the text: 'It is the kind of parody that protects seriousness by immediately going away from intensity. Love cannot be discussed without peril, but Bloom has nobly named it' (p. xiii). The problem with 'satire' is that if it 'always implies respect for some sort of reason and a positive if implicit order',[18] then the identification of the source of this order has involved critics of this episode in some embarrassing and contradictory manoeuvres. Philip Herring proposes that the moral opposite of the citizen is not really suggested by Joyce's book at all:

> It ought to be safe to infer that his position was diametrically opposite to the one he satirized; in other words, if the Citizen's political view is stupid and provincial, Joyce's must presumably be liberal and enlightened. Ironically enough, his view was closer to Homer's Cyclops than the Citizen's, because Joyce too was politically nearsighted: he believed those things closest to him were the most important.[19]

For Herring, then, Joyce's politics are even more regressive than those of the nationalists: the episode's supposedly entirely obvious moral satire is evidently open to challenge. David Hayman's account draws the astonishing conclusion that the narrator, the so-called 'Nameless One', is intended to stand as the source of moral order, simply because he is too lazy to attack Bloom himself. Hayman reads 'Cyclops' with attention only to the question of violence, and therefore the most inert person present, because the most physically passive, naturally wins his approval. Of the narrator's remark that the citizen might have been charged with assault and battery if he had managed to hit Bloom (*U*, p. 282), Hayman comments:

> For all the absurdity of the moment, we are not immersed in folly when a speaker can reflect on the legal consequences of a violent action in the midst of an excited re-enactment . . . . Clearly loyalty

to reason and accuracy outweighs even prejudice while the love of a good story and lively malice outweigh loyalty to any cause.[20]

In this way, traditional accounts of 'Cyclops' are in general rendered incoherent by their refusal to attach *any* positive qualities to the citizen or the kind of language that he speaks, in spite of the fact that his voice is one of the most 'interesting' in literary terms, and probably the funniest in the book. What I hope to re-examine here is how Joyce stands in relation to the 'satirical' portrait of the citizen, or more accurately, how the text as a whole is related to the procedures and experiments here. This will encompass the question of how Bloom is represented and what he represents, and the reverberation of the assault on him through the rest of the text, when it becomes closely involved with further reflections of themes of sexual dispossession, passivity and 'abnegation'. I want also to address the broadly post-structuralist emphasis on the opposition between Bloom and the citizen as one between multivocal dialogism and a monolingual monocular bigot, and suggest the inadequacy of this on the basis of a close reading of the text. In the first place, this will involve an account of the progress of the debate which is conducted between or inside the interpolated parodies, and an account of what the parties involved actually say, before attempting to relate what happens in Joyce's parodies to what happens at the level of content. I hope ultimately to bring these themes together in an account of how they relate to the question of 'injustice', even if this issue is addressed only at a purely verbal level – as is suggested by the quotation from Leopold Bloom which provides the title of this chapter.

THE CYCLOPS

In *The Consciousness of James Joyce*, Richard Ellmann concludes of 'Cyclops': 'Bloom fully supports Irish independence, but he challenges the citizen on the use of force'.[21] However, I can identify in this chapter no expression of support on Bloom's behalf for any such project – what he refers to in the cabman's shelter as 'that consummation devoutly to be or not to be wished for' (*U*, p. 524) – and consider that many contentious issues other than that of violence arise during the course of the debate. Indeed the entire critical history of reading Bloom's as the sole rational voice in this episode, and as a brave advocate of liberalism (or in a more up-to-date idiom, 'dialogism') which is encapsulated by Ellmann's summary, seems to me to be deeply flawed.

The citizen, as we have seen, first attacks Bloom's association with the *Freeman's Journal*. The drinkers then begin to discuss capital punishment, in a fashion which oscillates between neutrality, prurient curiosity and condemnation of the viciousness of the applicant executioners; according to the narrator, Bloom too comes out 'with the why and the wherefore and all the codology of the business' (*U*, p. 250). He specifically *defends* capital punishment because of its 'deterrent effect' – most ironically, if the post-1916 context of this dramatisation of Irish nationalist politics is kept in mind. Alf Bergan comments casually that one thing it doesn't have a deterrent effect on is the 'poor bugger's tool that's being hanged'. Bloom turns to a scientific explanation of this phenomenon, while the citizen, latching on to 'the wink of the word' (Bergan's mention of the execution of one of the Invincibles, the gang responsible for the Phoenix Park murders in 1882), starts 'gassing out of him about the invincibles and the old guard and the men of sixtyseven and who fears to speak of ninetyeight'. Here *both* the citizen and Bloom depart, along with everyone else who makes a contribution, from the obvious flow of the conversation. The new themes of science (Bloom) and nationalism (the citizen) clash, but Bloom as surely and to the equal boredom and irritation of the narrator has seen the wink of *his* word as well, in his account of the 'philoprogenitive erection *in articulo mortis per diminutionem capitis*.' Bloom and the citizen have 'an argument about the point' which culminates in the citizen's first threat to Bloom: '– The memory of the dead, says the citizen taking up his pintglass and glaring at Bloom' (*U*, p. 251).

Bloom's discourse is subsequently marked by quite specific evasions. When the conversation turns to Blazes Boylan, he proceeds with his discussion of the benefits to be gained from moderate physical exercise (*U*, p. 261); when the citizen becomes belligerent about 'strangers in our house' (*U*, p. 265), Bloom continues to tell Joe that 'for an advertisement you must have repetition. That's the whole secret' (*U*, p. 265). In this sense, Bloom himself is no less a 'monologist' than the citizen. Clearly the latter is also given to speechifying as well, but those remarks which he does make in conversation with others have been critically disregarded. For example, during a discussion of Belgian imperialism the following exchange occurs:

> – Well, says J.J., if they're any worse than the Belgians in the Congo Free State they must be bad. Did you read that report by a man what's this his name is?
> – Casement, says the citizen. He's an Irishman.

This kind of comment apparently entirely confirms David Hayman's estimate of the citizen, and serves merely to supply another illustration of the fact that:

> Grotesque chauvinism makes him a joke, a lunatic has-been who must be humoured or gently edged towards sanity and whose

> fixations inhibit free discussion. If he is not always wrong, he is never original or stimulating . . . foot and mouth disease is the only serious issue he raises.[22]

Even when critics modify the charge of mendaciousness against the citizen, then, they still insist, like Hayman here, that he is exceptionally boring. The question of the relative interest of Bloom's statements is affectionately dismissed : 'Poldy serious is Poldy dull as we see in Eumaeus'.[23] This judgement in turn makes possible a critical effort to produce the citizen as merely the mirror-image of Mr Deasy in Chapter 2, the Ulster Unionist who is indeed pilloried as being both wildly factually inaccurate in what he says, and extremely tedious. Norman Vance remarks of 'Cyclops': 'This allows Joyce to identify narrow Catholic nationalism with Deasy's Protestant Unionism, a witty effect underlined as Bloom and Stephen find themselves united in their estrangement from both these modes of Irishness'.[24] What is particularly 'Catholic' about the citizen's blasphemous obscenity remains unspecified by Vance, but the vital point here is the critical assertion that the citizen's version of history is no more imaginatively compelling or credible than that offered by Deasy. Matthew Hodgart provides a helpful gloss on what the citizen has to say:

> Incidentally the version of history given by the Citizen is hardly at all exaggerated from that favoured by the IRA today and only a little more from that taught in some Irish schools. It is not, however, a totally false view: the account of the English attitude to the Famine has some basis in truth.[25]

The citizen, in fact, reproduces the familiar Irish nationalist charge of genocide against the English for their policy during the potato famine of the 1840s:

> They were driven out of house and home in the black '47. Their mudcabins and their sheilings by the roadside were laid low by the batteringram and the *Times* rubbed its hands and told the whitelivered Saxons there would soon be as few Irish in Ireland as redskins in America. (*U*, p. 270)

This version of events may tend towards mythology in its black-and-white view of Anglo-Irish relations, but the straightforward charges of lying, ignorance or triviality scarcely apply to the citizen at this point. It is in fact true that some million Irish people starved to death in a disaster which by general agreement was very significantly mismanaged by the British authorities. The editorials which were published by the London *Times* during the time of the most atrocious starvation and suffering still provide harrowing reading for historians of Ireland today, which perhaps helps to explain why contemporary Irish 'revisionist' historiography is so notoriously silent on this period.[26] The citizen's view of history concurs with Joyce's own rehearsal of the Irish nationalist historical case in his 1907 essay, 'Ireland, Isle of Saints and Sages':

> The English now disparage the Irish because they are Catholic, poor and ignorant; however it will not be so easy to justify such disparagement to some people. Ireland is poor because English laws ruined the country's industries, especially the wool industry, because the neglect of English governments in the years of the potato famine allowed the best of the population to die from hunger. (*CW*, p. 167)

The citizen's discourse echoes quite specific details of Joyce's:

> There's no-one as blind as the fellow that won't see, if you know what that means. Where are our missing twenty millions of Irish should be here today instead of four, our lost tribes? And our potteries and textiles, the finest in the whole world? And our wool that was sold in Rome in the time of Juvenal and our flax and our damask from the looms of Antrim and our Limerick lace, our tanneries and our white flint glass down there by Ballybough and our Huguenot poplin that we have since Jacquard de Lyon and our woven silk and our Foxford tweeds and ivory raised point from the Carmelite convent in New Ross, nothing like it in the whole wide world . . . . What do the yellowjohns of Anglia owe us for our ruined trade and our ruined hearths? (*U*, p. 268)

The fact that Joyce publicly sponsored this view of Irish history in an early journalistic piece should not, of course, be taken as implying that he expected it to be taken at face value from the citizen in Chapter 12, over a decade later. It should, however, at least be recognized that there is nothing in the representation of Deasy that approximates to the imaginative and verbal force of this rhetoric, which in so far as it has once been the language of the writer himself inevitably takes on other implications and suggestions, in its parodied form, beyond those of mere repudiation and mockery. As Bahktin comments:

> A conversation with an internally persuasive word that one has begun to resist may continue, but it takes on another character: it is questioned, it is put in a new situation in order to expose its weak sides, to get a feel for its boundaries, to experience it physically as an object. For this reason stylizing discourse by attributing it to a person often becomes parodic, although not crudely parodic – since another's word, having been at an earlier

stage internally persuasive, mounts a resistance to this process and frequently sounds with no parodic overtones at all.[27]

Richard Ellmann reports that Joyce took the writing of such articles as 'Ireland, Isle of Saints and Sages' very seriously, and at one stage contemplated publishing them as a book, telling a prospective publisher that 'though these articles have no literary value, I believe they set out the problem sincerely and objectively'.[28] The citizen's speech, we could say, is exactly the opposite – interesting in literary terms but for many critics evidently intended by Joyce to be read as completely hypocritical and fallacious. However, the question of how the history which the citizen expounds at the level of content has a possible bearing on the experimentation with language which characterizes the chapter can only here be addressed in literary terms, and independently of questions about Joyce's 'sincerity' or 'objectivity'. I propose to examine this shortly in an investigation of the relation between the citizen's discourse and the other kinds of writing we find in the episode. For the moment, the observation that in some respects the views of Joyce and of the citizen may actually *coincide*, and the very fact that this has not been previously indicated, merely serves to illustrate further the inequality between extraordinarily generous critical estimations of Bloom and typical accounts of the citizen. This critical bias is very blatant indeed in readings of 'Cyclops'. It also, as I will argue, relates very precisely to the themes of colonial politics and anti-colonial resistance that are raised here, both at the level of content by the citizens, and by the necessarily political implications of Joyce's representation as a whole.

Much of the confrontation between the citizen and Bloom in fact unfolds in the presence of others. Very few of these are in full sympathy with the citizen, and they serve to qualify our estimate of Bloom's loneliness and bravery. Hayman comments (in *James Joyce's Ulysses: Critical Essays*, p. 252) that 'the more responsible make their entrances only after the stage has been set and Bloom has been exposed to the citizen for eighteen pages. By their number and power they gradually tip the scales in Bloom's favour'. These individuals arrive later, of course, because unlike their friends they are employed, and their jobs involve them in one of the few areas where there were jobs to be had in Dublin at the turn of the century, the English administration. This helps to lend them their power and authority in the pub. J.J. O'Molloy, a lawyer, attacks the citizen's singlemindedness and advocates the policy of what would later in 1904 be described by Arthur Griffith as 'Sinn Fein'. The narrator remarks:

> So J.J. puts in a word, doing the toff about one story was good till you heard another . . . . drawing up a bill of attainder to impeach a

> nation, and Bloom trying to back him up moderation and botheration and their colonies and their civilisation. (*U*, p. 266)

O'Molloy, that is to say, believes that political progress might be made in Ireland if England's guilt were internationally recognized through peaceful actions and campaigns. He preserves a faith in the 'European family' (*U*, p. 267), and the possibility of reform through negotiation with British democracy. In this he speaks, as in 'Aeolus', for constitutional nationalism. Bloom supports him with a quite specific *defence* of England's empire. J.J. O'Molloy and the citizen continue to argue about 'law and history' with Bloom, as the 'Nameless One' says, 'sticking in an odd word' (*U*, p. 267). In response to Ned Lambert's question the citizen begins to talk about corporal punishment in the British Navy. Bloom argues 'But . . . isn't discipline the same everywhere'; and that an Irish Navy would be as bad if it ever came into existence: 'wouldn't it be the same here if you put force against force?' (*U*, p. 270). It has generally been supposed that Bloom's apparent defence of aspects of the British administration during this discussion is merely strategic. He tries, that is, to convince the citizen that he cannot accuse the English of savagery unless he is more peace-loving and tolerant himself. In the light of this, David Hayman draws an analogy between Bloom's case here and Stephen's defence of Jewish merchants to Deasy in Chapter 2:

> – A merchant, Stephen says, is one who buys cheap and sells dear, jew or gentile, is he not?
>
> Not theirs: these clothes, this speech, these gestures. Their full slow eyes belied the words, the gestures eager and unoffending, but knew the rancours massed about them and knew their zeal was vain. (*U*, p. 28)

However, Stephen's is an accusation of the rich and powerful for forcing the dispossessed to do their business and to behave according to their own values while then hypocritically condemning them for doing so.[29] Bloom's abstractly universal system of morality takes no account of the relations of power (in this case, between the English and the Irish) in the way that Stephen's attack on anti-Semitism certainly does. Instead, he implicitly condemns the Irish nationalists for making the kind of response to British violence which their powerlessness has constrained them to make.

Bloom's central statement of this philosophy is his definition of love:

> – But it's no use, says he. Force, hatred, history, all that. That's not life for men and women, insult and hatred. And everybody knows that it's the very opposite of that that is really life.
> – Love, says Bloom. I mean the opposite of hatred. (*U*, p. 273)

Bloom first considers these words as he listens to the ballad 'The Croppy Boy' in 'Sirens':

> He bore no hate.
> Hate. Love. Those are names. Rudy. Soon I am old . . . .
> Ireland comes now. My country above the king. (*U*, p. 234)

In the song, the young rebel announces his creed: 'I bear no hate against living thing, but I love my country above my king'. Therefore it is *both* Bloom and the young croppy who claim to 'bear no hate': the text which provides the source of Bloom's definition, it could be argued, denies that to act out of love necessarily involves hatred, undermining Bloom's assertion that they are merely each other's 'opposites'. Just as the narrative parodies Bloom's stress on love, in the 'twaddle' which Ellmann is anxious to dismiss, the citizen too reflects on love, as both word and as concept. He responds bitterly to Bloom's gospel of 'universal love' by positioning the creed it represents in a specific historical context: 'What about sanctimonious Cromwell and his ironsides that put the women and children of Drogheda to the sword with the bible text *God is Love* pasted round the mouth of the cannon?' (*U*, p. 273–4). This is a move, as we have seen, entirely typical of Stephen's subversive strategies early in the text. It is not exactly a counter-argument to the idea of 'universal love', merely an appropriate and fleeting image of the past, which as Stephen has already learnt, is sometimes all that a broken history can yield us.

The dominant conception of Chapter 12, however, as straightforwardly satirical in its treatment of the citizen facilitates a conventional reading of the episode as simply the tale of a 'Dark tavern dominated by a mad fool'; a feast of 'gaga patriotism' in a 'den of nonsense'.[30] C.H. Peake, in similar vein, states that these 'foolish topers' discuss 'matters about which they are both ignorant and indifferent . . . with no genuine convictions at all'.[31] Such reading can see nothing positive in, for example, the specific parallels the drinkers draw between the position of Ireland and the plight of other colonised countries. Rather than, like Professor MacHugh, identifying the Irish with the ancient Greeks, European Catholicism or the Celts, these individuals identify themselves with the black subjects of British imperialism. Irish nationalism has by no means always been comfortable with this association, as the racist repudiation of it by Arthur Griffith makes plain. The nationalists here also display considerable sympathy for both the people whom they see as the powerless lackeys of imperial might – the whipped sailors of the British Navy – and also its labourers, the British working-class. The citizen states:

> The fellows that never will be slaves, with the only hereditary

> chamber on the face of God's earth, and their land in the hands of a dozen gamehogs and cottonball barons. That's the great empire they boast about of drudges and whipped serfs . . . . The tragedy of it is, says the citizen, they believe it. The unfortunate yahoos believe it. (*U*, p. 270)

This is dramatized vividly by a parodied account which the citizen reads aloud from the newspaper of the visit of a 'Zulu chief' to the cotton magnates of Manchester to receive 'the heartfelt thanks of British traders for the facilities afforded them in his dominions' (p. 274). The 'dusky potentate', the paper reports, delivered a speech which was 'freely translated' by the British chaplain. During this address, he announces that his dearest possession is a Bible, 'the volume of the word of God and the secret of England's greatness', dedicated to him by 'the great squaw Victoria'. Subsequently, His Majesty visits the chief cotton factory of Cottonopolis and makes his mark in the visitors' book (p. 274). To claim that the writer of this parody makes this black man appear stupid or childlike is equivalent to asserting that Joyce's parody of the citizen makes him seem like a mad fool. The racist discourse that so stereotypes the 'Zulu chief' is not directly represented, but it none the less provides the essential context for understanding the parody at work in the satirical newspaper report. The document which the citizen reads is a *protest* against the African's subjection to the protocols of British manners, and the pretended equivalence between languages, customs and cultures, the illusion of 'free translation' when the question of power is disregarded. 'Hypocrisy', as Conor Cruise O'Brien notes, is 'the permanent and universal element in the ideologies of ruling classes', and 'seeks to mask the gap between profession and action, to cover the realities of social and political struggle with the illusion of harmony. Irony uses the language of hypocrisy . . . with calculated excess, so that, as the realities show through, the pretences come to seem ghastly'.[32] The men in the pub appear to appreciate this distinction as they proceed to sympathise with the African, rather than, say, laugh or scoff at his 'barbarism': 'Wonder did he put that bible to the same use as I would', as Ned Lambert, one of the 'moderates' present remarks, and J.J. O'Molloy comments on the general cruelty of imperialism: 'flogging the natives on the belly to get all the red rubber they can out of them'. Their attitudes are in marked contrast to the benign racism of their social superiors, such as the Jesuit priest, bosom friend of David Sheehy, MP:

> Father Conmee thought of the souls of black and brown and yellow men and of his sermon on saint Peter Claver S.J. and the African mission and of the propagation of the faith and of the millions of black and brown and yellow souls that had not received

the baptism of water when their last hour came like a thief in the night. (*U*, p. 183)

However, perhaps the citizen's most important statement is made during a discussion of a letter from an English hangman to the British authorities in Dublin, offering his services to carry out an execution in Kilmainham jail. (The leaders of the 1916 Rebellion were also executed in Kilmainham.) The citizen concludes of H. Rumbold, the hangman: '– And a barbarous bloody barbarian he is too, says the citizen' (*U*, p. 249). Here we find side by side both terms of the opposition between Irish barbarian and English citizen which the citizen is attempting to invert. To deny the citizen any success in this, as every critical account of the chapter has done, can result in a restatement of the familiar stereotype that centuries of English investigation of Irish culture had been concerned to promote. It seems strange and inconsistent, to say the least, to conclude that Joyce's massive creative effort in 'Cyclops' should ultimately be read as proposing the idea of the barbarism of the Irish, the hoariest stereotype in all of Irish colonial history, and one which he very frequently publicly attacked. Inexorably, the description 'barbarian' in relation to the citizen crops up in the critical discourse which surrounds the episode, as when Matthew Hodgart offers the mistranslation 'Ourselves Alone' for the slogan 'Sinn Fein', and comments on its suitability for the 'barbarous insularity of the Cyclops'.[33]

In his essay 'Civilians and Barbarians', Seamus Deane describes how this ancient figure, 'the most disabling opposition in the history of the relations between the two nations', received a new inflection in nineteenth-century English political discourse, in response to modern forms of disciplinary power and racial theory:

> Races like the French and the Irish, in their resistance to the English idea of liberty, had now become criminalized – *inferno-human* beings . . . the specifically Protestant resistance to the characteristics of these races became more pronounced. In the case of the French, the sin was lasciviousness; in the case of the Irish, it was drunkenness.[34]

This same shift from folly and intemperance to insanity and criminality is legible in criticism of Chapter 12. Hugh Kenner, for example, opens his account of the episode with a quotation from the father of W.B. Yeats, who wrote that the English should never have executed the leaders of the 1916 Rebellion, because had they not been transformed into martyrs: 'Ireland would have pitied and loved and smiled at these men, knowing them to be mad fools. In the end they would have come to see that fools are the worst criminals'.[35] Michael Long, reading Joyce as 'the saving humanist of English-language modernism', in whose work we discover 'no hate, no contempt, no foulness of mouth', states that 'Joyce published no credo, but his writing is implicitly liberal, democratic and tolerant'.[36] It is not difficult to appreciate how attractive Joyce must appear to an English critic who wishes to appropriate a body of Irish literature for the 'mainstream' tradition, for Joyce's work seems to offer a superlative example of Celtic linguistic energy along with a devastating critique of Irish political incompetence. Joyce provides the blarney and the terrorism together, with the latter already satirized and condemned as a consequence of his supposed spontaneous allegiance to the values of English liberalism. The warning issued by Mathew Arnold, that the values of 'Irishness' must always be counter-balanced by the solid principle of English political order, becomes conveniently redundant once it is understood to be issued by the Irish writer on behalf of his own people. I believe that Joyce's relation to 'foul language' must be explored a little more deeply than this. Indeed I consider that Joyce employs the barbarian/citizen trope merely comically to undermine one specific attempt to invert it: the very inversion, in fact, which is offered by the discourse of Celticism.

In his introduction to the curse of Garryowen, the poem recited by the citizen's dog in one of the parodied interpolations –

> *The curse of my curses*
> *Seven days every day*
> *And seven dry Thursdays*
> *On you, Barney Kiernan,*
> *Has no sup of water*
> *To cool my courage,*
> *And my guts red roaring*
> *After Lowry's lights.* (*U*, p. 256)

Joyce imitates the polite newspaper-column chit-chat typical of what he saw as the genteel coteries of Celtic Revivalism:

> Our greatest living phonetic expert (wild horses shall not drag it from us!) has left no stone unturned in his efforts to delucidate and compare the verse recited and has found it bears a *striking* resemblance (the italics are ours) to the ranns of the ancient Celtic bards. We are not speaking so much of those delightful lovesongs with which the writer who conceals his identity under the graceful pseudonym of the Little Sweet Branch has familiarised the bookloving world but rather . . . of the harsher and more personal note which is found in the satirical effusions of the

> famous Raftery and of Donal MacConsidine to say nothing of a more modern lyrist at present very much in the public eye.

This is in blatant contrast to the actual content of the verse, of course, with its harsh, personal and satiric note. In this sense, Joyce may seem to suggest that Garryowen's poem is in fact closer to the native Irish tradition than the kind of work produced by the translators of the revival. The names of Gaelic poets are juxtaposed with that of Douglas Hyde ('Little Sweet Branch'), not in order to suggest that Joyce had any interest in substituting a more authentically Gaelic verse for the contemporary translations, but merely to exploit the humour inherent in the earthy content and uncouth sentiments that the journalese *glosses* over, in several senses of that term. The Revival's mission to recover and reclaim the Irish literary tradition through the medium of English depended, of course, on a faith in such translation: 'The metrical system of the canine original, which recalls the intricate alliterative and isosyllabic rules of the Welsh englyn, is infinitely more complicated but we believe that our readers will agree that *the spirit has been well caught*'.[37] Joyce comically mocks this illusion of 'free translation' with an illustration of the violence occluded by the levelling modern discourse of the newspapers. In a similar way, the violence signified by 'Cyclops' as a whole is not just the crude words and physical force of the citizen, but also the violent clashes it demonstrates between different languages. Far from different ways of signifying the world being grasped as mutually interchangeable and presented without distinction or hierarchy, *pace* MacCabe, we find instead a dramatisation of their confrontation and irreconcilability. The parodies expose the limitations of the translations they perform. When, for example, we are offered such a version of the events which take place in Kiernan's as the following –

> A most interesting discussion took place in the ancient hall of *Brian O'Ciarnain*'s in *Sraid na Bretaine Bheag*, under the auspices of *Sluagh na h-Eireann*, on the revival of ancient Gaelic sports and the importance of physical culture, as understood in ancient Greece and ancient Rome and ancient Ireland, for the development of the race . . . . L. Bloom, who met with a mixed reception of applause and hisses, having espoused the negative the vocalist chairman brought the discussion to a close, in response to repeated requests and hearty plaudits from all parts of a bumper house, by a remarkably noteworthy rendering of the immortal Thomas Osborne Davis' evergreen verses (happily too familiar to need recalling here) *A Nation Once Again*, in the execution of which the veteran patriot champion may be said without fear of contradiction to have fairly excelled himself. (*U*, p. 260)

– we cannot, I would argue, grant this equal authority or credibility with other ways of narrating the violent disagreement between Bloom and the citizen. This is not necessarily to say that the language of demotic violence – 'Gob, Jack made him toe the line. Told him that if he didn't patch up the pot, Jesus, he'd kick the shite out of him' (*U*, p. 258) – is presented straightforwardly as a 'true' way of speaking, but rather to point out that it is this speech which is continuously used to mock and combat the endlessly levelling discourse of the modern which appears unable to render the reality of conflict. This is in direct contrast to another major formal strategy of the novel, namely the attempt, primarily through the figure of Bloom, to use this modern discourse to demystify and secularize other kinds of 'high' styles or languages. Here the text cannot parody the citizen by these means, for his language of violence is its language as well. His discourse, in its relentless parody and destructive energy, resembles the modernism of sheer textual production exemplified by the interpolations; but it also resists the consequent assimilation of all styles into empty and abstract equivalence which is suggested by such a practice of parody: 'How's that for low?', Joyce used to ask gleefully when he read aloud from Chapter 12.[38]

A closer reading of the language of the parodies also throws doubt on, for example, Hugh Kenner's influential judgement that they are merely slightly exaggerated versions of the kind of translated epics which were very popular in Ireland in Joyce's time. Kenner believes that it was their pseudo-heroism and savagery which inspired the politics of the GAA, the IRB and the Rebellion of 1916. For him, the interpolated parodies resemble versions of Irish mythology 'tumbled together at an early stage of the Irish revival by someone with no ear, as the total absence of a speakable rhythm indicates . . . heroes cobbled in translatorese that Ireland was exhorted to thrill to'.[39] However, in Joyce's day these stories were often presented in rather refined versions. Lady Gregory begins her translation of the tales of Cuchulain with the admission:

> I left out a good deal I thought you would not care about for one reason or another . . . . I have told the whole story in plain and simple words, in the same way my old nurse Mary Sheridan used to be telling stories from the Irish long ago, and I a child at Roxborough.[40]

The suspicious modern reader might guess correctly that Gregory has omitted a lot of sex and violence. However, she also edits a lot of material which for the modern reader may have been genuinely boring. For example, Gregory's account of one incident from the *Tain* reads: 'And he made a round of the whole army, mowing men down on every side, in revenge for the boy troop of Emain'.[41] Thomas Kinsella's recent translation of the same passage tells:

> After this Medh sent out one hundred of her own followers to kill Cuchulainn but he slew them all at the fort of Cet Chuile – the crime of One Hundred. From this episode come the names Glais Chranl – the stream of blood; Cuilenn Cinn Duin – the Crime (some say) of Cinn Duin . . . .
>
> This slaughter on the Tain was given the name Seisrech Bresligi, the Sixfold Slaughter. Any count or estimate of the number of rabble who fell there is unknown and unknowable. Only the chiefs have been counted. The following are the names of these nobles and chiefs: two called Cruaid, two named Calad, two named Cir, two named Ciar [Kinsella's translation lists twenty eight more names].[42]

One of the sources of Joyce's comedy in this chapter is the fact that for his parodist, as for the ancient epic poet, nothing is 'too numerous to be enumerated' (*U*, p. 241). Here again, within modern mechanical reproduction some suggestion of an originary energy is retained: Joyce appears paradoxically closer to the source texts, in his exhaustive repetitions and inclusiveness, than the nineteenth-century versions of them which he parodies. The endless lists of 'Cyclops' can be seen as catalogues in the modern sense – they very often quote the language of advertising – and in the medieval sense, which is described by Umberto Eco as part of 'the encyclopedic approach to knowledge: the Inventory . . . or, in classical rhetorical terms, the *Enumeratio*'. As Eco goes on to explain, these lists may now seem amusing to the modern reader in their apparent failure to distinguish between the sacred and the merely curious or grotesque. In the Treasury of the Duc du Berry, Eco reports, were 'a stuffed elephant, a hydra, a basilisk, an egg within an egg found by an abbot, mana from the wilderness, the horn of a unicorn, the wedding ring of St. Joseph, and a coconut'.[43] The comic potential is inherent in the medieval source for the modern reader: Joyce is making fun of a modern form by, perhaps unwittingly, exploiting the potential for the absurd and grotesque within the source document, in his lengthy heterogeneous lists in this chapter. In this way Joyce challenges and subverts the language of the modern from the inside, as it were, as well as by its juxtaposition with the language of the citizens. His repetitiousness, and apparently mechanical piling up of detail –

> The figure seated on a large bolder at the foot of a round tower was that of a broadshouldered deepchested stronglimbed frankeyed redhaired freelyfreckled shaggybearded widemouthed

> largenosed longheaded deepvoiced barekneed brawnyhanded hairylegged ruddyfaced sinewyarmed hero. (*U*, p. 243)

– indicate not merely the 'unspeakable rhythms' of translators, but also the conventions of an original oral and formulaic poetry.

This interchange between traditional and modern also characterizes the speech of the citizens. One of the first parodies in 'Cyclops' is of a medieval poem, 'Aelfrid's Itinerary', which lists the delight and plenty of the four provinces of Ireland and was known to Joyce in a nineteenth-century version by James Clarence Mangan. It is particularly appropriate here because the men are sitting in the market area of Dublin, where animals and vegetables arrive in the city from the rest of Ireland:

> Thither the extremely large wains bring foison of the fields, flaskets of cauliflowers, floats of spinach, pineapple chunks, Rangoon beans, strikes of tomatoes, drums of figs, drills of Swedes, spherical potatoes and tallies of iridescent Kale, York and Savoy . . . and red green yellow brown, russet sweet big bitter ripe pomellated apples and chips of strawberries and sieves of gooseberries, pulpy and pelurious, and strawberries fit for princes and raspberries from their canes . . . sheep and pigs and heavyhooved kine from pasturelands of Lusk and Rush and Carrickmines and from the steamy vales of Thomond . . . their udders distended with superabundance of milk and butts of butter and rennets of cheese and farmer's firkins and targets of lamb and crannocks of corn and oblong eggs in great hundreds, various in size, the agate with the dun. (*U*, p. 242)

Here the syntax of mechanical reproduction is applied to the processes of natural production. The citizens, too, dwell constantly on themes concerning agriculture and industry, speculating about the natural resources of the country, on Ireland's supposedly extraordinary fertility and the possibility of building up the nation so it might regain its former splendour and wealth. In this they look beyond Dublin and towards a totalising vision of Ireland as a whole: as their physical situation suggests, they strain at the very formal limits of *Ulysses*, in its confinement to a narrow and purely urban space, and point towards the transcendence of those limits. They also, like the parodies, attempt to wrest some meaning from a modern form of production which might otherwise appear as merely dizzyingly proliferating and as purely contingent. A glass of stout, for example, is imagined to have come directly from the Guinness brothers:

> a crystal cup full of the foamy ebon ale which the noble brothers Bungiveagh and Bungardilaun brew ever in their divine alevats,

> cunning as the sons of deathless Leda. For they garner the succulent berries of the hop and mass and sift and bruise and brew them and they mix therewith sour juices and bring the must to the sacred fire and cease not from their toil, those cunning brothers, lords of the vat. (*U*, p. 246)

In its witness to the determination of the citizens both to use the language of the modern world and to make its productive possibilities carry the weight of other aspirations, Chapter 12 is closely analogous to the discourse of nationalism itself. Nationalism, as we have seen, always seeks to enable the people to enter into fully-fledged modernity, but tries to do so by reinventing modernity on its own terms, by retaining something from an archaic, pre-modern form of community.

The speech represented in 'Cyclops' has generally been described by critics as 'low-class' or 'plebeian'. However, this should not be exaggerated, as we are here still very definitely in a lower middle-class milieu. What is perhaps unusual is the wealth of Hiberno-English expressions and idioms and the profusion of Anglicised Gaelic words.[44] In this we can recognize a culture which bears the evidence of the efforts of language revivalism, its inadequate result being the few token words of Irish on everyone's lips. However, it is also a way of speech that bears the mark of a past effort to learn language, and in this case the English language. This is especially evident in the high proportion of malapropisms in the episode:

> – Who made those allegations? says Alf.
> – I, says Joe. I'm the alligator . . . .
> – Me, says Alf. Don't cast your nasturtiums on my character. (*U*, p. 263)

A.J. Bliss identifies malapropism as one of the most noteworthy features of the Anglo-Irish dialect, and while observing that it can be noticed in any part of Ireland, claims that it appears to be especially frequent in Dublin. He attributes the tendency to the fact that most English-speaking Irish people first learnt the language from individuals who were not themselves native speakers; errors in pronunciation which arose in this way were transmitted uncorrected.[45] The true significance of Joyce's deployment of Anglo-Irish dialect in this chapter is not in any way a contribution to a stereotype of the Irish 'gift of the gab'. Rather, in its creative estrangement from two cultures and two languages, it provides a parallel to literary modernism. It also, however, succeeds in resisting the illusion of 'free translation' which might seem the appropriate way of speech for such a polyglot modern world, in its dramatisation of a modern version of language wielded as an instrument of revenge, a deployment of 'style' that bursts through the limits of dialogue, and approaches as near as possible to action.

Faith in law, however, depends on confidence in 'free translation'. A court is, after all, a place where injury is described in language, and where claims and counterclaims are assessed by a judge who proposes himself as a master reader, a sound interpreter, who can then issue the command for punishment or redress. It assesses cases through the medium of language and rhetoric, which is why it is at once so appealing and so dangerous for the kind of political claims that, for example, the men in the office of the *Freeman's Journal* desire to make in Chapter 7. In a 1907 essay 'Ireland at the Bar', Joyce used the image of an Irish-speaking peasant in an English court of law as an image of the cause of Irish nationalism before world opinion. In the district of Maamtrasna in the west of Ireland, four or five apparently innocent members of a family named Joyce were arrested and charged with murder. James Joyce describes the scene in the courtroom:

> On one side was the excessively ceremonious interpreter, on the other the patriarch of a miserable tribe unused to civilised customs, who seemed stupefied by all the judicial ceremony. The magistrate said:
>
> 'Ask the accused if he saw the lady that night'. The question was referred to him in Irish, and the old man broke out into an involved explanation, gesticulating, appealing to the others accused and to heaven. Then he quieted down, worn out by his effort, and the interpreter turned to the magistrate and said:
>
> He says no, 'your worship'. (*CW*, p. 197)

The frenzied verbal activity of this peasant, Myles Joyce, remains entirely opaque to his English judge. Joyce depicts the unintelligibility of the national cause of Ireland to the English and the international community in similar terms:

> The figure of this dumbfounded old man, a remnant of a civilisation not ours, deaf and dumb before his judge, is a symbol of the Irish nation at the bar of public opinion. Like him, she is unable to appeal to the modern conscience of England and other countries. (*CW*, p. 198)

Between such legal means of redress and language understood as 'the hard word' (*U*, p. 241), used as an instrument of violent retaliation in satire and invective, much of the action of the 'Cyclops' chapter is played out. In the first paragraph the narrator complains about the sweep who nearly puts his eye out with his broom and remarks that 'I turned around to let him have the weight of my tongue . . . I'm on two minds not to give that fellow the charge for obstructing the thoroughfare with his brooms and ladders' (*U*, p. 240).

The condition of being 'on two minds' characterizes Joyce's representation of Irish nationalism throughout the chapter: the narrator, like the group in Chapter 7, as we have seen, in general opts for the latter, legalistic response. Throughout 'Cyclops', however, it is the historical context of issues about law, history and government which is at stake, and not merely 'law and order' as an abstract given category that can be unproblematically employed to assess issues of satire or moral order. When Matthew Hodgart announces

> The Cyclops-Citizen rejects established law and offers only the violence of terrorism and muscle. The IRB was an ancestor of the modern IRA and used bombs and other forms of murder to assist the liberation of Ireland. They did not recognise the law-courts of the established government, or indeed any authority except their own elected leadership[46]

he neglects to mention the fact that 'established' is not at all equivalent in the society represented to 'elected', 'agreed' or 'democratic', and indeed was not popularly believed to be justly instituted at all. The authority which such a government could command did not flow from consensus and was not marked by benevolence.

The essential political demand of nationalism is that the territory of the nation should coincide with that of the state. Any nationalism which is not already the official ideology of a state presents itself as a protest on behalf of those who, for reasons of cultural or especially linguistic difference, feel themselves to be unjustly treated by the state as it is currently instituted. Therefore, nationalist ideology is centrally concerned with the promotion of the culture and language of those who seek secession from the state, and advocates a vernacular language which can serve all citizens, on equal terms, as the medium of social communication and political administration. In practice, of course, premodern communities rarely offer such a language ready-made, and the vernacular which nationalism consolidates or disseminates is usually obliged to come to terms with a number of pre-existing languages or dialects.

A particularly bland version of formal English serves Joyce in *Ulysses* as representative of the official language in the society that he depicts. In Chapter 10 ('Wandering Rocks'), for example, the procession of the vice-regal carriage through the streets of Dublin is a symbolic manifestation of a state power which is palpably alien and intrusive, and which imposes an artificial, formal cohesion on the city it traverses. Nonetheless, its reception is reported as uniformly courteous – 'The viceroy was most cordially greeted on his way through the metropolis' (*U*, p. 207) –

even when these civil tones are comically at odds with the content of Joyce's descriptions: 'From its sluice in Wood quay wall under Tom Devan's office Poodle river hung out in fealty a tongue of liquid sewage'. Like his counterparts in the Literary Revival, Joyce concentrated on varieties of Hiberno-English, rather than on Irish, in his search for an alternative national vernacular. More explicitly than Yeats, Gregory or Synge, however, Joyce's dialect also bears the weight of crucial political questions. This is because his depiction of this vernacular as the medium of communication in a well-defined social group – as in 'Cyclops' – obliges him to engage with the associated demands made from within that community for political recognition and autonomy.

FORGIVENESS AND FORGETFULNESS

If it cannot be fairly concluded in this context that *Ulysses* offers an explicit vindication of the use of force, none the less it can be demonstrated that it provides, in the figure of Bloom, an important insight into the pacificism of the oppressed. His sexual masochism is more clearly revealed in Chapter 15 than elsewhere, but at a different level in Chapter 16 ('Eumaeus') we can observe a related strategy, a narrative mechanism by which an experience of defeat is transmuted into a story of success. This can be understood, like masochism, as a ploy by means of which gratification is gained from humiliation, thus transmuting pain into pleasure.

Recognizing the nationalist rhetoric of the cabman's shelter's keeper (reputed to be Skin-the-Goat, who was the getaway driver for the Invincibles after the murders in the Phoenix Park in 1882), Bloom tells Stephen how he has recently heard the 'same identical lingo' (*U*, p. 525), in an obvious reference to what happened in Barney Kiernan's. He announces to Stephen his rhetorical victory over the citizen, telling him how 'he simply but effectively silenced the offender' and commenting that this illustrates how 'a soft answer turns away wrath'. Clearly, this summary completely contradicts Bloom's recent experience: his 'soft answer' has not succeeded in protecting him from the consequences of the citizen's rage. Just as the citizen claims a possibility of victory when there seems to be none evident, except in the force of his rhetoric –

> – It's on the march, says the citizen . . . . (*U*, p. 266) We'll put force against force . . . . Ay, they drove out the peasants in hordes. Twenty thousand of them died in the coffinships. But those that came to the land of the free remember the land of bondage. And they will come again and with a vengeance, no

> cravens, the sons of Granuaile, the champions of Kathleen ni Houlihan. (*U*, p. 270)

– so too Bloom creatively misinterprets his history, in order the better to play the role of paternal adviser to Stephen. He behaves, to a smaller audience, and in a lower key, exactly as the citizen.

The sailor to whom Stephen and Bloom listen in the shelter stands as the last of the storytellers of *Ulysses*. His art is the final sorry provider of an experience of social community in the collective experience of narrative in the novel, and his violent one-liners are comically reduced even further by their translation into a recognizably Bloomian idiom:

> – Pom! then he shouted once.
> The entire audience waited, anticipating an additional detonation, there being still a further egg.
> – Pom! He shouted twice.
> Egg two evidently demolished, he nodded and winked, adding bloodthirstily:
> – *Buffalo Bill shoots to kill,*
> *Never missed nor he never will.* (*U*, p. 510)

Just as narrative art has been pared down by this stage simply to tales of violence – '– And I seen a man killed in Trieste by an Italian chap. Knife in his back. Knife like that . . . . Like that. *Prepare to meet your God*, says he. Chuk! It went into his back up to the butt' (*U*, p. 514) – so too the 'Story of Ireland' has culminated merely in a series of speculations about violence, and in particular a meditation on the Phoenix Park murders of 1882: 'They're great for the cold steel, somebody who was evidently quite in the dark said for the benefit of them all. That was why they thought the park murders of the invincibles was done by foreigners on account of them using knives' (*U*, p. 514). Bloom recognizes that the history which inspires the arguments in the cabman's shelter remains a source of interest and amusement. He exploits the comic potential of a vigorous and lively clash of opinions and wills for its entertainment value but shies away from the possibility of its physical manifestation: 'Then they began to have a few irascible words when it waxed hotter, both, needless to say, appealing to the listeners who followed the passage of arms with interest so long as they didn't indulge in recriminations and come to blows' (*U*, p. 524). In the same way, Bloom claims to have given the citizen '(metaphorically) one in the gizzard' (*U*, p. 536) revealing again, at a stroke, both his interest in violence and its sublimation:

> Quite apart from that he disliked those careers of crime and wrongdoing on principle. Yet, though such criminal propensities had never been an inmate of his bosom in any shape or form, he

> certainly did feel and no denying it (while inwardly remaining what he was) a certain kind of admiration for a man who had actually brandished a knife, cold steel, with the courage of his political convictions (though personally, he would never be party to any such thing). (*U*, p. 524)

As the men in the shelter comment, there had been some suggestion that the murders in the Park had been committed by 'foreigners' because the use of knives was considered to be so brutal as to be 'un-Irish'. Such a conjunction of cold steel and violent heat of passion was evidently not considered characteristic of the native temperament. Bloom associates this violent passion with sexual love and vengeance, and both, again, with 'foreign' temperaments: 'On the contrary that stab in the back touch was quite in keeping with those italianos' (*U*, p. 520). These themes converge around the figure of Parnell, with his public image of cool, aloof leadership, icy patriotism and hatred for the English, in apparent contrast to the intensity of his private love for Katharine O'Shea. Parnell's lover, according to Bloom, had Mediterranean blood, like his own wife Molly, who is also 'half-Spanish':

> off the same bat as those love vendettas of the south, have her or swing for her, when the husband frequently, after some words passed between the two concerning her relations with the other lucky mortal (he having had the pair watched), inflicted fatal injuries on his adored one as a result of an alternative postnuptial *liaison* by plunging his knife into her (p. 525) . . . it was just the wellknown case of hot passion, pure and simple, upsetting the applecart with a vengeance and just bore out the very thing he was saying as she also was Spanish or half so, types that wouldn't do things by halves, passionate abandon of the south, casting every shred of decency to the wind. (*U*, p. 532)

In this analysis of the Parnell case, then, Bloom sides with the one who breaks the marriage bond, rather than the cuckold. What is in the blood is, apparently, inarguable: 'simply a case of the husband not being up to scratch, with nothing in common between them beyond the name, and then a real man arriving on the scene' (*U*, p. 532). In this, he embraces a notion of masculinity which has been previously used to denigrate and deride him: 'Half and half, I mean, says the citizen. A fellow that's neither fish nor flesh (*U*, p. 263) . . . . Do you call that a man? says the citizen' (*U*, p. 277). In an effective reversal of Chapter 12, Bloom is now talking of racial traits and innate characteristics:

> Spaniards, for instance, he continued, passionate temperaments like that, impetuous as Old Nick, are given to taking the law into their own hands . . . . It comes from the great heat, climate

> generally (*U*, p. 520) . . . . Just bears out what I was saying, he, with glowing bosom said to Stephen, about blood and the sun. (*U*, p. 532)

Bloom is, of course, injured in two ways during the course of the day: by the citizen's attack on him and by Molly's affair with Blazes Boylan. Because Irish nationalism employs a variety of images of domestic security and purity, insisting on the need to banish all 'strangers in the house', Bloom as a co-operative cuckold and non-patriarchal husband is frequently read as providing a positive image of racial and national inclusiveness as well. However, as emerges in Chapter 16, he is also very intent on cordoning off this realm of political and sexual passion. He is a hygienist, concerned with the licensing of prostitutes by the proper authorities (*U*, p. 517) and the medical inspection of all eatables, as much as he is with the preservation of the distinction between the domestic realm and that of tales 'verging on the tropical calculated to freeze the marrow of anybody's bones'. His preference, as described in Chapter 17 ('Ithaca'), is for 'discussion in tepid security of unsolved historical and criminal problems' (*U*, p. 587). He constructs a story of exclusion and racial purity as surely as the citizen does in his anti-Semitic rantings:

> – Those are nice things, says the citizen, coming over here to Ireland filling the country with bugs. (*U*, p. 265)
>
> Saint Patrick would want to land again at Ballykinlar and convert us, says the citizen, after allowing things like that to contaminate our shores. (*U*, p. 277)

As we have seen, Bloom considers the Phoenix Park murders to be evidence of pure criminality, with which his relationship is nevertheless significantly ambivalent. He asserts that the Irish are, as it were, biologically resentful because of some organic weakness, their quarrels the consequence of a pathological reflex: 'All those wretched quarrels, in his humble opinion, stirring up bad blood, from some bump of combativeness or gland of some kind' (*U*, p. 526). Material interests, he here asserts, work against political extremism. He defends Jewish people because of their proven devotion to commerce: 'Because they are imbued with the proper spirit. They are practical and proved to be so' (*U*, p. 526). This attitude he aligns with his own pragmatic philosophy of 'Where you can live well, the sense is, if you work'. However, in the same breath he claims of Irish quarrels that they are all 'very largely a question of the money question which was at the back of everything greed and jealousy, people never knowing when to stop' (*U*, p. 526).

This symptomatic contradiction again testifies to the ambiguous impulses which, as he lies in bed beside his wife in Chapter 17, finally work to produce his sense of resignation and apparent tolerance of her infidelity. This is a resolution achieved at that point in the text where, as Fredric Jameson points out, the vision of the complete subjugation of the natural world by instrumental reason is most blatantly juxtaposed with a sense of the futility and meaninglessness, not just of the works of humankind, but of nature and human life themselves.[47] Bloom's scientific speculations culminate, that is to say, in his both terrifying and consoling sense of 'the apathy of the stars', which are: 'in reality evermoving wanderers from immeasurably remote eons to infinitely remote futures in comparison with which the years, threescore and ten, of allotted human life formed a parenthesis of infinitesimal brevity' (*U*, p. 573).

These meditations bring some comfort to Bloom because they reassure him of the futility of any effort whatsoever. In the same way, we are told that he dreams regularly of 'schemes so difficult of realisation' (*U*, p. 591) in order to induce passivity and sleepiness. The catechist of 'Ithaca' asks of his response to the knowledge of his wife's infidelity:

> Why more abnegation than jealousy, less envy than equanimity?
> . . . the incongruity and disproportion between the selfprolonging tension of the thing proposed to be done and the selfabbreviating relaxation of the thing done
> . . . . the natural grammatical transition by inversion involving no alteration of sense of an aorist preterite proposition (parsed as masculine subject, monosyllabic onomatopoeic transitive verb with direct feminine object) from the active voice into its correlative aorist preterite proposition (parsed as feminine subject, auxilliary verb and quasimonosyllabic onomatopoeic past participle with complementary masculine agent) in the passive voice. (*U*, pp. 603–4)

Bloom's achievement of this acceptance of Molly is one of the two crucial events in *Ulysses* that can be read as proving that something actually happens on 'Bloomsday', and that it marks a decisive change in the lives of the characters; Molly's supposed rejection of Boylan and decision to devote herself to Bloom is the other. Both events, if that is what they are, take place without any kind of communication between the partners and without each other's knowledge. None the less, Marilyn French represents a long tradition in Joyce studies with her claim: 'Bloom's attitude permits him to remain the "unconquered hero" right to the end of the novel, and it is one of the few things in *Ulysses* that Joyce clearly labels "right".'[48] Bloom's enabling rendition to himself of the events of the day, 'the natural grammatical transition by inversion' in the quotation above, can only plausibly be decoded as the critical difference between 'He fucked her' and 'She was fucked by him'. It resembles the translation into 'the passive voice' also conveniently accomplished by Haines's 'It seems history is to blame'; it is an act of translation which obscures agency and responsibility, of a kind which is repeatedly dramatised and exposed by Stephen Dedalus early in the text, and by Chapter 12. Joyce's presentation of Bloom's passivity precisely as such an act of translation enables us radically to reinterpret its implications in the light of the text as a whole.

In conclusion, we can say that readings of *Ulysses*'s 'political' chapter tend to identify two kinds of discourse at work here: the multivocal, playful and dialogic which characterizes the interpolated parodies and the speech of Leopold Bloom, and the monological stream of 'Fenian shibboleths'[49] associated with the citizen, in whom we can observe the conjunction of scandalous metaphysical presumptions, verbal ugliness and bodily violence. As we have seen, some readings ascribe moral value to Bloom's statements in a relatively unproblematic way, insisting that they are not subjected to the same kind of parody as the other styles. Alternatively, Bloom is understood to be the marker of a racial difference and of a discursive inventiveness and mobility which align him with the other stylistic experiments of Bakhtinian levelling and carnival in the episode. This is a polarity which is significantly analogous to the one which contemporary Irish cultural criticism has employed to characterize modern Irish culture. Typically, an argument such as Kearney's in *Transitions* describes Ireland as a place where nativist, mythological and violently exclusive modes of thought clash with modern demythologizing rationality and internationalism. Chapter 12, then, appears to offer a microcosmic version of this opposition. In general, as we have seen, contemporary Irish writers tend to call neither for one mode of thought and writing or the other to be adopted uncritically, but rather point to the possibility of a creative dialogue between them. However, in *Ulysses*, as I have argued, we witness the migration of a potentially critical practice of parody and demystification into the realm of postmodern pastiche, which indiscriminately absorbs and levels all kinds of language or ways of speaking. But this does not mean that it is only this practice of postmodern stylism which is at stake in *Ulysses*, and specifically in this episode. Critics have invariably presumed that multivocal modernity in this chapter is embodied by the internationalist Bloom: 'A nation is the same people living in the same place' (*U*, p. 272). I have been concerned here both to demonstrate the presuppositions which prejudge criticism of the citizen's discourse, and to show the affinity between the speech of the citizens generally and the parodic interpolations. At the simplest level, it is they, after all, who make jokes, talk excessively and compose their own parodies: in their more global interests in imperialism and in politics they actually transcend the narrow focus of the novel itself on the Irish situation. Their very words bear the mark of their colonial experiences, and expose the grounding of the modernist textual experiments in a specific and brutally material history. We can see that Bloom does not bring 'multivocality' to the scene, but that this is already there, produced by the colonial situation itself, but for the moment locked into that situation. The liberation it signifies in terms of language could only ever enter into material existence if the other, significantly related, language it produces – that of nationalism – were to be promoted and its project successfully carried through.

4

JOYCE'S REPRESENTATION OF POLITICAL VIOLENCE

TERRORISM IN *ULYSSES*

As my reading of *Ulysses* demonstrates, both the progress of Joyce's novel and the language of the individuals who constitute its primary focus are implicated in a practice of verbal or symbolic violence. The text establishes linkages between form and content in this regard by means of its dramatization of verbal inventiveness, invective and parody as aggressive responses to colonial power. In Joyce's persistent foregrounding of this linguistic forcefulness, I have argued, *Ulysses* testifies to the existence within the community it depicts of strategies of resistance to imperialist domination, and not merely - as a conventional reading proposes - examples at the level of form of its comic demystification and subversion.

However, the political praxis denoted by the text in this way remains at such a symbolic level: as we have seen, *Ulysses* is as far short of explicitly sponsoring political violence as it is from the explicit condemnation of that violence which has traditionally been uncovered by its commentators. But such a literary-critical reading of the text as I have elaborated here does not in itself exhaust the political implications of Joyce's novel: *Ulysses*'s notorious silence regarding the major political events of early twentieth-century Ireland remains unaddressed. Karl Radek, for example, castigates Joyce's failure to represent revolutionary history directly:

> But it is sufficient to consider the picture that he gives, in order to see that it does not fit even those trivial heroes which he depicts . . . . But these Blooms and Dedaluses, whom the author relentlessly pursues into the lavatory, the brothel and the pot-house, did not cease to be petty bourgeois when they took part in the Irish insurrection of 1916. The petty bourgeois is a profoundly contradictory phenomenon, and in order to give a portrayal of the petty bourgeois, one must present him in all his relations to life . . . . For him, the national revolutionary movement of the Irish

> petty-bourgeoisie did not exist, and consequently the picture he presents, despite its ostensible impartiality, is untrue.[1]

Nonetheless, as a number of recent critics have noted, *Ulysses* does contain *some* reference to 'real' Irish history, in its repeated – not to say obsessive – allusions to a few apparently isolated incidents from the late nineteenth century. I hope to reassess the significance of these in conjunction with a critical articulation of Joyce's account of Irish political history in his early non-fictional writings.

Joyce's Italian lectures and articles (written between 1907 and 1912) have been described by, for example, Dominic Manganiello as offering an intelligent and even-handed assessment of Irish nationalism, and they have played a major part in the recruitment of the writer as 'soft' Irish nationalist by Richard Ellmann and later commentators on Joyce's politics. I will be concerned to demonstrate here that Joyce's critics have in fact been over-generous in their estimate of Joyce as political commentator on Ireland: his essays, it can be argued, give an ambivalent, confused and even contradictory account of Irish nationalism, and in this way are complementary to the representation of nationalism in the text of Joyce's major novel. It is paradoxically by virtue of these failings that the non-fictional writings give a fuller and more complex testimony to the ironies of modern anti-colonialism than critics have appreciated. Their simple appropriations of Joyce's remarks are paralleled by their moralistic readings of *Ulysses* itself. Terrorism in particular, I will argue, as itself a kind of symbolic or aestheticized violence, has a particular relevance to Joyce's writing which is clearly too scandalous for his commentators to contemplate: I will be especially concerned to question their assumption of Joyce's essentially diagnostic view of Irish terrorists as pathological deviants.

The interchange between symbolic and real violence which characterises Joyce's representation of terrorism in *Ulysses* also underlies the bizarre drama of Chapter 15. In the second part of this chapter, I will examine 'Circe' as an ironic representation of the Easter 1916 Rebellion, an event which, as Radek complains, otherwise stands as the novel's most noteworthy historical elision. This chapter, unique in the text for being staged in the heart of the Dublin slums (where fully one third of the population of the city lived in 1904[2]) dramatizes an encounter with colonial power utterly unlike that evoked, for example, by the serene procession of the viceregal cavalcade in Chapter 10. It concludes – at least in Stephen's hallucination – like the Rebellion in violent conflagration as Dublin, under heavy military bombardment, erupts in flames:

> *(Brimstone fires spring up. Dense clouds roll past. Heavy Gatling guns boom. Pandemonium. Troops deploy. Gallop of hoofs. Artillery. Hoarse commands.*

> *Bells clang. Backers shout. Drunkards bawl. Whores screech. Foghorns hoot. Cries of valour. Shrieks of dying. Pikes clash on cuirasses . . . . The midnight sun is darkened. The earth trembles. The dead of Dublin from Prospect and Mount Jerome in white sheepskin overcoats and black goatfell cloaks arise and appear to many.)* (p. 488)

In 'Circe', as I will show, Joyce lays bare the material basis of slum poverty and disease which lurks beneath (and helps to generate) the episode's surrealist fantasies. In its carnivalesque extravaganza and terrifying raising of ghosts – both personal and historical – it offers an analogy to the symbolism and theatricality of the 1916 Rebellion itself. By the same token, however, Joyce's text demonstrates the insufficiency of any merely aestheticizing or 'theatrical' resolution of these conditions. Hence, *Ulysses* attests to, in Radek's words, the 'profoundly contradictory' nature of this bourgeois 'national revolutionary movement' more successfully than it could possibly have done by the merely realistic depiction of it which Radek demands.

We have already observed how often assessments of Joyce's political views have traditionally been obliged to depend on such formulations as Manganiello's 'Joyce must have thought'; establishing Joyce's 'thoughts', especially about political issues, however, is by no means straightforward. For example, Richard Ellmann reports in his biography that Joyce's response to news of the 1916 Rebellion was 'complex . . . balanced between bitterness and nostalgia', and that Joyce demonstrated some 'inconsistency' in his statements: 'although he evaluated the rising as useless, he felt also out of things'. Ellmann's description is characteristically generous. Joyce apparently shouted 'Erin go bragh' ('long live Ireland') as the citizen does in Chapter 15, when he heard that the British had decided to drop their planned policy of conscription in Ireland, and predicted that he and his son would wear shamrocks in a free Ireland. When asked, however, whether he would visit an independent Irish state he responded: 'So I might declare myself its first enemy?'[3]

In *Stephen Hero*, Joyce outlines Dedalus's rejection of the policies of Arthur Griffith and early Sinn Fein. Stephen condemns Griffith's so-called 'Hungarian policy' as based too loosely on superficial resemblances between the two countries, and faults Ireland's politicians for the absurdities which follow from their lack of a 'just sense of comparison': 'The intelligent centres of the movement were so scantily supplied that the analogies they gave out as exact and potent were really analogies built haphazard upon very inexact knowledge' (*SH*, p. 66–7). However, it could also be argued that Joyce's own political judgements rely on precisely such styles of superficial or analogical thought. His very enthusiasm for Griffith, indeed, itself owed to the fact that Joyce reckoned him to be a figure comparable to the Italian socialist Arturo Labriola, simply on the basis of their shared opposition to Parliamentary politics.[4] Much of his essay 'Fenianism' (1907) is concerned with a summary account of the differences between the 'two traditions' in Irish nationalism – constitutionalism and physical force – which he portrays in similarly schematic form. Thus he describes the latter:

> This party under different names: 'White Boys', 'Men of '98', 'United Irishmen', 'Invincibles', 'Fenians', has always refused to be connected with either the English parties or the Nationalist parliamentarians. They maintain (and in this assertion history fully supports them) that any concessions that have been granted to Ireland, England has granted unwillingly, and, as it is usually put, at the point of a bayonet. (*CW*, p. 188)

In 1882, the year of Joyce's birth, Parnell and Gladstone concluded the 'Kilmainham treaty'. Under its terms, Parnell agreed to use his influence to control the activities of the militant Land League in return for the Liberal Party's commitment to instituting Home Rule for Ireland. As Joyce records, this agreement between the two leaders marked an important shift from violent agrarianism to constitutionalism in Irish politics. Joyce proceeds to outline the fate of 'Fenianism' in the first decade of this century:

> Now, it is impossible for a bloody and desperate doctrine like Fenianism to continue its existence in an atmosphere like this, and in fact, as agrarian crimes and crimes of violence have become more and more rare, Fenianism too has once more changed its name and appearance. It is still a separatist doctrine but it no longer uses dynamite. (*CW*, p. 191)

In his account of the genesis of Arthur Griffith's Sinn Fein, Joyce revealingly emphasises its 'Irreconcilable' heritage, in spite of its refusal to sponsor political violence, presumably because Griffith, like the Republicans, shunned the politics of Westminister. Although Griffith's policy was 'separatist' in its advocacy of parliamentary autonomy for Ireland, his conception of Irish independence was radically at odds with that of Republican tradition: Griffith campaigned for the restoration of the constitution which had existed in Ireland before the Act of Union (1800), while radical separatist nationalism demanded a total severance of the link with Britain. In this light, it is strange that Joyce anticipates the revival of 'a bilingual, *republican*, self-centered, and enterprising island' (*CW*, p. 173, my emphasis) on the foundation of Griffith's programme. Either Joyce is simply inaccurate in his assessment of early Sinn Fein, or his concern neatly to delineate an actually existing

Republican heritage leads him to exaggerate certain features of that movement. He goes on to claim that the subterranean continuation of the separatist, violent tradition between the Fenian rebellion and the emergence of Arthur Griffith was demonstrated by two events:

> After the dispersal of the Fenians, the tradition of the doctrine of physical force shows up at intervals in violent crimes. The Invincibles blow up the prison at Clerkenwell, snatch their friends from the hands of the police at Manchester and kill the escort, stab to death in broad daylight the English Chief Secretary, Lord Frederick Cavendish, and the Under-Secretary, Burke, in Phoenix Park, Dublin. (*CW*, p. 190)

The attack on Clerkenwell prison in 1867 and the Phoenix Park murders of 1882: these are undoubtedly the two most infamous acts of Irish political violence in the second half of the nineteenth century. They are also the historical events to which most space is devoted in *Ulysses*. If Joyce's purpose was to expose and condemn the excesses of separatist nationalism, he could have chosen no more explicit illustrations of the random cruelty involved in terrorism. Alternatively, if the summary historical narrative which he traces in his essay also governs his representation of Irish history in the novel, then the attention he devotes to these incidents suggests that they are intended to connote more than aberrant, unrepresentative and cruel acts, and indeed symbolise the persistence of a tradition once more at the forefront. It is, in fact, Joyce's interest in these manifestations of 'Fenianism' which obliquely determine his pro-Griffith pronouncements.

In Chapter 3, Stephen Dedalus recalls his visit to Kevin Egan (Casey), in Paris. Casey had taken part in the attack on the police van in Manchester, and the attack on Clerkenwell had been intended to rescue him from prison. In his focus here on Egan, Malcolm Brown suggests, Joyce 'spotlighted a small, lurid, half-mad fragment that did exist, right enough, but did not represent much but itself'.[5] (In his 1907 essay Joyce employs the same imagery of light and darkness to *defend* the Fenian movement, which he describes as: '*not* one of the usual flashes of Celtic temperament that lighten the shadows for a moment and leave behind a darkness blacker than before' (*CW*, p. 189, my emphasis).) The death-toll at Clerkenwell was extremely high, largely due to the incompetence of the bombers. Brown reports:

> The explosion blew out nearly two hundred feet of brick wall and hurled forty tons of masonry across the exercise yard. It would have killed Burke and Casey if they had been there. It shattered every window in the jail, and across the street it demolished a

> block of tenements, killing twelve persons and maiming a hundred and twenty others.[6]

Hence Joyce's fictional rendition:

> Lover, for her love he prowled with colonel Richard Burke, tanist of his sept, under the walls of Clerkenwell and, crouching, saw a flame of vengeance hurl them upward in the fog. Shattered glass and toppling masonry. In gay Paree he hides, Egan of Paris, unsought by any save by me . . . (*U*, p. 36). They have forgotten Kevin Egan, not he them. Remembering thee, O Sion. (*U*, p. 37)

The English public was shocked by these killings. Such a reaction of outrage inspired the 'Dynamitards' – a break-away Fenian group – to make acts of terror in England its main pursuit; their belief in the efficacy of so-called 'propaganda by the deed' was shared by a number of anarchist groups of the time. Norman Sherry details how public revulsion at Fenian and anarchist attacks in London, together with the dissemination of new criminological theories, led to the inculcation of powerful criminal stereotypes in the popular mind. Joseph Conrad, he reports, drew on stereotypes of both Irish terrorists and anarchists for his pseudo-medical or scientific portrait of political criminality in *The Secret Agent* (1907).[7] Malcolm Brown attributes similar political motives to Joyce in his description of the Clerkenwell episode from Chapter 3 as a 'vignette heavy with disgust' for 'an addict of a demented nostalgia for a cause long dead'. Brown suggests that Joyce represents 'patriot compulsion' as 'a symptom of voyeurism, cuckoldry, homosexuality and nympholepsy'. Joyce, he reports, wrote in the same psychoanalytical age that inspired Dr Ernest Jones's Freudian interpretation of 'the Irish problem': 'those eccentric people who live on the lesser islands yearn for a motherland rather than a fatherland'.[8] Tom Paulin, however, draws a startlingly opposed conclusion on the basis of the same passage from 'Proteus', announcing: 'Thus Stephen, the artist-hero, is the inheritor of a long tradition of political rebellion'.[9] It may seem scarcely credible that Brown and Paulin are glossing the same passage. Brown clearly anticipates that Joyce's representation of the Clerkenwell explosion will be imbued with a profound moral disgust. As we can note in this case, however, this response is not obvious enough to impress itself on *every* informed reader of the text: Joyce's depiction of Egan is sufficiently oblique to enable critics to remark on it in directly contradictory ways, in apparent harmony with their own political dispositions.

Paulin's claim that a comradeship exists between aesthete and terrorist is sanctioned by the verbal parallels which Joyce draws between Stephen's attempt to destroy chronology in art, and the explosion which he associates with Egan. Stephen reflects in Chapter 2: 'A phrase, then, of impatience, thud of Blake's wings of excess. I hear the ruin of all space, shattered glass and toppling masonry, and time one livid final flame. What's left us then?' (*U*, p. 20). These words correspond with Joyce's description of Clerkenwell: 'Shattered glass and toppling masonry'. However, it could also be argued – in opposition to Paulin – that Stephen is troubled and disturbed, rather than inspired, by Egan's treatment of him as 'yokefellow', 'our crimes our common cause' (*U*, p. 36).

It is also interesting to note, in this context, that the origin of 'propaganda by the deed' in the philosophy of anarchism in fact aligns the Fenian terrorists with thinkers for whom – according to Manganiello – Joyce had a great deal of respect. He writes: 'The anarchists, like Bakunin, fascinated Joyce because, whereas Marx dictated an impersonal class warfare, they sought to liberate the individual from those forces that smothered human potentialities'.[10] Indeed Engels condemned the Phoenix Park murders precisely as 'Bakuninist' violence:

> But the Fenians themselves are being drawn increasingly to a type of Bakuninism; the assassination of Burke and Cavendish could have pursued the sole aim of thwarting the compromise between the Land League and Gladstone . . . . In this light the 'heroic deed' in Phoenix Park appears as a purely Bakuninist, boastful and senseless 'propagande par le fait' (propaganda by deed), if not as crass foolishness.[11]

Manganiello circumvents the embarrassment of reconciling Joyce's anarchist interests with his putative hatred for violence by asserting that, as a pacifist, he was really keener on such writers as Benjamin Tucker and Proudhon than Bakunin, although he records no evidence in support of this claim.[12] The *a priori* assumption that Joyce must always gravitate towards the position of moderation is by now familiar from commentary on his attitude to nationalism.

Malcolm Brown, as we have seen, self-consciously employs a discourse of criminal pathology in relation to Egan. This is based on the assumption that the Fenian's interest in the lasciviousness of the French reveals his own sexual perversity, and that this is symptomatic of political corruption: 'The *froeken, bonne à tout faire,* who rubs male nakedness in the bath at Upsala. *Moi faire,* she said, *tous les messieurs*. Not this *monsieur,* I said. Most licentious custom. Bath a most private thing' (p.36). As in *The Secret Agent,* a close association is drawn between sexual and political deviance: Egan, according to Brown, is implicated by the terms of his own discourse. Yet when this vocabulary of criminal pathology enters critical discussion about *Ulysses,* its application is invariably limited to the figures in the background of the text. This is in disregard of the fact that none of Joyce's characters provides more symptomatic evidence of what Brown details as 'voyeurism, cuckoldry, homosexuality and nympholepsy' than Leopold Bloom, in whom such foibles are apparently dissociated from the disease of 'patriot compulsion'. How convincing, then, is the critical ascription of this criminological purpose to Joyce, if elsewhere he parodies such a discourse or uses it in very different ways?

Joyce's explicit borrowings from modern codifications of sexual deviance and degeneracy occur mainly in the courtroom scenes from Chapter 15. When Bloom is accused of being 'a wellknown dynamitard, forger, bigamist, bawd and cuckold and a public nuisance to the citizens of Dublin' (*U*, p. 384), a number of legal and medical experts speak in his defence. Malachi Mulligan, 'sex specialist', announces:

> Born out of bedlock hereditary epilepsy is present, the consequence of unbridled lust. Traces of elephantiasis have been discovered among his ascendants. There are marked symptoms of chronic exhibitionism. Ambidexterity is also latent. He is prematurely bald from self-abuse, perversely idealistic in consequence, a reformed rake and has metal teeth. In consequence of a family complex he has temporarily lost his memory and I believe him to be more sinned against than sinning. (p. 402)

J.J. O'Molloy, in barrister's wig, offers an apologia in similar style:

> The trumped up misdemeanour was due to a momentary aberration of heredity, brought on by hallucination, such familiarities as the alleged guilty occurrence being quite permitted in my client's native place, the land of the Pharaoh . . . . I would deal in especial with atavism . . . . His submission is that he is of Mongolian extraction and irresponsible for his actions. Not all there in fact. (p. 378)

These speeches demonstrate, in a comic mode, how apparently enlightened scientific classifications quickly begin to betray connotations of genetic determination and racism. Joyce's interest in the scientific investigation of atavism and degeneracy is evinced by his citing of the work of the Italian criminologist Cesare Lombroso in *Stephen Hero* as the counterpart of an advanced and enlightened art. Recent studies of Joyce have offered voluminous evidence of his continuing fascination with sexology, deviance and the new science of contraception.[13] However, this has generally been marshalled to argue for Joyce's deconstruction of 'normal' sexuality, and particularly his valorization of Bloom as the hero of sexual modernity. Tony Tanner argues that *Ulysses* collapses all traditional oppositions between perversion and normality, as a text in which perversity is the 'normal' mode of procedure:[14] Bloom is not then condemned for his sexual peculiarities, but exonerated from any 'crime'. If this consensus is accepted, then the critical assumption that Joyce employs categories of pathological perversity in purely negative form when it comes to extreme nationalism must surely be treated with scepticism.

There are also a number of revealing inconsistencies in critical accounts of the significance of the other major incident of political violence in *Ulysses*, the murders in the Phoenix Park. These killings, as we have seen, directly followed Parnell's successful negotiation with Gladstone and the 'Kilmainham Treaty' of 1882. The leader of the Irish Parliamentary Party was so horrified at the news of the deaths that he feared that all the progress he had made with the British would be overturned, and considered offering his resignation to the Prime Minister. Manganiello announces that this incident 'forced Joyce to take a stand against political violence and against the physical force tradition in Irish history':[15] if so, Joyce faced this painful dilemma, and manifested this admirable level of political maturity, at the tender age of three months. Matthew Hodgart describes the significance of the Phoenix Park murders in Joyce's novel:

> The gang made a successful getaway, but were later caught, thanks to an informer, one Carey, who was himself later assassinated. I have given space to this sordid incident, which except for the eminence of its victims has been paralleled hundreds of times in Ireland, because it haunted Joyce. Some reference to the murders appears in almost every chapter of *Ulysses*, and it is typical of the violence from which Joyce recoiled and from which Bloom is meant to offer some kind of deliverance.[16]

When Hodgart states that the Phoenix Park murderers were apprehended '*thanks* to an informer', it is safe to infer that this locution expresses gratitude and approbation, as well as simply causation. Criticism of the novel more typically revolves on the unstated paradox that Joyce censures both nationalist violence, and the betrayal of its perpetrators, with admirable even-handedness. However, it is not entirely clear how the Irish tradition of informing can be condemned so confidently if a commitment to the cause served by the men of violence is also deemed to be morally reprehensible. Even Bloom seems to disdain the betrayer of the Invincibles when he compares him to the notably unsavoury Mr Kelleher: 'Never know who you're talking to. Corny Kelleher he has Harvey Duff in his eye. Like that Peter or Denis or James Carey that blew the gaff on the invincibles' (*U*, p. 134).

This is a paradox not, however, clarified by Joyce's own pronouncements. Indeed I would argue that it represents just the kind of symptomatic ambiguity in his political thought which has been so misleadingly simplified to an idea of impeccable fair-mindedness. Such ambiguities abound in essays like 'Ireland, Island of Saints and Sages'. Ellmann and Mason, in their prefatory remarks to this piece, point out that in spite of the sympathetic audience Joyce enjoyed when he delivered the original lecture in Trieste, and the obvious sympathy to the nationalist case his argument displays, Joyce none the less 'felt compelled to point out that his country had its history of betrayals, of eloquent inactivity, of absurd and narrow belief'. However, Joyce's editors, at least, do not proceed to judge that in this Joyce represented the voice of moderate common sense, but rather refuse him his self-appointed position of what he calls an 'unprejudiced observer': 'His attitude, though he calls it objective, wavers between affectionate fascination with Ireland and distrust of her' (*CW*, p. 153).

In this lecture, Joyce refers to Ireland as 'a country destined by God to be the everlasting caricature of the serious world', and claims 'that it is rather naive to heap insults on England for her misdeeds in Ireland'. In apparent exasperation with nationalist laments, he states that he cannot understand 'the purpose of bitter invective against the English despoiler, the disdain for the vast Anglo-Saxon civilisation, even though it is almost entirely a materialistic civilisation'. However, one could equally construct a very differently nuanced argument on the basis of his remarks, emphasising instead its attack on 'the phrasemakers of Fleet Street', and the caricature of Ireland propagated by British culture. Joyce bitterly attacks the representation of the Irish in the popular press, 'the unbalanced, helpless idiots about whom we read in the lead articles of the *Standard* and *Morning Post*', and questions the validity of the stereotype of Irish political separatists as 'madmen'. He also, however, insists that the Anglo-Norman invasion (the originary 'English' occupation of Ireland, in nationalist mythography) was instigated by an Irish king, and that the Act of Union was legislated by an Irish Parliament. As an Irish citizen, Joyce demands an explanation for these two monstrous blunders before the country in which such shameful events occurred 'has the most rudimentary right to persuade one of her sons to change his position from that of an unprejudiced observer to that of a convinced nationalist'. But this proclamation, too, is immediately qualified:

> On the other hand, impartiality can easily be confused with a convenient disregard of facts, and if an observer, fully convinced that at the time of Henry II Ireland was a body torn by fierce strife and at the time of William Pitt was a venal and wicked mess of corruption, draws from these facts the conclusion that England does not have many crimes to expiate in Ireland, now and in the

> future, he is very much mistaken. When a victorious country tyrannizes over another, it cannot logically be considered wrong for that other to rebel. (*CW*, p. 163)

In the face of this series of rather inconsistent arguments, a judgement such as that offered by Philip Herring may appear plausible. Herring concludes his discussion of Joyce's lecture with the exemplary remark: 'The near extinction of Irish culture and language and the systematic persecution of Catholics were effectively counterbalanced by Ireland's history of self-betrayal'.[17] The idea of the 'effective counterbalance' which Herring proposes, with the implication that the moral wrong of imperialist violence is cancelled out by the failure of the Irish to respond effectively and consistently to it, is among the most influential critical ideas which have been used to make sense of Joyce's attitude towards Irish nationalism. But what his critics see as detached ambivalence was experienced as painful deadlock by Joyce. His writings about Ireland may not provide a coherent critique of either colonised or colonialist; but their very ambiguities and hesitations testify to the uncertain, divided consciousness of the colonial subject, which he is unable to articulate in its full complexity outside his fiction.

Joyce's last substantial treatment of the Irish situation in essay form is 'The Shade of Parnell' (1912). He writes at the culmination of decades of campaigning and negotiation for Home Rule at Westminister, and in tones of unprecedented bitterness:

> The century which began with the transaction of buying and selling the Dublin parliament is now closing with a triangular pact between England, Ireland and the United States. It was graced with six Irish revolutionary movements which, by the use of dynamite, rhetoric, the boycott, obstructionism, armed revolt, and political assassination, have succeeded in keeping awake the slow and senile conscience of English liberalism. (*CW*, p. 224)

Parnell, Joyce prophesies, will be the shade at the banquet for the celebration of this meagre achievement, which he refers to derisively as the mere 'appearance of autonomy'. Of course, Home Rule was never to arrive in the form in which Joyce anticipates it. The outbreak of war delayed implementation of the change, and in the meantime the Easter Rebellion was radically to change the Irish political situation.

However, as Marx reminds us in 'The Eighteenth Brumaire', ghosts often walk at such revolutionary times, paradoxically just when women and men are most intently occupied in creating for themselves entirely new futures. If the banquet for the miserable prize of Home Rule is significant enough to enjoy such a noble haunting, then the 'carnival with masked licence' (*U*, p. 399) in the 'Circe' episode of *Ulysses*, merits the visits of numerous ghosts. These festivities, in fact, are preyed on by the accusations and recriminations of revenants, alternatively tragic and farcical. In this, 'Circe' proves analogous to Marx's description of bourgeois revolutions which

> storm swiftly from success to success; their dramatic effects outdo each other; men and things seem set in sparkling brilliants; ecstasy is the everyday spirit; but they are short-lived; soon they have attained their zenith, and long crapulent depression lays hold of society before it learns soberly to assimilate the results of its storm-and-stress period.[18]

If we read 'Circe' as both Joyce's acknowledgement of Ireland's revolution and his testimony to its limitations, it may be easier to judge whether the shade of Parnell – which haunts all of Joyce's texts – is merely the measure of his inability to move with the political times, his commitment to a lost cause of history even 'in the face of practical alternatives'.[19] Perhaps Parnell, who by 1912 functions for Joyce – however erroneously – as a symbol of the futility of constitutionalism, compromise and pragmatism, can alternatively be read as the image of a *real* past out of which a better future might have been built.

'CIRCE' AND 1916

Joyce designated 'the locomotor apparatus' – a term for those parts of the human body specifically adapted for movement – his 'Organ' for Chapter 15, although in Nighttown, arms and legs are more noticeable for their failure to move bodies about properly than they are for efficiency or mobility. The limbs of the human and sub-human creatures in 'Circe''s nightmarish procession seem to be afflicted by the venereal ailment 'locomotor ataxy' (*U*, p. 425), about which the prostitute Florry comments so knowingly. Diseased and broken human bodies litter these streets; gnomes, bandy and scrofulous children, armless, dwarfed and simian figures lurch, tremble and dribble. The 'technique' – and the subject matter – of 'Circe' is 'hallucination', which produces, as Patrick McGee claims, 'a groundless and objectless writing'[20] in its divorce from any reference to external or material reality. But Joyce's consistent linkage between perceptual disturbance and sickness in fact works to ground the linguistic fantasia of the chapter in very specific social conditions, which, for example, Kitty's remarks suggest:

> And Mary Shortall that was in the lock with the pox she got from Jimmy Pidgeon in the blue caps had a child off him that couldn't swallow and was smothered with the convulsions in the mattress and we all subscribed for the funeral. (*U*, p. 424)

Bloom reflects during this escapade that Molly often said that she would have liked to visit Nighttown – 'Slumming. The exotic, you see' (*U*, p. 362) – and the chapter, for both the revelling participants and the reader, is pervaded by the exoticism of both the brothel and of the tenement.

On one level, then, Joyce's subversive attention to limbs, apertures, mouths and bowels in his portrayal of the expressionistic Circean body –

THE HOBGOBLIN

> *(his jaws chattering, capers to and fro, goggling his eyes, squeaking, kangaroohopping with outstretched clutching arms, then all at once thrusts his lipless face through the fork of his thighs) Il vient! C'est moi! L'homme qui rit! L'homme primigène! (he whirls round and round with dervish howls).* (*U*, p. 413)

– answers very precisely to Mikhail Bakhtin's description of the importance of the productive 'material bodily lower stratum' in folk humour and satire:

> Thus the artistic logic of the grotesque image ignores the closed, smooth and impenetrable surface of the body and retains only its excrescences (sprouts, buds) and orifices, only that which leads beyond the body's limited space or into the body's depths.[21]

At the same time, however, 'Circe' registers the suffering and humiliation associated with the loss of bodily unity and control: 'Hey, shitbreeches' (*U*, p. 355), the motorman calls after Leopold near the beginning of the episode. Equally, Bloom's fantastical alibis and aliases are first produced in response to the aggressive obstruction of his passage through the streets of Dublin, and his interrogation by figures in authority who patrol them. From the moment Bloom follows Dedalus into Nighttown, these alternative identities are designed as a strategy for evading 'identification' – in a legal and political sense – by watchmen, policemen and spies.

Hence, for all of 'Circe''s subversions – the reversal of gender hierarchies, obliteration of class distinctions, interruptions of linear time, confusions between public and private, conscious and unconscious – the very notion of carnival is also located and dramatized within a recognisable political and cultural context in this episode. We learn in 'Circe' that the consequence of many of these inversions is ultimately the re-establishment of the pre-existing power relations. Bloom's incarnation, as 'the new womanly man' (*U*, p. 403), for example, is only made possible by virtue of his projection of Bella Cohen as a sadistic, fetishistic figure. Her cruelty to him then serves to justify his misogynistic dismissal of all the prostitutes when the reverie is over. 'Fool someone else', he tells her, 'not me. (*He sniffs.*) Rut. Onions. Sulphur. Grease' (*U*, p. 452). The revolution enacted by this carnival is fictive and transient: the phrase, in Marx's formulation, goes beyond the content. I will argue that Chapter 15 also makes a number of related attempts to recreate or transcend the social conditions it describes, thus demonstrating the analogies which obtain between this practice of writing and such Utopian strategies. Joyce's writing cannot help but indicate their limits: however, the text's intimacy with – and implication in – the resolutions that it simultaneously travesties, makes any straightforward notion of satire or critique untenable in this context. Moreover, some of these ideas – both about politics, mainly the focus of Bloom's interventions, and about aesthetics, mainly Stephen's concern – run significantly parallel to the kinds of ideological solutions to Ireland's problems which inspired the rebels of 1916. More precisely, 'Circe' stages the question of whether an Irish version of British capitalism is really the appropriate fulfilment of Irish nationalist aspiration. I propose that the issue of the cultural meaning of economic and political modernisation – the central topic of nationalism – can here be addressed in conjunction with the *modernist* quest for a universal language, one which would transcend the realm of cultural and political contestation.

If all bourgeois revolutions are flawed by the contradiction between form and substance which Marx identifies, then the Easter Rebellion of 1916 surely demonstrates the farcical implications of this in a particularly privileged form. It was a revolution organized by myth-makers and poets: activists who could not even decide on what day the uprising was to take place, and some of whom had to interrupt their rehearsal of a play by W.B. Yeats to participate; insurgents who even forgot to bring the glue to paste up copies of their Proclamation of the Irish Republic. Indeed, no signed original of this document now exists and, in true Derridean style, there may never have been one: all the copies were printed copies, the names of all the signatories printed reproductions. On Easter Monday morning, Patrick Pearse read the Proclamation from the steps of the GPO to a largely indifferent crowd, many people attempting to go about their daily business as usual. If the Irish Revolution was particularly 'surreal' in one sense, then, it certainly failed to unleash the dizzying libidinal intensities in the general populace that Kristin Ross describes as typically the experience of modern revolutionary subjects: Wyndham Lewis's remarks about its 'artificial, psuedo-historical air' might seem more appropriate to the hostile observer.[22] Nonetheless, as Edgar Holt reminds us, for the ordinary citizens of Dublin the night of 24 April was quite literally a drunken carnival:

> With no policemen to stop them, men, women and children poured out of the city slums and were soon breaking the windows of shops in O'Connell Street and helping themselves to the goods displayed . . . slatternly children broke into sweet shops and came out loaded with boxes of chocolates, while their elders sat on the pavements trying on looted boots and shoes. Gold watches were taken from a jeweller's shop and offered for sale at a shilling each, girls put gold bangles on their ankles, and at a big store men delved eagerly into boxes of shirts and pyjamas . . . . The bars were crowded with looters of both sexes . . . . The day that had brought Pearse's heroic proclamation of Ireland's destiny ended with Irishmen reeling drunkenly home through the Dublin streets and unkempt women staggering back to the slums with heavy loads of stolen finery.[23]

The tenement dwellers failed to respond heroically to the high-sounding rhetoric of the Rebellion, but it could also be pointed out that they were prescient in their cynicism. For them, the revolution was indeed to change very little, as whatever social content it possessed was drastically compromised during the process which led to the Treaty, partition and the Free State. The theatricality of the Rebellion may have signalled its success as modernist artifice, but it is also the index of its failure to transform the underlying material reality of the lives of the people it claimed to represent. The fact that the uprising was celebrated in an orgy of consumerist fantasy in O'Connell Street also, as we will see, proves suggestive in the context of 'Circe'.

Cheryl Herr argues that Chapter 15 represents the most direct treatment in *Ulysses* of the contradictions shaping daily life in early twentieth-century Ireland:

> 'Circe' is as much the world of an imperialized experience as it is of the unconscious. It is no exaggeration to state that although critics have tended to focus on the significance of the episode for the purgation of various psychic problems of Stephen and Bloom, 'Circe' insists on being read as a portrait of cultural psychosis.[24]

The relation between this 'cultural psychosis' and Irish history is illuminated if we recognize the degree to which 'Circe' confounds and confuses cultural and national identities, as well as ones of class and gender. At the level of content, Joyce stages a confrontation between urban Irish culture and British popular culture through his citations of British popular songs and his unflattering rendition of the English working-class speech of Privates Carr and Compton. These mingle with working-class Dublin accents, which predominate here for perhaps the first time in *Ulysses*. And, as Herr records, the form of 'Circe' is indebted to popular entertainments – pantomime and music hall in particular – which were British in origin, and indeed commonly charged in Ireland with being 'anti-national': a contributor to D.P. Moran's *The Leader* denounced the music halls as 'regular night-schools for Anglicisation'.[25] According to Herr, the episode both alludes to and simultaneously undermines the Utopian impulses of modern popular culture, in its ironic borrowings of such pantomime devices as the transformation scene. She remarks: 'That society went for its answers to the realm of fairyland and folklore suggests the strength of the underlying resistance to significant socio-economic changes; that Joyce refused to do the same indicates an active critique of this programming for social inactivity.'[26]

Moreover, there is in Joyce's text a consistent identification of modern consumer culture with *Englishness* or – more or less interchangeably – Britishness: nationalist ideology, as we have seen, invariably attempts to wrest the promise and potential of modernisation out of its initial association with such cultural domination. In, for example, Bloom's vision of a commodified Utopia, British and Irish motifs are superimposed:

> *An acclimatised Britisher, he had seen that summer eve from the footplate of an engine cab of the Loop line railway company while the rain refrained from falling glimpses, as it were, through the windows of loveful households in Dublin city and urban district of scenes truly rural of happiness of the better land with Dockrell's wallpaper at one and ninepence a dozen, innocent Britishborn bairns lisping prayers to the Sacred Infant . . . all with fervour reciting the family rosary round the crackling Yulelog while in boreens and green lanes the colleens and their swains strolled what times the strains of the organtoned melodeon Britanniametalbound, with four acting stops and twelvefold bellows, a sacrifice, greatest bargain ever.* (*U*, p. 377)

This hallucinatory vision of cultural integration is not sustainable: at the end of his speech Bloom begins to mumble incoherently, and the audience shouts that they can no longer hear him. When open hostility breaks out between Stephen and the soldiers, the nursery rhyme refrain 'London's burning! London's burning!' – previously cited in a neutral way – is redeployed to describe the night sky: 'Dublin's burning! Dublin's burning!' (*U*, p. 488). When Bloom, in another of his Circean transmogrifications, is asked 'When will we have our own house of keys?' (i.e. Parliamentary independence), he replies:

> I stand for the reform of municipal morals and the plain ten commandments. New worlds for old. Union of all, jew, moslem and gentile . . . . Tuberculosis, lunacy, war and mendicancy must now cease. General amnesty, weekly carnival with masked licence,

> bonuses for all, esperanto the universal language with universal brotherhood. No more patriotism of barspongers and dropsical impostors. Free money, free rent, free love and a free lay church in a free lay state. (*U*, p. 399)

Bloom, that is to say, calls for these reforms to be instituted immediately: there is no need for the intervention of those he believes to be charlatan nationalists, and perhaps no need even for political autonomy – after all, he does fail to answer the question addressed to him. Bloom's speeches in 'Circe' are commonly regarded as central statements of Joyce's own political credo. Such judgements about Joyce's politics cannot be deemed either accurate or inaccurate in the context of this phantasmagoria. The sentiments expressed by Bloom, we might say, are the most radical the text is capable of articulating: however, the limitations of these well-meaning proposals are also displayed within it. The drawbacks of a 'carnival for all with masked licence' are here clearly demonstrated; and it is apparent that there can be no 'universal language with universal brotherhood' in the present conditions of conflict which obtain between languages and cultures. Translating all human communication into the apparently neutral medium of 'esperanto' will not in itself bring such conflicts to an end: even the esperanto of 'Circe' – the hallucinatory compound of England and Ireland, man and woman, rich and poor – proves explosively unstable. Bloom, then, both projects his culture's Utopian fantasies and exhibits its ideological insufficiencies; his position is not satirized by the text of 'Circe', but neither is it presented without considerable irony. Bloom offers no resolution of the contradictions which emerge during 'this scuffle on a Dublin street'.[27]

If Bloom faces audiences in this episode which oscillate between adulation and hostility with remarkable rapidity, then Stephen – like Pearse on Easter Monday morning – addresses a baffled and indifferent one. As Dedalus arrives on the scene in Nighttown he '*chants with joy the* introit *for paschal time*', intoning the the Easter antiphon '*Salvi facti sunt*' (*U*, p. 353) – 'they were made whole (saved)': he thus introduces an appropriately triumphalist Paschal note for this 'festivity' or 'sacrament' (*U*, p. 399). This also blends with a Pentecostal motif: at Pentecost, Christ's disciples were granted 'the gift of tongues', the ability to speak a version of human language that would be comprehensible to each of their listeners in his or her own language. Stephen expresses his desire for such a dialect, a universal language which closely parallels Bloom's notion of esperanto: 'So that gesture, not music not odour, would be a universal language, the gift of tongues rendering visible not the lay sense but the first entelechy, the structural rhythm' (*U*, p. 353). We more usually associate Joycean modernism with a celebration of the *felix culpa* of linguistic multiplicity, in its waging of what Jacques Derrida describes as 'a Babelian act of war'.[28] However, the characteristically modernist search for deep structures, which Stephen articulates here, also seeks to frustrate the punishment of Babel not by uncovering some pre-lapsarian or originary tongue but by confounding all languages – which is of course, Joyce's startling achievement in *Finnegans Wake*. This universal language, in which all languages are equally at home, does indeed function as an origin to the extent that it enfolds all potentialities – past and future – within itself. All languages are one language; all places one place, the world becomes one and has one history: this is the logic of modernity. Nationalism, as we have seen, cunningly attempts to make the best of both worlds, the traditional and the modern; Bloom opts contentedly for the new; but Dedalus seeks an equivalent compromise, and aspires to create a new world-language which will accommodate within itself the old language. Stephen Heath, however, is anxious to deny the existence of any quest for origins or closures in Stephen's pronouncements, instead claiming that 'Circe' enacts 'a constant theatralization of language in its productivity'.[29] To the extent that this drama necessarily encounters issues of class and gender, and demonstrates them to be materially grounded in economic deprivation and sexual exploitation, it may indeed point to the text's transcendence of the politics with which it is complicit. A nationalist revolution which does not take sufficient account of the differences within the community which it defines risks merely preserving old forms of oppression, as the inheritors of the tradition of 1916 found to their cost.

The effects of this carnivalesque explosion, then, are by no means straightforward or controllable. Among the visitors here are many of our old friends, the Irish Romantic nationalists: the Croppy Boy, the citizen, a creature called 'The End of the World' who sounds suspiciously like George Russell, and especially Old Gummy Granny, who hands Stephen a dagger and prays for him to be killed. However, Joyce's deployment in this comic extravaganza of the tragic motifs of blood sacrifice and apocalypse, dear to those whom George Watson describes as 'the teleologists of Irish nationalism', does not merely enable them to be securely satirized, 'spoofed', or in Watson's terms, 'specifically mocked'.[30] Chapter 15 is no more a 'spoof' of an aestheticized, apocalyptic history than it is a spoof of Bakhtinian carnival or popular culture. These ghosts are not laid to rest so easily. Moreover, tragedy and farce are not in any case so conveniently distinct. Wyndham Lewis calls Joyce and Yeats 'the prose and then poetry respectively of the Ireland that culminated in the Rebellion'.[31] If so, then Yeats's poetic account of what happened at Easter 1916 apparently takes the form of a celebration of this heroic apocalypse:

> When Pearse summoned Cuchulain to his side,
> What stalked through the Post Office?[32]

In a comic, demystifying and demotic mode, 'Circe' provides the prose version of that same question. Its ghosts are not 'summoned' in some grand rhetorical gesture: they are, like the British soldiers in the tenements, uninvited guests (*U*, p. 479). None of the revellers seeks out the bitter and vengeful voices of the past, but they none the less make themselves heard, apparently thrown up spontaneously by the merry round of drinking, dancing and sex. In this, they perhaps stand not only for the nightmares of history that cannot be forgotten; but also as reminders of a revolutionary promise which, having been disappointed, refuses to be appeased.

5

'POOR LITTLE BRITTLE MAGIC NATION'[1]

Finnegans Wake as a post-colonial novel

Contemporary nationalisms from the so-called Third World depart from nineteenth-century European nationalist tradition in their disavowal of what Edward Said has called the 'heroic narratives' of the Romantic and imperial nation. In the work of present-day post-colonial novelists, according to Timothy Brennan, the 'nation' none the less persists as a vital 'discursive formation' – 'not simply an allegory or imaginative vision, but a gestative political structure which the Third-World artist is very often either consciously building or suffering the lack of' – and in the naturally cosmopolitan form of the novel, Brennan claims, it often finds expression in a fiction where

> the contradictory topoi of exile and nation are fused in a lament for the necessary and regrettable insistence of nation-forming, in which the writer proclaims his [*sic*] identity with a country whose artificiality and exclusiveness have driven him into a kind of exile – a simultaneous recognition of nationhood and an alienation from it.[2]

Irish literature, of course, encompasses a significant body of Romantic nationalist writing. This, from Thomas Davis – who specifically acknowledged his indebtedness to German Romantic thought – to the poetry of W.B. Yeats, has played a major role in a project of cultural decolonisation. Joyce's work, as we have seen, alludes to these heroic overtones of nation only sporadically and in a very muted register, and partakes instead of a more quotidian, secular and novelistic conception of the time, space and plots of the nation state. As a result of this, Joyce might be interpreted as sharing, from the very outset, in Brennan's 'nationalism of mourning' which is so typical of anti-imperialist writers *after* national independence has been achieved, when the heroism of struggle recedes and the divisions strategically suppressed in the interests of a putative national unity come to the fore. If Joyce's writing testifies to 'nation-forming' in this fashion, then we might anticipate that this would be intensified in the case of *Finnegans Wake*: Joyce's last book was written in the aftermath of the institution of the two presently existing Irish states – 'New South Ireland and Vetera Uladh' (*FW*, p. 78), as the *Wake* calls them – and during the rise of continental fascism, which permanently discredited nationalist modes of thought for so many European thinkers and writers.

Perhaps the main question which we confront here, then, is how to trace this potentially more sympathetic, dialectical and recognizably post-colonial response to nationalism in a work which so relentlessly dismantles all national languages and freely confounds historical epochs, events and individuals. In Philippe Sollers' well-known account of *Finnegans Wake* as 'the most formidably anti-fascist book produced between the two wars', for example, Joyce's attack on nationalism, his repudiation of any pure national language and of any 'imaginary' human collectivity are viewed as intimately related:

> Joyce's refusal to indulge in the slightest dead pronouncement is exactly *itself* the political act, an act which explodes at the heart of the rhetorical *polis*, at the heart of the narcissistic recognition of the human group: the end of nationalisms decided by Joyce at the time when national crises are at their most virulent . . . . What Joyce is in the process of constructing with *Finnegans Wake*, from 1923 to 1939, is an active transnationalism, disarticulating, rearticulating and at the same time annulling the maximum number of traces – linguistic, historical, mythological, religious. In what he writes, *nothing remains but differences*, and so he calls into question all and every community (this is referred to as his 'unreadability').[3]

Joyce's apparent assault on the narcissism of community, however, has more often been assimilated to a facile universalism, exemplified by William York Tindall's prefatory remark to his explication of the text: '*Finnegans Wake* is about anybody, anywhere, anytime.'[4] While it is futile to deny the basis of these interpretations of the *Wake* in Joyce's experimental fiction, I am concerned here to question the detached and historically transcendent view-points which both Sollers and Tindall – from very different critical perspectives – ascribe to the author, and offer to the commentator. Ironically, Joyce's Wakean 'unreadability' is insistently presented in the text itself as a protest against the too-easy apprehension of any merely written history. It is a complaint against what Samuel Beckett calls 'the rapid skimming and absorption of the scant cream of sense':[5] the assumption of a passive relationship not merely with the historical *text*, but also with the history it purports to represent. One of the central critical encounters repeatedly dramatized

– and satirized – in the *Wake* is that between antiquarian historian and the annals of the past. As Joyce writes:

> So, how idlers' winds turning pages on pages, as innocens with anaclete play popeye antipop, the leaves of the living in the boke of the deeds, annals of themselves timing the cycles of events grand and national, bring fassilwise to pass how. (*FW*, p. 13).

So, at the further level of the encounter between reader and the text of *Finnegans Wake*, this leisurely idleness is challenged by the fact that the reader is obliged to labour at interpretation, and indeed forced to participate in the production of the text, although, of course, this readerly praxis necessarily remains symbolic and private. Taking on this burden of interpretation, however, apparently discharges the critic from any engagement with that historical praxis with which the text as a whole is concerned. In this way, *Wake* readers have failed to appreciate that the book of the deeds of the dead is still continuous with the stories and the actions of the living: in the absence of this further level of implication and participation, this conflictive and contradictory history is reduced to a mere game by the complacent commentator. Too many readers have merely taken the text at its word, enthusiastically embracing its vision of a cyclical human history in which all conflict is ultimately subsumed and cancelled in a comic vision of eternal recurrence. Hence all antagonists in the end find themselves agreeing, and spatial confrontation dissolves back into a temporal flux: consequently, as one critic puts it, 'Joyce ridicules all patriotic aspirations and portrays the outcome of independence-seeking . . . as a matter of Tweedledum and Tweedledee'.[6] Our task here is to attend to Joyce's unquestionable success in enabling the critical enjoyment of such a comic and cyclical history, while not neglecting the specific history which he draws into his writing in order that it might be transcended at the level of form. In this way a corrective may be supplied to the surprising insensitivity to issues of colonial politics so often displayed by commentary on the text.

During the early months of 1922 – to quote Richard Ellmann's rather sanguine account – 'Ireland was achieving independence just as *Ulysses* was achieving publication':[7] a few months later, the new Irish Free State had broken down in civil war. At stake was the Anglo-Irish Treaty, which had been negotiated by representatives of Eamon De Valera's government in December 1921, and which instituted the separation of the southern twenty-six counties from the northern six counties: the supporters of De Valera, who rejected the constitutional arrangements agreed at the London meeting, clashed violently with the pro-Treaty forces under the command of Michael Collins. Critics such as John Garvin and Dominic Manganiello have exhaustively explicated the enormous volume of allusion to the war in *Finnegans Wake*.[8] Joyce makes copious reference both to the Treaty, and to De Valera's alternative, the so-called 'Document Number Two', which he attempted to have ratified by the Dail in place of the original text. Many of the disputes which led ultimately to military conflict revolved around questions about texts and writing, oaths and proclamations, and these debates about authorship, authority, language and reality evidently appealed strongly to Joyce's literary imagination. Manganiello points out that Parnell's declaration to the Irish people, 'When you sell, get my price', to which Joyce repeatedly alludes in the book, also influences his treatment of the Treaty negotiations and of partition in *Finnegans Wake*. It lurks behind the numerous representations of bungled and dishonest transactions in the text, and its description of post-partition Dublin as: 'A phantom city, phaked of philim pholk, bowed and sould for a four of hundreds of manhood in their three and three-score fylkers for a price partitional of twenty six and six' (*FW*, p. 264). This, according to John Garvin, represents Joyce's cynical 'verdict' on independent Ireland:[9] 'At the cost of the death of her own people Ireland did not get the full price in her negotiations with Britain', Manganiello concludes.[10] Whether or not we question the specificity of these remarks made on behalf of Joyce by his political critics, it remains significant that even at this allusive level, the fact of partition is treated in tones of apparent regret and lament throughout *Finnegans Wake*. These echo even in ALP's concluding meditations on the 'invision of Indelond . . . though dev do espart' (*FW*, p. 626). In one of his earliest letters to Harriet Shaw Weaver about *Work in Progress*, in October 1923, Joyce schematically indicated his plans to incorporate representative figures for the four provinces of Ireland, and samples of the dialects of the North, South, East and West (*SL*, p. 297), into his book. In his deployment of the figures of the Gaelic Four Masters, and in his placing of the 'Yawn under Inquest' chapter (III.3) at the very centre of ancient Ireland – The Hill of Uisneach, sacred site of the Middle or Fifth Province, in present-day Co. Westmeath – Joyce manifests a drive towards integration and unification which is by no means politically innocent.[11] His imaginative recuperation of 'Irrland's split little pea' (*FW*, p. 171) parallels in its inclusiveness the Irish nationalist vision of one green island, against which, for example, Ulster Unionists have so consistently protested. This is an interesting anomaly in a text which has always been read as celebrating difference and the destruction of any unitary identity: as in Flann O'Brien's novel *The Poor Mouth*, the ghost which haunts this comic text is revealed as bearing the familiar 'shape of the pleasant little land which is our own'.[12]

The Irish Civil War also forms an integral component of the fraternal antagonism between the sons of the Wakean family. As David Pierce states:

> Just as *Ulysses* belongs to a period of expectancy that found its now perennially hopeful expression in the one day in June in 1904, in a parallel way *Finnegans Wake* gives voice to the disorder and disillusionment that befell Irish politics in the immediate aftermath of the Anglo-Irish War, when civil war and internecine feuding broke out between the warring brothers Shem and Shaun.[13]

This is emphasized by the persistent identification of the figure of Shem the Penman with Joyce himself, and that of the Shaun-figure with De Valera, an opposition which grows especially poignant as the exiled artist hears 'through deafths of durkness greengrown deeper . . . . [the] vote of the Irish, voise from afar' (*FW*, p. 407) in the third book of the text.[14] De Valera, at this point, is no longer the republican leader of the twenties but rather the constitutional politician of the following decades: after his defeat in the war, De Valera entered the Dail at the head of a new party, and set about dismantling the Treaty – apart from its provision for partition – from within. It is as the guiding spirit and virtually the sole author of the 1937 Constitution of the Irish Republic, which enshrined the special position of the Catholic Church in the life of the nation, that De Valera is memorialized by Joyce in the figure of the pious and sermonizing Shaun or 'Kev'. As a dramatisation of the painful dislocation between the motifs of 'exile' and 'nation', therefore, this geminal conflict could scarcely be more precisely historically located. Nonetheless, at the beginning of the Civil War, Joyce told Harriet Shaw Weaver that he was preparing to write a book which should be a kind of 'universal history':[15] its consummate internationality, then, must be understood as bearing the imprint of very local disappointments and failures. As Seamus Deane argues:

> *Finnegans Wake* is Joyce's Irish answer to an Irish problem. It is written in a ghost language about phantasmal figures; history is haunted by them and embodies them over and over again in specific people, places and tongues. If Ireland could not be herself, then, by way of compensation, the world would become Ireland. Thus is the problem of identity solved. Irish history is world history *in parvo*.[16]

Finnegans Wake is Joyce's reflection on his 'wastobe land' (*FW*, p. 62), in which 'all that has been done has yet to be done and done again' (*FW*, p. 194).

We face major difficulties, however, in critically describing Joyce's translation of the apparently marginal and local into the idiom of the universal. As *Ulysses*'s successive styles are replaced by what one critic calls the 'simultaneous polyphony'[17] of *Finnegans Wake*, the specifically colonial determinations of Joyce's text are occluded. Often what J. Colm O'Sullivan describes as 'the invasions, assimilations, changes of sides, betrayals, assassinations and braggadocio' of Irish history are regarded simply as 'a superb metaphor' for Joyce's essentially wider and more generally relevant interests and preoccupations.[18] Irish experience stands merely as an apt microcosmic representation of all the inevitable strife and turmoil of human history, and hence the specifics of cultural and political domination are naturalised. Alternatively, the relation between coloniser and colonised is assimilated to the paradigm of the psychic development and maturation of a single individual. Here, the necessity for the 'native' Id to be subdued by the mature Ego is acknowledged, and we are invited to appreciate that the unreflective, primitive and indigenous being is launched into a productive dialectic with its advanced counterpart by means of the experience of colonization. As Kimberly Devlin writes:

> This imperialistic warfare can be interpreted as another version of the self/other conflict, because it entails a 'native' or original personality defending itself against interference from external or 'foreign' forces. The goals of socialization and imperialist conflict, after all, are strangely similar: the 'civilized' interloper desires to repress and finally subsume the identity and impulses of the 'native' or primal self . . . . In short, the repressive 'other' consistently appears as a representative of external authority, as one of many societal hierarchs. He embodies symbolically those codes and laws that give civilization its shape and order, and that the inchoate self must inevitably confront.[19]

Hence, both the options of reading the text as a 'universal' or as an 'individual' history tend to universalize the historical experiences out of which it is produced. These two interpretative strategies are, of course, by no means irreconcilable: indeed they may even be seen as complementary and interchangeable. Sollers' denunciation of nationalism as a 'twofold obstruction – to the unconscious and to the area of the international' might be understood as encompassing them both, in a call to recognize the 'truth' of the unconscious which is both trans-individual and trans-cultural.[20] However, the possibility of examining the text in a broader context of post-colonial culture has tended to be neglected by its critics. I would not seek to argue that such dominant readings are entirely at odds with the text's own strategies and procedures: *Finnegans Wake* undoubtedly can be viewed as a text in which historical contradictions are presented as always already overcome. Rather, I wish to attend to the violence and repression to which it also attests, and account for the ways in which Joyce's hard-won solution to the 'Irish question' has proved so acceptable to readers entirely oblivious to the politics of anti-imperialism. Moreover, surprising configurations of native and exile, invader and nationalist, emerge on the basis of a re-examination of some of the scenes of fraternal conflict which are so significant in the post-colonial context: this will serve to contextualize a critical tradition which lays the stress merely on 'the livelier ironies' of Irish nationalism, contributing to a sense of that political ideology's hopeless self-contradiction. This also will open up the question of the significance of Joyce's deployment of the theories and philosophies of Giordano Bruno (1548–1600) and Giambattista Vico (1668–1744) in the text. On the basis of Samuel Beckett's remarks in *Our Exagmination*, we can call into question the predominantly idealistic interpretations of these bodies of thought which have been offered by later Joyceans. Hence, although certain features of *Finnegans Wake* can usefully be read as anticipating the later development of 'magic realism' in, for example, the work of Indian and South American writers, we do not have to rely on these alone to articulate the specificity of an Irish post-colonial fiction. Indeed, I will argue that while the importance of colonialism in 'magic realist' texts is relatively obvious even to their metropolitan and First World readers and critics, this is in part due to their participation in postmodernism: what we have in *Finnegans Wake* is perhaps the unique instance of a post-colonial *modernist* text, but we are not in the habit of considering the colonial determinations of such literature.

As Fredric Jameson remarks, what is at stake in post-colonial postmodernism is 'not a realism transfigured by the "supplement" of a magical perspective but a reality which is already in and of itself magical or fantastic . . . in the social reality of Latin America, realism is already necessarily a magic realism'.[21] *Finnegans Wake* reflects on and jokingly excuses its own implausible excesses in similar terms: 'we are in for a sequentiality of improbable possibles . . . for utterly impossible as are all these events they are probably as like those which may have taken place as any others which never took person at all are ever likely to be' (*FW*, p. 110). The text also shares with Timothy Brennan's 'post-colonial cosmopolitans' extensive treatment of current political events, including satirical representations of disguised but identifiable political figures. Its garrulous, repetitive narrative style, which retains some suggestions of fable and fairy-story is – like the work of Salman Rushdie – clearly engaged in a dialogue with traditional oral narratives, and the *Wake*, together with such texts, embodies a Rabelaisian sprawling inclusiveness at the level of form. Like Rushdie's *Midnight's Children* (1980), Joyce's novel relates the adventures of, in particular, a pair of boy-children whose lives are in some senses co-extensive with the history of the new independent nation: the Wakean sons are, in addition, explicitly presented as the product of the union between invader-father and native earth-mother, quite literally the offspring of the imperialist encounter. And as we will see, the fashion in which Rushdie's characters Saleem and Shiva represent 'the two valid forms of creation' of Hindu myth is also illuminating in the context of Shem and Shaun.[22] However, for Brennan, the 'revisionist spirit with which Rushdie and others enter the postmodern scene' is also indissociable from a sense of urgent engagement, an embrace of the moral responsibility of remembering and bearing witness, and a confidence in the functional role of art in political and social life.[23] While these features could also, although less plausibly, be ascribed to Joyce, his text also self-reflexively describes itself as 'antilibellous and nonactionable and this applies to its whole wholume' (*FW*, p. 48): its extreme inaccessibility means that the book is hardly likely to be read as conveying a sense of polemical urgency, or the desire to popularize – although it might appear to desecrate – high culture. *Finnegans Wake* does not, then, in any sense set out to destroy the self-confident aura of modernist fiction.

Finnegans Wake's major divergence from this paradigm, however, is its reluctance to concern itself exclusively, at the level of content, with a specifically post-colonial era. As many explicators since Beckett have pointed out, all historical times are simultaneously present at any given point in the text. Usually, no single set of correspondences which might be employed to construct a distinct storyline can plausibly be extracted from its polyvalent circulations and meanderings. Equally, as the progress of history is chiefly figured by the progress of the five-member nuclear family, we can also say that at each point of the family's story, every conceivable aspect of inter-familial emotion – marital devotion and sexual love, Oedipal ambivalence, sibling rivalry, resentment by the parents of their children etc. – is involved. The sons, for example, are perpetually engaged in conflict with their father, as well as with each other, although from time to time different phases of these struggles come to the fore, in harmony with the Viconian structure of the text as a whole. Hence, when these familial adventures are matched up with their Irish historical counterparts, we can see that the arrival of HCE in Dublin (the 'originary' moment of colonisation), the parricidal ambitions of his sons (anti-imperialist war) and the fraternal antagonism or succession disputes (post-colonial power-struggles) are not at all clearly dissociable. In this sense, the Wakean vision corresponds to the 'long view' of history, which has so often been ascribed to the so-called 'Irish historical imagination'; as the old joke goes, the Irish have to keep remembering their history, because the English keep forgetting it.

Another significant consequence of Joyce's all-inclusiveness is that the various stages of opposition to invasion or colonization blend together, both in the text and in commentary upon it. Indeed, it could be argued that critics of the *Wake* have even proved unable to distinguish *between* invasion and colonization. Their sanguine remarks about 'Ireland's legendary propensity towards assimilation of its invaders'[24] and their view of tenth-century conflicts as essentially the same as those of the nineteenth and twentieth centuries effectively disregard the cultural significance of modern colonialism. In this, of course, they might be excused for merely rehearsing Joyce's own historical account, which does indeed seem to suggest a monotonous sequence of one invasion after another. But it is inappropriate to employ Joyce's aesthetic *response* to colonialism to insinuate in this fashion that Ireland's colonial experience was never really all that serious or tragic. *Finnegans Wake* could not have been produced out of any encounter between 'native' and 'invader' save that of Irish culture and British imperialism. If Ireland has ever managed to overcome this history by means of engulfing and absorbing English language and culture, it has perhaps done so *only* within the confines of Joyce's novel.

As a result of Joyce's narrative strategies, the initial hostility to HCE as Invader, for example, displayed by the *Wake* citizenry – 'the hoolivans of the nation' (*FW*, p. 6) – appears readily to merge into a nationalist xenophobia. Indeed the scurrilous 'Ballad of Persse O'Reilly' has echoes of the citizen's anti-semitism in *Ulysses*:

> Sweet bad luck on the waves washed to our island,
> The hooker of that hammerfast viking,
> And Gall's curse on the day when Eblana bay
> Saw his black and tan man-o'-war . . . .
>
> Then we'll have a free trade Gaels' band and mass meeting
> For to sod the brave son of Scandiknavery.
> And we'll bury him down in Oxmanstown
> Along with the devil and the Danes,
> (*Chorus*) With the deaf and dumb Danes,
> And with all their remains. (*FW*, pp. 46–7).

Finnegans Wake, in its enthusiastic embrace of the language and cultures of all the various settlers whose descendants are numbered among the present-day inhabitants of Ireland, is therefore read by Colin MacCabe as a straightforward *celebration* of this history which has resulted in 'Miscegenations on Miscegenations' (*FW*, p. 18).[25] Resistance to 'invasion', then, merely masks racist fears concerning sexual contact between different peoples. MacCabe, however, does not ask how we can logically occupy an anti-imperialist position while claiming that there is *nothing* to regret in Ireland's history. Certainly, Joyce associates invasion with sexual violence from the outset: 'What chance cuddleys, what cashels aired and ventilated! What bidmetoloves sinduced by what tegotetabsolvers! (*FW*, p. 4). . . . And they fell upon one another: and themselves they have fallen' (*FW*, p. 15). Here, 'fell upon' can be read as either aggressive or affectionate. The 'fall' of the invaders is prophesied: they will be absorbed by the natives in the process of interbreeding. Joyce's formulation, however, does not entirely write out the violence of this encounter:

> What clashes here of wills gen wonts, oystrygods gaggin fishygods! Brékkek Kékkek Kékkek Kékkek! Kóax Kóax Kóax! Ualu Ualu Ualu! Quaouauh! . . . . Sod's brood, be me fear! (*FW*, p. 4)

In 'Ireland, Island of Saints and Sages' he had described Ireland during the conflict with the Danes and Norwegians as 'a veritable slaughterhouse', a period of strife when 'the culture necessarily languished' (*CW*, pp. 159–60). In this context, it would be surprising if this epoch had been presented in this text solely in the positive terms of cultural and racial interchange which MacCabe's comments suggest. *Finnegans Wake*, he writes, is 'anathema to those nationalists who wished to promote doctrines of Celtic purity'.[26] However, Joyce's refusal of any notion of 'purity of descent' (which even Fichte discounts as a criterion of national belonging[27]) does not apparently deter him from analysing and describing this 'compound' – but none the less identifiable – quality of 'Irishness'.[28] If the very notion of national characteristics was genuinely irrelevant to Joyce's thought, it could be argued, the observation that present-day Irish people have Scandinavian ancestors would only be worth making to demystify xenophobes: for Joyce, by contrast, it is an aspect of Irish historical experience which still enables us to explain certain features of contemporary Irish political character and life (*CW*, p. 160). As Frank Budgen reports:

> Believing that human nature is, in the main, subdued to what it works in, like the dyer's hand, I always regarded trade or caste as primary influences in forming character. Joyce, on the other hand, attached greater weight to race, nation, and to some real yet indefinite thing one might call type.[29]

It can be argued that the virulent racism of fascism was in part produced out of the intersection of Fichtean nationalism with post-Darwinian pseudo-scientific notions about evolution and race. It is interesting to note, then, that Joyce is more imaginatively attracted by the latter than he is ever by the originally benign basis of nationalism in a Herderian celebration of rustic folk-culture. 'Irishness' is heterogeneous for Joyce, but it also represents a kind of originary heterogeneity: its definitive characteristic is its quality of eluding definition. In this context, it is entirely self-consistent for the internationalist Joyce to describe *The Book of Kells* as 'the most Irish thing we have',[30] and for the critic to describe *Finnegans Wake* as a distinctly 'Irish' text.

Such conveniently imprecise formulations as MacCabe's both present a straw-target caricature of Irish nationalism, and utterly ignores its consistent professions of anti-sectarianism and its broader political concerns and preoccupations. In considering nationalism only as a philosophy of identity, any attack on the spurious purity of 'Ireland' – such as Joyce is understood to be enacting here – is valorized. A parallel might here be drawn with the critical treatment of the theme of incest in *Finnegans Wake*. In the Wakean family, it appears, we cannot clearly distinguish between the existence of incestuous desires and their enactment. HCE seems to be an incestuous father, and virtually every sexual permutation imaginable within the family group is realised. As Margot Norris writes:

> The social consequence of incest is the destruction of the social order . . . . Incest obliterates those distinctions that create a system of relationships in which every individual has a function and an identity . . . . Interference with the kinship laws causes the social fabric to unravel and identities to become indeterminate once again.[31]

It might be interesting to speculate, however, how the victims of sexual abuse would respond to the idea of incest as a radical subversion of the centered subject, or as a disruption of the proper order of patrilineal succession and patriarchal authority.

Rather, Joyce's determined Utopian recuperation of every violence, defeat and loss should be examined in the context of Freud's description of the representational strategies of the dream-work. Freud asserts in *The Interpretation of Dreams* that the dreaming mind, in pursuit of the fulfilment of ungratified desire, confuses temporalities, converts optatives into present tenses, dispenses with such logical connections as 'if', 'because', 'just as', 'although', and 'either-or', and disregards contradictions and contraries.[32] As a number of critics have remarked, this is virtually a description of Joyce's procedures here. In this, of course, the *Wake* also assents to the doctrine of *coincidentia oppositorum* – the co-incidence of apparent contraries – which Joyce claimed to have derived from Nicholas of Causa through the writings of Giordano Bruno. These writers viewed the universe as a continuum, rather than a hierarchy, in which 'contrary and diverse mobile parts converged to constitute a single continuous motionless body'. As Bruno writes:

> Our philosophy . . . . reduceth to a single origin and relateth to a single end, and maketh contraries to coincide so that there is one

> primal foundation of both origin and end. From this coincidence of contraries, we deduce that ultimately it is divinely true that contraries are within contraries; wherefore it is not difficult to compass the knowledge that every thing is within every other.[33]

If colonizer and colonized converge in this way, of course, then neither can really either succeed or fail. As Joseph Valente argues:

> In this 'letter selfpenned to one's other', the individual and his opposite number, the attitude or idea and its antithesis, desire and its inversion, force and counterforce, the colonist and colonised are all indissolubly bound together, synergetic, each divided within and doubled without.[34]

Joyce has therefore, as Valente claims, created a conceptual condition in which violence and exploitation are always *literally* self-defeating. This, however, does not imply that in this his text reflects a truth about political reality. Thus, if Salman Rushdie describes the history of Pakistan as representing 'the failure of the dreaming imagination' in his novel *Shame*, Joyce's book seeks to assert the potency and the *success* of dreams. In translating the 'manifest content' of the Wakean dream into its 'latent thoughts', though, we must appreciate that historical failure, analogous to the one with which Rushdie engages, is the essential precondition of this aesthetic victory.

While virtually any part of *Finnegans Wake* might be fairly described as obscure, one of its most explicit *representations* of incomprehension and of the breakdown of communication occurs early in the text, during the exchange between Mutt and Jute in the opening chapter. These two figures are usually read as avatars of Shem and Shaun respectively, and they also stand as the first native and invader figures in the series which culminates in the dialogue between Muta and Juva in the final chapter. Mutt (the Shem-like figure) is taken to be the native here. This is noteworthy in itself as for much of the text it is Shem who is the figure of exile, and Shaun who is represented by the 'all-too-Irish' Jaun, who counsels the pupils of St Bride's to 'Be ownkind. Be kithkinish. Be bloodysibby. Be irish' (*FW*, p. 465), and who threatens to break his brother's 'outsider's face for him' (*FW*, p. 442). The expatriation of Shem, then, paradoxically represents the exclusion of the most native figure in the country; just as St Patrick, the patron saint of patriotic Irish Catholicism, appears as foreigner and an invader in the closing pages of the book. Moreover, although Mutt, a lonely cave-dweller, represents here the figure of the outsider, he is described in quite primitivistic terms, munching on bones and apparently drinking alcohol out of the skull of some creature. He appears physically malformed and hunchbacked: 'Forshapen his pigmaid hoagshead, shroonk his plodsfoot

. . . . his mammamuscles most mousterious . . . . Me seemeth a dragon man' (*FW*, p. 15). Jute, that is to say, resembles a 'Mousterian' or a Neanderthal human being, or William Blake's dragon man.[35] Mutt, although he is the native and on home ground, is a polyglot, and offers to converse with Jute in any of several suitably hybrid languages he names: 'scowegian . . . anglease . . . phonio saxo?' (*FW*, p. 16). Jute merely protests indignantly: 'I can beuraly forsttaand a weird from sturk to finnic in such a patwhat as your rutterdamrotter' (*FW*, p. 17). As a Shaun-figure, Jute is oriented towards the spatial and visual, and is therefore rather deaf. We also learn that Mutt is unable to make himself understood because he has 'became a stun a stummer', which seems to indicate that he has started to stammer, a 'hauhauhauhaudible thing', as Jute mocks him. Stammering, throughout *Finnegans Wake*, is a sign of original sin, or a symptom of some more obscure primordial guilt. Mutt's utterance 'Hasatency?' is also a sign of such guilt, as it resembles the word which exposed the forger Richard Pigott, who had tried to destroy Parnell's career in the 1880s. In Vico's *The New Science*, stammering is also associated with the very origins of human language.[36] Pre-historic men and women, according to Vico, startled while making love in the open by thunder, interpreted this great celestial noise as a divine voice of rebuke and, filled with shame, retired into caves. There, they falteringly attempted to imitate the sound and hence began to speak. In this way, the First Great Age, that of Theocracy, was inaugurated. Mutt's stammering, then, suggests that he is a representative First-Age human (Book I of *Finnegans Wake* is devoted to the Theocratic Age), and, as he tells Jute, he started his stuttering at 'The Inns of Dungtarf': possibly a Dublin pub, but also the Battle of Clontarf, where the Irish forces under Brian Boru won a great victory against the Danes in 1014. The sound which impels Mutt into the Viconian cycle of development is no natural or meteorological one, but the chance event of war *between* cultures and societies.

Mutt suddenly recognizes his interlocutor as a Viking when Jute attempts to bribe him with fake money: 'cross your qualm with trink gilt'. 'How wooden I not know it, the intellible greytcloak of Cedric Silkyshag!', Mutt cries. This encompasses allusions to 'Wood's ha'pence', a debased coinage for Ireland against which Swift protested, to Harold Graycloak, who ruled Norway in the tenth century, and to Sitric Skilkenbeard, who led the Danish force at Clontarf. Recognizing Jute as an associate of the Danes, then, Mutt points out to him the 'viceking's graab' – i.e. both their spoil and their grave; the word 'Howe' here similarly evokes both the meanings of Parliament and burial ground. Money and Parliament – both introduced into Ireland by the Danes – are characteristic elements in Vico's Third Age, that of Democracy, of which the burial mound is also the most important symbol. Mutt is apparently introduced to these things by a stranger, while in his own land. If Jute's word 'One eyegonblack' includes the meaning 'One eye gone black', then there may here be a suggestion here that he has just struck Mutt, or blackened his eye. The blows, then, with which Shaun the patriot later threatens Shem the cosmopolitan, stand revealed as a repetition of the violence first inflicted by the invader. So an alternative temporal priority is established between the violence of invasion and the violence of nationalism, which replaces the received critical view of an essentially pacific settlement and aggressively exclusivist response.

These pages, then, dramatize a dialogue – or an attempt at dialogue – across cultures, and, more importantly, across historical epochs, as they are associated with stages of the Viconian cycle. Indeed a variety of both Viconian and Brunian motifs comes into play in this passage. Mutt's confident overview of the eventual merging of Viking and Irish – 'Let erehim ruhmuhrmuhr. Mearmerge two races, swete and brack. Morthering rue. Hither, craching eastuards, they are in surgence: hence, cool at ebb, they requiesce' (*FW*, p. 17) – recalls the *coincidentia oppositorum*, and his lecture on human history to Jute concludes with a suitably Viconian stress on repetition and cyclicalism: 'This ourth of years is not save brickdust and being humus the same roturns' (*FW*, p. 18). In fact, the two narrative (or anti-narrative) paradigms supplied by Joyce's borrowings from Bruno and Vico could be said to be structurally analogous. As Northrop Frye states: 'Vico's cyclical conception of historical process is really a vision of time within a spatial metaphor, and Bruno's conception of the identity of polarized opposites is a vision of the spatial subject-object confrontation dissolving back into a temporal flux'[37] However, Vico, unlike Bruno, also supplies a *methodology* for *Finnegans Wake*. This is suggested here by the description of the 'middenmound', the heap of earth and waste which is the substratum of *Wake* history: '(Stoop) if you are abcedminded, to this claybook, what curios of signs (please stoop), in this allaphbed! Can you rede (since We and Thou had it out already) its world?' (*FW*, p. 18) In order to 'a gain control of the circumcentric megacycles, ranging from the antidulibnium onto the serostaatarean'(*FW*, p. 310),[38] the Wakean investigator must examine the letters of the past, enabling the history of human culture to be unravelled from within the history of its language. In a parallel way, Vico's philological method holds out the promise of the ultimate legibility or meaningfulness of history, based on his belief that what is made by humans must be decipherable and comprehensible to them: the 'true' and the made are equivalent, *verum et factum convertuntur*. The resolutely anti-Cartesian Vico proposes, in Martin Jay's words, 'a participatory rather than a spectatorial link' between the subject and the object of cognition.[39] In this sense, then,

Samuel Beckett employs Viconian arguments when he condemns those who 'qualify as the "ravings of a Bedlamite" the formal structure raised by Mr Joyce after years of patient and inspired labour'.[40] Beckett argues:

> It follows that History is neither to be considered a formless structure, due exclusively to the achievements of individual agents, nor as possessing a reality apart from and independent of them, accomplished behind their backs in spite of them, the work of some superior force, variously known as Fate, Chance, Fortune, God . . . . History, then is not the result of Fate or Chance – in both cases the individual would be separated from his product – but the result of a Necessity that is not Fate, of a Liberty that is not Chance.[41]

I will shortly consider the relevance of this Viconian notion of 'Providence' to other parts of *Finnegans Wake*. But I would first like to examine the role of Vico's history in the interchange between Mutt and Jute. Is his philosophy of history a useful resource, we might ask, for the individual in Mutt's historical situation? Rather, I would argue that aspects of Joyce's representation of the identifiably Irish context of the exchange may serve to interfere with his appropriation of Vico, and with any critical assimilation of the native/invader conflicts to the paradigm of a history of perpetual recurrence.

There appears to be distinction – if not a contradiction – between the rigid design of Vico's four-part schema of the course and recourse of historical events, and the wealth of heterogeneous cultural detail which *The New Science* offers as evidence of this pattern. As Edward Said states:

> Although Vico's subject is the common law of nations, and his ambition to find a common beginning – a genealogical project – his 'topical' method is everywhere to amass evidence by correlation, complementarity, and adjacency. Although his desire is to locate a primeval beginning, a line of direct filiality, the material testimony of language and his learning restrain his desire, engaging it instead with the susceptibility of language to divination and poetry.[42]

Said argues that Vico, in this way, startlingly anticipates certain modernist forms of narrative which share with his work a determining interest in human collectivity, and in relationships of parallelism and adjacency. However, among the problematics which Said believes is opened up by his own study of modernism is: 'the question of the domination of one intellectual or national domain over another (one culture is more "developed" than – having begun earlier and "arrived" before another)'.[43] This is a question, of course, which clearly anticipates Said's later writing on colonial discourse in *Orientalism* (1979), although he does not suggest whether or not Vico has any particular relevance to the theme of cultural imperialism. In his 'Survey of the Ancient and the Modern World of Nations in the Light of the Principles of this Science', the conclusion to *The New Science*, Vico provides an overview of his own historical time with apparent equanimity:

> Today a complete humanity seems spread abroad through all the nations, for a few great monarchs rule over this world of peoples . . . . But Christian Europe is everywhere radiant with such humanity that it abounds in all the good things that make for the happiness of human life, ministering to the comforts of the body as well as to the pleasures of the mind and spirit.

Vico concludes this global tour with an outline of the history of European expansionism in America: 'Lastly, crossing the ocean, in the new world, the American Indians would now be following this course of human institutions if they had not been discovered by the Europeans'.[44] Here, Vico suggests that this 'discovery' has *impeded* the natural evolutionary development of these peoples: according to him, Mutt would be hindered rather than helped by his dialogue with Jute. The inadequacy of the Viconian paradigm to encompass 'native' and 'invader', when elements of 'primitive' and 'advanced' are superimposed on this opposition, becomes clear. The Viconian 'solution' to colonial conflict proposed by Joyce, and accepted by his critics, is therefore rendered insecure. Moreover, the encounter also raises problems at the level of *method*. While Vico's book has no ethical or moral preference for 'pure' or 'national' languages, they do possess a practical advantage in his scheme. As the 'sequence of human institutions sets the pattern for the histories of words in the various native languages', Vico writes:

> From this we infer the following corollary: that languages are more beautiful in proportion as they are richer in these condensed heroic expressions; that they are more beautiful because they are more expressive and because they are more expressive they are truer and more faithful. And that on the contrary, in proportion as they are more crowded with words of unknown origin, they are less delightful, because obscure and confused, and therefore more likely to deceive and lead astray.[45]

In this, he articulates a proto-Fichtean position: as in *Addresses to the German Nation* 'original' languages develop out of the common life of the folk, and learning a foreign word in an 'unnatural' manner involves a recapitulation of the entire previous linguistic development of a nation.[46] We have already seen how the historical placement of the

Mutt and Jute episode is suggested by the wealth of Danish and Germanic words, and depends on the Norse associations of the words 'Howe' and 'Thingmote': it proceeds on the basis of 'imported' words which evince the disruption of the 'natural' sequence of human institutions. A cyclical theory of history may, of course, remain scandalous to the linear plots of imperialism, which propose for all a single line of political development, and legitimate a single culture. As Yeats argues: 'Outside Anglo-Saxon nations where progress, impelled by moral enthusiasm and the Patent Office, seems a perpetual straight line, this "circular movement", as Swift's master, Polybius, called it, has long been the friend and enemy of public order'.[47] The mismatch between the Viconian and the colonial paradigm, however, in the case of Mutt and Jute, subverts the Utopian reading of Vico which *Finnegans Wake* has generally been seen to embody.

The figures of the Wakean brothers are incarnated as Butt and Taff in Chapter III.3. During this chapter, in the words of Campbell and Robinson's *Skeleton Key*, 'the brother battle becomes magnified to gigantic terms of imperial conflict'.[48] One of the many narratives discernible in this episode is the tale of Butt's assassination of a Russian general at the battle of Sevastapol. Joyce apparently based this storyline on an anecdote of his father's about an Irish soldier named Buckley who fought with the British forces during the Crimean War. Hence, the theme of conflict *between* imperial powers (the struggle between Russia and Britain for ascendancy in the Near East, 1853–6) is transformed both into one of anti-imperialist warfare – in the scenes where a quaking and reluctant Butt girds himself up to kill the corrupt General, who is a HCE or father figure – and into fraternal antagonism, as Butt, recounting his experiences, is teased and mocked by Taff. This section of *Finnegans Wake* also encompasses one of the most explicit representations of the convergence of contraries: first, the brothers partly exchange identity to become 'Tuff' and 'Batt'; subsequently they are described as 'now one and the same person', speaking in unison (*FW*, p. 354).

When the Russians invaded Finland in 1940, Joyce wrote to Eugene Jolas: 'The most curious comment I have received on the book is a symbolical one from Helsinki, where, as foretold by the prophet, the Finn again wakes, and volunteer Buckleys are running from all sides to shoot that Russian General'.[49] This remark, and in particular the interpretation of his title which Joyce supplies, has inspired some of the most straightforwardly political readings of *Finnegans Wake*, or 'Finnegans, Wake!' As Maria Jolas states:

> Finnegan, for Joyce, was the eternally comic Irishman, the fellow who, having started out in life as the great Finn, of heroic stature,

> had fallen to the position of the down-trodden drunken hod-carrier of the song, the man that everyone laughed at . . . . But Finnegan was also the under-dog, the common people, not only of Ireland . . . . but also the common people everywhere.[50]

But here I would like to consider why the Shem figure is recruited for this apparently heroic act of resistance, when, as Campbell and Robinson comment, 'the whole course of the book shows that an indisposition to stand up even for his own rights is Shem's norm of action'.[51] It is also one of the very rare points at which he enjoys the approval and respect of the general populace. The narrative, indeed, begins to unfold to their calls of: 'We want Bud. We want Bud Budderly . . . . For Ehren, boys, gobrawl!' (p. 337–8). In order to explore the possible political implications of this, we must also address the specific manner in which the union of the two brothers is effected, and consider why Joyce insists on this Brunian symbiosis. I will argue that the significance of these features is due to Joyce's attention to the problem of post-colonial succession. His concentration on these issues in what is apparently an anti-imperialist narrative demonstrates their priority in the interpretation of *Finnegans Wake*. It is by appreciating the specific ironies of the post-colonial condition that we can explain how, in the course of the brother-battle, 'native' becomes 'exile' to the exact extent that 'invader' becomes 'native', and neither Shem nor Shaun appear capable of properly defeating or succeeding their father. Otherwise, the questions raised by their antagonism or equivalence can be too easily appropriated for observations about ambivalence and symmetry *within* the imperial relationship itself.

Butt prevaricates for some time before he shoots the Russian General. During this period of doubt and uncertainty, he acquires a Celtic revivalist colouring and a distinctly Syngean turn of phrase:

> (*his face glows green, his hair greys white, his bleyes bcome broon to suite his cultic twalette*). But when I seeing him in his oneship fetch along within hail that tourrible tall with his nitshnykopfgoknob . . . . But, meac Coolp, Arram of Eirzerum, as I love our Deer Dirouchy, I confesses withould pridejealice when I looked upon the Saur of all the Haurousians with the weight of his arge fullin upon him from the travaillings of his tommuck and rueckenased the fates of a bosser there was fear on me the sons of Nuad for him and it was heavy he was for me then the way I immingled my Iremenial hairmaierians ammongled his Gospolis fomiliours till, achaura moucreas, I adn't the arts to. (*FW*, p. 344–5)

This scene evokes Stephen Dedalus's association of Celticist stereotypes with Hamlet-like paralysis in Chapter 9 of *Ulysses*: Here, however, it is the writerly – or 'Joycean' – figure who is accused of conforming to the Romantic cliché of artistic sensitivity. Taff mocks his brother's melancholy cowardice, and once again threatens him with violence: 'Weepon, weeponder, song of sorrowmon! Which goatheye and sheepskeer they damnty well know. Papaist! Gambanman! Take the cawraidd's blow!' (*FW*, p. 344). This is ironic, because Taff himself keeps well out of the action: *'sulphuring to himsalves all the pungataries of sin praktice in failing to furrow theogonies of the dommed'* (*FW*, p. 352–3).

Kimberly Devlin argues that the version of the brother-conflict narrated in the fable of the Ondt and the Gracehopper (*FW*, III.1) closely corresponds to the conflict between Butt and Taff here. In the later story, the pair are characterized by appetite and restraint respectively, reflected in the contrast between the self-indulgent, lascivious Shem-like Gracehopper and the self-denying, prudent Shaun-like Ondt. She goes on: 'So Butt and Taff reinforce the dichotomy between inhibition and license seen elsewhere in Joyce's works; as counterparts, they form another version of the primal, unsocialized self's interaction with civilizing structures of restraint'.[52] However, it might also be argued that this polarization is in fact not so neatly reproduced here. Indeed, whenever the war between Shem and Shaun is given a more recognisably social or political background, as, for example, in Book I.7 – the so-called 'Shem the Penman' episode – Shem's uncivilized lack of restraint translates into private excess and the pursuit of writerly *jouissance*, in contrast to the sober, civilized Shaun who is proud to do true battle for his nation. It is Shem who there is anxious to avoid 'anything anyway approaching a straightforward standup or knockdown row' (*FW*, p. 174). As the narrator, who appears to share Shaun's values, comments in exasperation:

> Talk about lowness! Any dog's quantity of it visibly oozed out thickly from this dirty little blacking beetle . . . . the yet unremuneranded national apostate, who was cowardly gun and camera shy, taking what he fondly thought was a short cut to Caer Fere, Soak Amerigas, vias the shipsteam *Pridewin*, after having buried a hatchet not so long before. (*FW*, p. 171).

Butt's prevarication, therefore, is in fact more characteristic of Shem than his sudden violent outburst. He overcomes his reluctance to shoot only on his third attempt, when he observes the General defecating and wiping himself with a sod of turf ('the old sod' being an affectionate name for Ireland): 'we insurrectioned . . . I shuttm (*FW*, p. 352) . . . . At that instullt to Igorladns! '(*FW*, p. 353). If Shem is seen as consistently impulsive and unrestrained, then this is the only place in the text where this takes on a social or a political meaning in terms of action. In this scene, we witness the point at which the modernist writer – the Viconian interpreter of history *par excellence* – is transformed into a Viconian participant in history. As Beckett points out, Vico is no idealist, but a 'practical roundheaded Neapolitan'.[53] Butt is impelled towards action by his reluctance to become a keening Celtic artist or a passive bystander. Once the General has been shot, the literally explosive effects of this assassination exceed Butt's capacity for interpretation. He may not have foreseen the consequences of what he does, but none the less it is this *intervention* which produces the '*abnihilisation of the etym*' (*FW*, p. 353). This is the moment of apparently perfect stasis during which everything and everyone is, as the stage-directions inform us: '*ideally reconstituted . . . . All the presents are determining as regards for the future the howabouts of their past absences which they might see on at hearing could they once smell of tastes from touch. To ought find a values for*' (*FW*, p. 355). Placed at the mid-point of the text, this represents a kind of mini-*ricorso*, a condition of both rest and infinite possibility. Taff salutes his brother: 'And may he be too an intrepidation of our dreams which we foregot at wiking when the morn hath razed out limpalove and the bleakfrost chilled our ravery!' (p. 338). This is the only explicit allusion in *Finnegans Wake* to the text by Freud which, as we have seen, sheds so much light on Joyce's night-time world. Freud, of course, is interested not merely in representing dreams, but in interpreting them. Is it possible, then, that his invocation here invites such a decoding; that this moment, rather than that of the apparent 'awakening' in the final chapter, is a key instance of lucidity and self-consciousness in the text? Shem must take on some of the features more characteristic of his brother, in order to make the conditions he habitually creates in writing actually prevail for all: 'the first till last alshemist wrote over every square inch of the only foolscap available, his own body, till by it corrosive sublimation one continuous present tense integument slowly unfolded all marryvoising moodmoulded cyclewheeling history' (*FW*, pp. 185–6). In spite of Taff's plea that the meaning of their dream not be forgotten, their exhilaration is short-lived. As the stage-directions describe: '*their fight upheld to right for a wee while being baffled and tottered* . . . . So till butagain budly shoots thon rising germinal let bodley chow the fatt of his anger and badley bide the toil of the tubb' (*FW*, p. 354). Until this action is repeated, Shaun must seethe and Shem, like his precursor Swift, must content himself with writing satires, venting his aggression in the labour of writing.

Campbell and Robinson may make an exaggerated claim when they declare that in this chapter we learn that –

> The diseases, mildews, and enslavements which Albion inflicts upon the bodies of men provoke the victimised to revolutionary

> explosion. Butt as the symbol of man degraded in the service of empire . . . participates in the obscene orgy, but driven to limit of endurance abruptly turns and destroys the oppressor[54] –

but such an interpretation at least makes sense of the political milieu in which the story is enacted, which a purely psychoanalytical account singularly fails to do. As Margot Norris writes: 'in the enduring struggle between the individual's anarchic psyche and the laws that make civilization possible, the psyche is momentarily triumphant only in the dream'.[55] She here reflects the critical view that the encounter between Butt and the Russian General mirrors the debate between Bulkily (Archbishop Berkeley, Idealist Irish philosopher, or a Celtic druid) and St Patrick in the final chapter. *The Skeleton Key* suggests:

> The name of the archdruid suggests . . . Buckley, who shot the Russian General; and this suggestion is supported by the designation of St Patrick as the Eurasian General. In the depths of sleep it was Buckley who won, but in the course of daylight history it will be the General . . . . Rome, Russia, England, and Japan coalesce as representatives of successful statecraft, in opposition to the Gnostic, Individualistic, Irish, Taoist combination of the druid. The former is Shaunish, the latter Shemmish; the former is lord of the day, the latter of night.[56]

If the accounts provided by Norris and *The Skeleton Key* are accurate, it is obvious that Shem cannot be victorious outside the realm of fantasy. His moment of glory is inevitably fleeting: as the most ALP-like of the two brothers, he entirely lacks the hard-headed, masculine virtues of his father which are needed to build up the world in his own image. The *Wake*, we could say, proposes the structural impossibility of the victory of the artist, or the succession of the child most closely associated with the life-giving 'Bringer of Plurabilities' (*FW*, p. 104). Similarly, no revolution made by the war-like Shaun will usher in an era during which Shem-like qualities will find a place. Indeed, it could equally be argued that the Viconian structure of the text as a whole militates against the succession of Shaun. Book III, the epoch of his ascendancy, is devoted to the Age of Democracy, or 'gossipocracy' as it is called here. This may be the most advanced of Vico's ages, but it is also the most degenerate, as it heralds the ultimate breakdown of ordered society and the beginning of the period of reflux.[57] Therefore, because Shem and Shaun are both merely partial emanations of their father, they can never add up to the man he was: 'a house he has founded to which he has assigned its fate' (*FW*, p. 136). As Timothy Brennan comments on the protagonists of *Midnight's Children*:

> As author, Saleem, like Brahma, imagines the whole of Indian history and contains it within him. His 'impotency' reflects his inability to change historical events except in so far as he convinces others to believe the doctored versions of his tales . . . . Saleem/Brahma displays the largely negative or inverted capacity of Shiva for generation: that is, his impotency (lack of practical political power) directly strengthens his fertility *as a writer*. For his part, Shiva, member of the angry masses, has the power to change events but uses it in ways that will not produce meaningful change.[58]

However, this politically pessimistic aspect of the brother-battle also has a potentially positive, or critical, side. Through the figure of 'Shem the Penman', the very incarnation of what J.M. Bernstein describes as the modernist 'subject-who-writes', we can also trace the *Wake*'s own self-criticism.[59] Shem's compulsive representations of the 'new Irish stew' remain haunted, as he tells his brother, by 'a convulsionary sense of not having been or being all that I might have been or you meant to becoming' (*FW*, p. 193). The success of the modernist artist in creating what virtually amounts to a parallel universe paradoxically produces anxiety about the insecurity and the baselessness of this very world: 'you have reared your disunited kingdom on the vacuum of your own most intensely doubtful soul (*FW*, p. 188) . . . . in honour bound to the cross of your own cruelfiction' (*FW*, p. 192) Shem's motto, 'This exists that isits after having been said we know' (*FW*, p. 186), as Seamus Deane points out, amounts to a declaration of the omnipotence and autonomy of language: 'That which exists depends for its existence on having being said'. In this, however, Joyce not only reveals 'the essentially fictive nature of political imagining',[60] but also, against the backdrop of war and rebellion represented in this episode, testifies to the ineffectualness and impotency of merely imagined solutions to political problems. In Shem's text, as in the *Wake* itself, it is impossible to distinguish between what we might describe as descriptive and performative utterances: the very act of giving witness, therefore, implicates the writer in guilt and responsibility. By this night-time paralogic, Shem is as implicated in post-colonial failure as the belligerent participants in the Irish Civil War:

> you, who sleep at our vigil and fast for our feast, you with your dislocated reason, have cutely foretold, a jophet in your own absence . . . death with every disaster, the dynamitisation of colleagues, the reducing of records to ashes, the levelling of all customs by blazes, the return of a lot of sweetempered gunpowdered didst unto dudst. (*FW*, pp. 189–90)

It might therefore be asserted that *Finnegans Wake* also provides a critique of the aesthetic transcendence of history which, at another level, it so successfully enacts. It is as important for Shem to become like Shaun as it is for Shaun to become like Shem.

So long as Shem and Shaun are understood as representing 'native' and 'invader' – or 'colonised' and 'coloniser' – then what I have called the Utopian reading of their interdependence and apparent interchangeability seems to predominate: 'Invader and native resister are linked forever and their most violent struggles bind them all the more tightly'.[61] The *Wakean* brother-battle, from this point of view, would seem to offer a good example of what Homi K. Bhabha describes as the 'colonial subject', a discursive unity which comprises both colonizer and colonized: authority and power, Bhabha suggests, are never exclusively or securely in the possession of the coloniser alone.[62] In *Finnegans Wake*, however, Joyce's conception of such a shared colonial discourse is demonstrably produced out of the experience of the colonized culture itself. Perhaps it is only in this context, as the distance between Joyce's text and its criticism illustrates, that any such assertion of colonial 'ambivalence' preserves its subversive implications.[63]

However, if the post-colonial provenance of the *Wake* is kept in mind, the distinction between invader/colonizer and native/colonized recedes in importance. After the departure of the imperialists, who are generally fairly recognisable, the most important distinction to be drawn – and it is a much more difficult one – is between those who are complicit with neo-colonialism, and those who are not, whether they be former natives or former settlers.[64] As Fredric Jameson points out, this is 'an aesthetic dilemma, a crisis of representation', which intensifies as the operations of external controlling forces become ever more difficult to understand or depict.[65] It is this which Shem and Shaun, and particularly the slippage between Shaun as invader and Shaun as nationalist, encapsulate. It is important, I would argue, that this dilemma should not be critically constructed as primarily a feature of the imperial relationship. In so far as Shaun inherits the constructive and expansionist qualities of HCE, he is both essential in the effort to slay the father, and better equipped for it than Shem. As an HCE-figure himself, he is not sufficiently distinct from his father to repudiate him totally: Shem's closeness to his mother distinguishes him much more sharply from his male parent. When the patriarchal qualities of Shaun are carried over into the new era, HCE's continuing presence and authority are revealed. There is no clear end to the imperialist era in *Finnegans Wake* because this force also shapes the destinies of HCE's and ALP's descendants. The succession issue may be unresolved in Joyce's art, but it has not been resolved in life. The Wakean vision may blur all these various epochs together, but we can also understand why this history should look blurred from Joyce's particular vantage point.

In his essay, 'Third-World Literature in the Era of Multinational Capital', Jameson argues that the structures of national allegory are not so much absent from the literature of the First World as unconscious within them. In contrast to 'our own cultural texts, third world national allegories are conscious and overt'.[66] *Finnegans Wake*, in its openness to such a reading, may therefore appear in this regard a *less* complex text than Joyce's earlier books, more 'theirs' than 'ours'.[67] Coincidentally, in his discussion of a Third-World literature which is mostly popular or socially realist, Jameson mentions that such writing 'will not offer the satisfactions of Proust or Joyce', or cater for our 'commitment to a rhythm of modernist innovation'.[68] It would be tempting to remark that in *Finnegans Wake* we get the best of both worlds. However, that would be to ignore how much has been lost by its readers' understandable failure to grasp the importance of its 'Third-World' status at all.

6

JOYCE, WOMEN AND NATIONALISM

PREFACE: 'THE FLESH THAT ALWAYS AFFIRMS'?[1]

Joyce concluded *Ulysses* with the 'female word *yes*', 'the least forceful word in the language', which for him denoted 'acquiescence, self-abandon, relaxation, the end of all resistance'.[2] It is evident that he sought to finish the book in a joyful, celebratory style – this 'affirmation' he here associates both with femininity and the refusal of conflict. For if Molly Bloom triumphs over the disappointment and exhaustion of 'Bloomsday', she appears to do so simply by acting out Leopold's declaration that love 'is really life' (*U*, p. 273) – except that for her this love is essentially sexual. Molly's wisdom, although it does not find expression in comparably quotable insights, lends her a privileged status within *Ulysses*. Despite her small vocabulary, frequent mistakes and obvious self-contradictions, her voice is not interrupted, imitated or parodied. Style, as Hugh Kenner observes, is no more than a system of limits, and as such implies constraint; here there are no limits, and hence 'no mockery . . . because for once, no style'.[3] Molly has, of course, been criticized as well as admired, arousing disgust along with desire, but for most commentators she remains 'contradictory and mysterious, yet magnificently convincing and satisfactory'.[4] In so far as her erotic vitalism supposedly transcends the partial, ideologically limited viewpoints of her fellow Dubliners, she can offer us respite after the stylistic battles of the earlier episodes, and relief from the struggles and frustrations they depict.

Although Joyce may have dismissed interior monologue as a bridge over which he would march his eighteen episodes,[5] many readers, including some influenced by contemporary feminist theory, have considered that the discourse of Chapter 18 ('Penelope') is rather more than an artistic convenience for his troops. This monologue, in its flagrant disregard for punctuation, syntactic order and the law of non-contradiction, can be read as a kind of womanly writing; indeed, Molly's language is explicitly associated with the female body and its libidinal pleasures. Suzette Henke, for example, while acknowledging that Joyce deploys a range of stereotypes of women in this episode (as 'Molly depicts herself to herself through the language of pornographic fantasy'[6]) considers that his real achievement is in successfully ventriloquizing a disruptive 'feminine' language: 'Although Molly's sinuous prose-poetry flows from a masculine pen, it none the less offers a linguistic paradigm of *écriture féminine*, as *jouissance* is deferred by the free play of a woman character's imagination over the elusive terrain of sexual difference'.[7]

My aim here, however, will be to look closely at such recent feminist accounts of Joyce's texts. In general, such readings – not least of Chapter 18 – associate this linguistic 'femininity' primarily with Joyce's female figures, but it also touches the lives of his male characters, especially in relation to infancy, sensuous pleasure and sexuality. Its counterpart, so the argument runs, is a fluid, decentred and supposedly anti-patriarchal mode of writing. Joyce had from the outset a troubled, ambivalent relationship with feminine sexuality and language. His early texts evince an occasional deep anxiety about women; the sufferings and ambitions of Stephen Dedalus, as we have seen, are bound up with a desire for mastery over unruly bodies and desires, and for Dedalus, as perhaps for his author, the surest way to achieve this is through art. Ultimately, however, Joyce himself is seen to adopt the voice and position of the marginalised woman, most notably in Chapter 18 and in those passages in *Finnegans Wake* which deal with the figures of mother and daughter. For many Joycean feminists, this progression from misogyny to semiotic carnival presents only one major political difficulty. This lies in judging whether Joyce genuinely surrenders authority to the 'feminine', or whether his practice of modernism represents its final appropriation. For if modernism is among other things a response to a general cultural crisis of masculine authority, this invocation of 'Woman' may be no more than a cunning strategy for maintaining dominion, rather than finally abandoning it.[8]

Those who defend the doctrine of *écriture féminine* point to the poetic, Utopian character of this notion of 'writing the body' – though they may concede that, as a feminist strategy, such a theory does not necessarily address the social or political conditions of women's oppression. Nevertheless, recent feminist readings of *Ulysses* often simply import distinctions between feminine and masculine discourse, *jouissance* and logocentrism, from contemporary French theory, which they then map on to Joyce's social world, in a manner that has quite direct political implications. In recognizably post-structuralist fashion, for example, Suzette Henke proposes that in Joyce's later texts 'polysemic and polyglottic iterations', work to 'challenge the name and law of the father by poetically subverting the univocal discourse associated with phallocentric master narratives'.[9] But to recruit Joyce as French feminist *avant la lettre* in this manner would seem to involve a chorus of approval for Molly's supposed rejection of the public world of *Ulysses*, as a realm of undifferentiated patriarchal discourse – ratifying her privatized separation from it. But what might it mean, in the context of *Ulysses*, straightforwardly to valorize Molly's disengagement, her acquiescent refusal of resistance, or to propose this as a model for feminism, in a world where master narratives are clearly not merely 'univocal' but in disagreement and competition with each other?[10] An Irish feminist, in particular, might want to emphasize that in Ireland, at the time 'Penelope' was written, a number of political discourses were vying for control over (among other things) the political destinies of Irish women – we cannot afford to reduce such conflict to mere masculine ideology, on which women have a supposedly privileged or transcendental perspective.[11] For if, taking our cue from contemporary theory, we attempted to generate an anti-colonial politics from gender alone, we might conclude with Patrick McGee that 'the crisis in Joyce the subject' emerges from the deeper contradiction between 'the desire of colonial Ireland and the law of the British Empire'.[12] Such a formulation merely reproduces a familiar opposition between a subversive 'desire' and an oppressive 'law', glibly superimposing the psychoanalytical paradigm on the colonial. The Irish may be flattered by this collective feminisation, but if they refuse altogether the laws of language and sociability, how are they to create a world in which they might live out their political desires?

For in such readings, Leopold Bloom typically emerges in the narrative as a man derided for his lack of masculinity, and one who provides instead 'a model of androgyny and male nurturing';[13] then, in this final chapter, we encounter the other partner in this unconventional marriage, whose candour and emancipated conduct contrast so starkly with the oppressive languages of Irish men. Bonnie Kime Scott even speculates that it may be thanks to Molly's influence that Leopold has outgrown this society of immature political enthusiasms:

> Molly is in general opposed to politics and violence, implying that she leaves war and political disputation to men. Interestingly, the mild-mannered, womanly Poldy is the subject of her disdain for early political posturings. Has she perhaps discouraged him over the years, thus contributing to this womanly or androgynous makeup?[14]

But it is surely problematic to deploy such a notion of 'feminine' pacifism to combat or evade 'politics and violence'. For if Leopold Bloom becomes more 'womanly' by virtue of his progressive political quietism, then such a judgement insists on an absolute divorce between the public world of Dublin and the private realm of value. Politically, this seems merely a fulfilment of Leopold's meek promise in 'Circe': '*he meant to reform, to retrieve the memory of the past in a purely sisterly way and return to nature as a purely domestic animal*' (*U*, p. 376). Perhaps if all Irish males, then, would only get out of the pubs and sit quietly in their own front rooms, their troubles would be over.

Such readings then align the feminine with the realms of domesticity, nurture and privacy, as opposed to a public world of dreary ideological illusion and male aggression. This, of course, coincides exactly with the bourgeois separation of spheres – perhaps the most important modern ideological support for the confinement and exploitation of women. It is true enough that in *Ulysses* the public sphere is largely, although not exclusively, inhabited by men, and dominated by their concerns; the domestic realm is available to both women and men, but is at least partially controlled and symbolized by the former. But in seeking to give sexuality (love) priority over politics (violence), some feminist critics simply accept a particular, naturalised version of the 'political' – one closely connected, whatever the radicalism of the theory, to Leopold's own tamely conventional politics. At the level of the public sphere, then, their readings would seem to uphold his vaguely humanitarian liberalism. But more damagingly, they imply that the interests of women are not at stake in the public discourse of Irish politics. They thus lead us to the startling conclusion that the specific interests of *Irish* women – obviously the only possible foundation for an Irish women's movement – are simply not involved in the discussions of politics, nationalism and the rest which can be heard in *Ulysses*. But that nationalism is sexist does not mean it is *irrelevant* to women. There is an immense distinction between arguing, on the one hand, that women's issues have not been adequately addressed in the public world (and they could not be if women are absent) and claiming, on the other hand, that such matters as colonialism, nationalism, or public politics are of little concern to women in the first place. We might well lament the fate of feminist women in nationalist movements, or the compromise of Irish feminism (and socialism) by a narrow nationalism. But these do not add up to, or imply, an intrinsic contradiction between feminism and nationalism. And these issues could never be addressed or resolved in the private sphere alone. For if Molly is emancipated, or if her emancipation is based on a possible reconciliation within her marriage, then she has apparently liberated herself by simply enunciating that 'female word, *yes*'. Molly may be an insubordinate wife, but her monologue is, after all, delivered from the conjugal bed in her own house – this is the position from which she issues such stirring declarations as: 'they call that friendship killing and then burying one another and they all with their wives and families at home' (*U*, p. 636).

Nationalist movements are notorious not only for marginalizing women, but also for their extensive symbolic deployment of femininity, especially in the form of feminine or maternal images of the national territory. In this context, feminist critics concerned to chart Joyce's progress away from sexism often link his enlightenment with departure from nationalist Ireland. Henke asks whether Joyce 'somehow manage[d] to transcend the limits of birth and education, of socialization and temper, to move in the direction of understanding the problems of contemporary sexual politics and the enigma of female desire.'[15] But here, in opposing parochial preoccupations to a supposedly trans-cultural 'desire', feminist readers may drastically underplay the ideological connections *between* national politics and sexuality already in place in the local discourses which Joyce cites. The overdetermination of images of domestic security by the colonial context, for example, is established by frequent references to those 'strangers in our house' (*U*, p. 265); a phrase often associated with the scapegoating of that 'dishonoured wife' (*U*, p. 266) who precipitated the Anglo-Norman invasion by her adultery. The eroticized figure of the faithless temptress ('And here she is', as Alf jokes to the citizen, pointing to a pin-up, 'in all her warpaint') is countered by the traditional allegory of Ireland as a woman. Joyce alludes to this symbolic tradition early in *Ulysses*, with the appearance of the milkwoman at the tower – 'Silk of the kine and poor old woman, names given her in old times' (*U*, p. 12) – and it reaches its apotheosis in the figure of Old Gummy Granny, who implores Stephen to die for his country: 'Remove him, acushla. At 8.35 a.m. you will be in heaven and Ireland will be free. (*She prays*) O good God, take him!' (*U*, p. 490). In particular, it is invoked whenever themes of sex, reproduction and the state enter the narrative – in relation to Mrs Purefoy in Holles Street Hospital, the prostitutes of Nighttown and the ghostly Mrs Dedalus. This persistent linkage between mother and motherland in Joyce's writing leads James Fairhall to declare: 'The ambivalence towards women ['the artist-hero'] develops as a child, crystallized in his confusion over whether or not to kiss his mother, parallels his ambivalence towards Ireland'.[16]

Joyce's borrowing of this nationalist imagery in *Ulysses* suggests that it may prove difficult to uncover here a realm of femininity, entirely innocent of ideology and violence, which could subsist as a site of infantile bliss, or more adult pleasures. For such conceptions of the feminine, and especially the maternal, are already part of a shared political discourse, explicitly invoked and exploited by Irish nationalism. Indeed, nationalist ideology shares many themes with recent feminist theory – nostalgia for the body of the mother, fantasies of an originary lost plenitude, a longing for unmediated relations with language and the flesh. Perhaps this conjunction should not surprise us in the light of

Julia Kristeva's view that nationalism offers individuals the opportunity to relive their early fantasy of the all-nourishing body of the pre-Oedipal mother. Nationalists, needless to say, regressively invoke 'this myth of the archaic mother . . . possessor of some mythical unity'[17] because they refuse to accept the fact of separation from the maternal body, whereas feminist theorists (some of whom are much less cautious about such formulations than Kristeva herself) attend to the irruption of the 'semiotic' as radically destructive of any certain origin or identity.[18]

But do Joyce's references to such stereotypes necessarily indicate that he approves of them? Might his allusions to the symbolic role of women in nationalism be read as *critique* – proof that he acknowledged, but repudiated, the incarcerating stereotypes of women prevalent in Irish society? Molly's happiest memories are of Gibraltar and the Mediterranean – the most subversive thing about her, as the heroine of an Irish novel, is that she is not really a native at all. Similarly, the polyglot Anna Livia does not sanction any exclusive, racist myth, but is instead the 'bringer of Plurabilities' (*FW*, p. 104). Joyce thus demonstrates that 'love is not national but international, articulated by the interacial Bloom and Molly'.[19] The 'feminine discourse' of Chapter 18 and ALP's monologue in *Finnegans Wake* grounds the entire human family in these night-time reflections, subverting the appropriation of 'Woman' by any small, self-obsessed group.

This may privilege women, but perhaps no more than the nationalist cliché. For allegorical transformation again places them on the borderline between culture and nature; women figure as 'the raw material for symbolisation – biology, reproduction, the body, mortality, cycles of growth and decay', rather than as equal participants in human culture.[20] In order to recognise 'female desire', we evidently must leave behind not just Irish mores, but any particular society. As Bloom instructs Cissy Caffrey in Chapter 15, women are the 'sacred lifegivers', 'the link between generations and nations' (*U*, p. 488), rather than politically and historically positioned subjects themselves. But we do not escape from stereotype by removing women from historical time – even from the nightmare of Irish history. Indeed, through Cissy, Joyce dramatizes this general stereotype in a specific historical situation. Her efforts to mediate between Stephen and the British soldier offer an ironic comment on the 'quick motherwit' (*U*, p. 285) she demonstrates earlier in the day; Cissy's very presence in Nighttown, as Irishmen and British soldiers meet in the context of their mutual sexual exploitation of Irish women, sheds a different light on her pacifying mission. Cissy fares well in Chapter 13, successfully quelling the babies' dispute over their sandcastles. As the narrator wryly asides, 'every little Irishman's house is his castle' (*U*, p. 285), thus reducing political rivalries and territorial disputes to sublimated instincts of infantile aggression: men are helplessly locked in unimportant conflicts, until women intervene, bringing tranquillity and salvation. In Chapter 15, however, Cissy again imagines herself, by virtue of her sex, to be the bearer of special symbolic significance. She first fantasizes that 'They're going to fight. For me!' (*U*, p. 487). But this is quickly revealed as a vulgar mistake, and she pleads instead with the soldier: 'Amn't I with you? Amn't I your girl?' (*U*, p. 488). As the paid servant of his sexual need, of course, she has no such status or authority: the futility of being the only the 'girl' – the object of symbolic exchange, or the stake of culture – when one is embedded in a particular conflict, is made abundantly clear.

Suzette Henke then articulates an important feminist preoccupation when she writes: 'Did Joyce persistently relegate the female to those narrow Catholic categories of virgin/whore, Mary/Eve, angel/temptress that proved so popular in turn of the century Ireland?'[21] But readers should not assume that familiar stereotypes will just be more 'popular' in Ireland, although they can anticipate that, due to local factors like Catholicism or colonialism, they may operate in distinctive ways. And if, in spite of our feminist revisions, we are obliged to conclude that Joyce ends his major texts with a progression from culture to nature, mediated through the figure of the woman, then we must decide whether we can distinguish between his exploitation of this cliché, and a general recourse to it in his own society. I will argue that Joyce fails to depart from stereotype in his representation of women, but he instead redistributes elements of feminine stereotypes among a variety of figures in a manner determined both by culturally specific notions of femininity, and by particular historical conditions. I hope to reposition the debate about Joyce's feminism, or his use to feminism, by showing how these female figures bear a function of protest and resistance, both in relation to patriarchy and to colonialism – they do not merely signify a passive 'affirmation'. But such fictional strategies originate (to paraphrase Patrick McGee) in the psychic and historical crisis of a particular male subject, and it would be absurd to claim that we could elaborate a theory of anti-colonial feminism solely on the basis of Joyce's texts. But equally, they contain no 'feminism', awaiting an eager recuperation by radical critics, if this is to be founded on the notion of Joyce's simple disengagement from the Irish scene – a variety of feminism which would, most perniciously, render nationalism simply synonymous with patriarchy.

WOMEN AND THE NATION

The story of Gretta and Gabriel Conroy, chief protagonists of 'The Dead', usefully illustrates some of the complex relations between femininity and nationhood in Joyce's early fiction. After the party on Usher's Quay, as Gretta is walking through the snowy Dublin streets, her husband reflects: 'She seemed to him so frail that he longed to defend her against something and then to be alone with her. Moments of their secret life together burst like stars upon his memory' (*D*, p. 244). Gabriel's fond protectiveness in his marriage perfectly complements his public role of educated, manly civility. But by the end of the night, Gabriel has come to realise that he is neither Gretta's guardian nor her true lover; and the bourgeois culture that he valued so highly, both personally and professionally, seems utterly bogus.

Critics of 'The Dead', as we have seen, are often tempted to read Gretta - a feminine representative of a vanquished culture - as an image of Irishness or Ireland itself. According to a well-established feminist critique of how such symbolic functions oppress women, Gretta is a victim of a cultural stereotype. But here we do not witness 'the power of nationhood to edit the reality of womanhood'[22] in any straightforward way. The nationalist stereotype, at least, does not associate the allegorical figure of Ireland simply with privacy or domesticity, unlike the more modern one embraced by Gabriel. Mother Ireland may expect Irish women to produce strong sons to die in the cause of freedom, but she herself is an image of distressed, marginalised womanhood, bereft of husband, land and family. The allegory thus reflects a historical truth of Irish family life: in a society of celibacy and late marriage (features directly related to the legacy of the Famine), it is surely notable that the Conroys are the only married couple at the Morkhams' party.[23] Gabriel imagines that he is a citizen of an ordinary modern city, but as a Dubliner, he cannot afford to make that assumption - indeed he is severely punished for entertaining merely the most conventional expectations of his private life.

Gretta's suitability as a symbol of Ireland, though, is partly due to her traditionally 'feminine' virtues of kindness, patience and extreme passivity. She makes no explicit complaint against Gabriel; she embodies the rebuking, demanding elements of Mother Ireland only in her distracted melancholy. She thus provides a good foil for another woman at the party, who is actively chiding and satiric: Gretta may represent the woman as nation, but Molly Ivors is an early type of the woman as *nationalist* in Joyce. Disturbed by Molly Ivors' harsh criticism, Gabriel faces a dilemma. He likes to charm and impress women, but when the education he generally advocates is extended to them, it apparently produces bossy, sexless individuals like Ivors. At the same time, the pathetic figure of Lily, ignorant, vulnerable and (so Joyce hints) pregnant, surely vindicates Molly's aggressive virginity. During this Epiphany feast Gabriel undergoes a sexual humiliation, or symbolic castration, at the hands of these three women. And although Joyce avoids the familiar tripartite image of woman as mother, virgin and whore, the splitting of 'femininity' here into three distinct figures serves equally well to contain, or manage, the sexual and political threats which Gabriel associates with women. Joyce's device is then analogous in structure, but not identical in content, to the general stereotype.

Gretta then represents the 'split-off' good bits of Irish womanhood; she may be sexually punishing, but she is also innocent and romantically sorrowful. Its more explicitly political elements, that is to say, have been attributed instead to the articulate and self-assured Miss Ivors. Gretta eludes the modernizing forces of both feminism, with its emphasis on what Gayatri Spivak describes as 'female individualism', and political nationalism.[24] Without those allies who inflict the first wounds on Gabriel – Lily in the role of victim, and Molly Ivors as feminist-nationalist – Gretta could not wield such enormous symbolic power in the final scene. But, by the same token, her passivity makes it all the easier for Gabriel to contemplate her mournfully, as an image of his own repudiated culture. Joyce's exploitation of cliché, then, is influenced by nationalism, both as it invoked femininity (Gretta) and as it involved women (Molly Ivors). But he does not simply permit the mythical 'body of the nation' to absorb the body of the actual woman, with the consequent eclipse of Gretta's own subjectivity. Rather, Gretta seems to enjoy secret and obscure modes of selfhood, which baffle her husband. By contrast, a disturbing complicity operates between nationalism, bourgeois modernity and aspects of Irish feminism. The feminist woman is not politically undercut, and her association with nationalism serves to dignify the latter. But for the young Joyce, the alliance is none the less disquieting.

The sexual independence of the modern woman may confuse Gabriel, but it horrifies Stephen D(a)edalus. The latter believes that women's emancipation, like his own, must encompass sexual liberation, but he is intensely annoyed that the feminists he meets seem more interested in saving Ireland than in *jouissance*.[25] Stephen suspects that Emma Clery rejects his offer of free love purely because of her 'middle-class affectations' (*SH*, p. 72); 'She wants a man and a little house to live in' (*SH*, p. 184), as his friend assures him. Emma ('EC', in *A Portrait of the Artist*) may be a Catholic and a Gaelic leaguer, but she is also a fellow student who enquires curiously about Stephen's ideas and aesthetic theories. His reasons for loving her, however, are apparently unconnected with her personal interests or ambitions. Rather, he considers that physical and emotional submission to him – in Lawrentian style – will release her from her sterile selfhood.

Stephen muses that his beloved is: 'a batlike soul waking to the consciousness of itself in darkness and secrecy and loneliness, tarrying awhile, loveless and sinless, with her mild lover and leaving him to whisper of innocent transgressions in the latticed ear of a priest' (*P*, p. 225). This echoes his earlier description of the peasant woman who invites his friend Davin to her bed.[26] But while the peasant was 'a type of her race and his own' (*P*, p. 186), EC is 'a figure of the womanhood of her country' (*P*, p. 225). The two are then linked, but there is also an important distinction between them: the first woman represents an inchoate racial substratum, while the second is more clearly gendered, individualised and nationalised. Ironically, there is a greater possibility of a sexual alliance between Stephen, the modern 'heretic' (*P*, p. 224), and the native pagan, than between the two undergraduates. Stephen would like to blame this on Emma's religious principles, but it is also undeniably connected to her sense of personal autonomy. Young women, who are given the choice, do not generally end up barefoot and pregnant in mud cabins. Simply because of women's relation to reproduction, as Stephen acknowledges – 'A woman's body is a corporal asset of the State: if she traffic with it she must sell it either as a harlot or as a married woman or as a working celibate or as a mistress' (*SH*, p. 207) – his views of sexual politics are absurdly Utopian.

So the young artist, too, faces a sexual dilemma. He may surrender to the native temptress, but the dark forces of sex would then draw him back into 'racial' consciousness, and in Ireland, this has a very different political significance than it might for a Rupert Birkin. The modern woman, on the other hand, threatens to imprison him in convention. Sexual pleasure cannot be simply opposed, in the style of contemporary theory, to a contained bourgeois self – indeed, it may even be at odds with those varieties of feminism actually available to women in the society which Joyce depicts. We already glimpsed some of these complications in our discussion of Chapter 11 of *Ulysses* ('Sirens'). Joyce there describes the intoxicating fluidity of the barmaid's bodies, but their 'femininity' is nevertheless associated with the loss of male selfhood, not just in erotic delight, but in patriotic sacrifice, blood and death. Even in Dublin bar-room fantasy, as Colin MacCabe reminds us, you cannot be sure of politically safe, post-nationalist sex.

But the assertive, punishing woman is not merely repressed or eliminated in Joyce's fiction. To begin with, her pursuit of individuality is too embarrassingly close to Dedalus's own escapist project. She may not be his ideal companion in his quest for self-fulfilment, but then he is not much interested in a feminine version of himself. Indeed perhaps she troubles him, philosophically and personally, precisely because she echoes his own facile declarations of autonomy – just as Molly Ivors unnerves Gabriel because he has more in common with her than with anyone else at the party. But in so far as Stephen's aesthetic ideals remain communal, feminism cannot be ignored. Joyce's fidelity to realism alone suffices to make apparent the justice of its claims. This is reflected in the pitiful life of Mrs Dedalus, modelled on that of his own mother. As Joyce wrote to Nora Barnacle:

> How could I like the idea of home? My home was just a middle-class affair ruined by spendthrift habits which I have inherited. My mother was slowly killed, I think, by my father's ill-treatment, by years of trouble, and by my cynical frankness of conduct. When I looked on her face as she lay in her coffin – a face gray and wasted with cancer – I understood that I was looking on the face of a victim and I cursed the system which had made her a victim. (*SL*, p. 25)

But there is an immense distinction, as Stephen Dedalus learns, between 'cursing the system', and making sense of one's relationships of dependence, resentment and desire with the victims. The first level of response, one might say, is adult and political, the other infantile and largely unconscious. (In this sense, the man who respectfully announced that the emancipation of women was 'the greatest revolution in our time in the most important relationship there is', can perhaps be reconciled with the man who pointedly told Mary Colum, 'I hate intellectual women'.)[27] For Stephen is both a fellow victim of patriarchy, colonialism and Catholicism, and heir to a certain position of patriarchal power. His feeling of deprivation conflicts with his sense of guilty privilege. Increasingly, this is a contradiction for which the mother herself is blamed: 'where would they all of them be', asks Molly Bloom, 'if they hadnt a mother to look after them?' (*U*, p. 640), but Joyce's Dubliners seem in any case to inhabit a world in which mothers are most noticeable by their absence. But since good mothering ends in happy separation, it is ironic that the mother who has failed is perpetually desired, and never forgotten.[28] Stephen, in particular, links his present physical and moral debility with early deprivation; at the tower in Sandycove, Mulligan's 'wellfed voice' hails the sea 'as a great sweet mother' (*U*, p. 5), but Dedalus feels greater empathy with Sargent, his sickly pupil. For a mother's love may be the 'only true thing in life' (*U*, p. 23), but it is of little account if her body is too frail to nourish her child's. Equally, if the mother is so insubstantial that she scarcely even exists, she cannot confer identity on another person. The mutual dependence of mother and baby then becomes shameful, as the male infant is forced to share in a humiliating, feminine powerlessness: 'With her weak blood and wheysour milk she had fed him and hid from sight of others his swaddling bonds' (*U*, p. 23). Moreover, a deep association may linger for the child between the mother, food and the phallus (or its absence). Freud was not at all surprised that women in analysis reproached their mothers for not having given them a penis, but he was perplexed when they insisted also that they had not been given enough milk. It seems that females in particular, as Maud Ellmann comments, 'see the penis and the milk as interchangeable, as gifts at the disposal of the mother; girls don't just lack the penis, but the very pabulum of life'. In certain circumstances, evidently, this is an experience of 'femininity' which is not exclusive to women.[29]

In the Dedalus family, as it is depicted in *A Portrait of the Artist*, worldly or political impotence is initially associated with male authority figures. During the fateful Christmas dinner, men seem obsessed with public politics, but the women, including Mrs Dedalus, evidently give a higher priority to religion. But already, the men prove unexpectedly vulnerable: 'Stephen, raising his terrorstricken face, saw that his father's eyes were full of tears' (*P*, p. 41). Later, the young boy is surrounded by 'the constant voices of his father and of his masters', as they summon him into their patriarchal order:

> urging him to be a gentleman above all things and urging him to be a good Catholic above all things. When the gymnasium had been opened he heard another voice urging him to be strong and healthy and manly and when the movement towards national revival began to be felt in the college yet another voice had bidden him to be true to his country and help to raise up her fallen language and tradition. In the profane world, as he foresaw, a worldly voice would bid him raise up his father's fallen state by his labours. (*P*, p. 86)

But if this is Stephen's invitation to assume a position of male authority, it is less an extension of right than an admission of failure. Dedalus is called upon to exercise power, but all that has been transmitted to him, in preparation for this responsibility, is a history of defeat. The Irish preoccupation with 'manliness', in this sense, bespeaks its actual absence; and instead of inheriting patriarchal privilege, the boy is implored to re-establish it. Nevertheless, in so far as these appeals coincide with those of nationalism, they are firmly linked with the paternal line. By *Ulysses*, however, the figure of the demanding *mother* has become, for Stephen, the primary bearer of images of nationality, even if this runs contrary to his own familial experience. For in psychic terms, the castrated mother precedes the ineffectual father.

In *Ulysses*, Mother Ireland appears as a 'witch on her toadstool', a crone with 'old shrunken paps', who steals 'rich white milk, not hers'

(*U*, p. 12). Significantly, she too is a mother who has starved her children, *'the deathflower of the potato blight on her breast'* (*U*, p. 485). Her disease, like an infection in the maternal breast, has poisoned the nation. Both the ghostly, biological mother and Old Gummy Granny now articulate the father's demands, calling on Stephen to be true to his church and his country. But because these injunctions conflict with the son's sense of identity at a fundamental level, this is for him a radically unsettling scene. Although Mrs Dedalus, at the outset, speaks gently and lovingly to Stephen, he answers her 'The ghoul! Hyena! . . . . (*strangled with rage, his features drawn grey and old*) Shite!' (*U*, p. 474–5). His furious rejection of his real mother would seem more legitimate as a response to Mother Ireland, but then Mrs Dedalus could not credibly be presented as murderous towards her son if the two figures were not in some way analogous. Whether the women are to blame for their own illness, or whether they are themselves victims of an external 'system', is no longer relevant. Stephen is merely the man that they have made of him, and yet they place on him demands for which he is drastically unfitted. The infant which these mothers failed to nourish and protect cannot now be transformed into their champion – it is much too late for Old Gummy Granny to hand him the dagger of phallic authority. Stephen's relationship with his mother and his relationship with Ireland are more than just 'parallel', as James Fairhall states. Anxieties about femininity and about nationhood overlap, and the sexual crisis is thus inescapably political.

The repulsive national mother of 'Circe' anticipates similar attacks on the woman-as-nation allegory by later post-colonial writers – Salman Rushdie's portrayal of Indira Ghandi in *Midnights' Children*, for instance. (Indeed such writers' frequent presentations of the female body in luridly misogynistic terms should serve to remind us that, no matter how legitimate their political satires, post-nationalists can be as sexist as nationalists. Feminists should be careful to consider whether *every* 'subversion' of the symbolic use of femininity is actually progressive for women.) But Joyce also insists on the proximity of this degraded Mother Ireland to the decaying flesh of the real mother, and it is the phantom's revolting *materiality* which really disturbs Stephen. Both mothers may then belong to what Julia Kristeva has named the realm of maternal 'abjection'; they prey on that 'primordial fear situated at the point where the subject first splits from the body of the mother'.[30] Kristeva's notion of the abject mother effectively inverts the lyrical image of the maternal body, familiar from the writings of other French women theorists, by describing how the infant – who is not yet an independent 'subject' – discovers that it must separate itself from its mother's body – a body which is not yet an 'object', in the sense of an external support that would allow the subject to become detached or autonomous.[31] So, if there is a kinship between nationalists and French feminists, in terms of their mutual idealisation of the maternal body, then Stephen's political impasse and his terror of his mother's body may also be fundamentally linked.

Although Dedalus's difficulties are vividly dramatised in the Nighttown episode, they are not resolved. However, psychoanalytic commentators on *Ulysses* assert that his sexual problems are also addressed at the larger level of the text as a whole. Release for Stephen (and here such critics as Mark Schechner and Frances Restuccia draw enthusiastically on a wealth of information about Joyce's own sexuality) comes through sexual masochism. The male masochist creates in fantasy a dominant woman, who is supplied with a fetish; this eroticized object substitutes for her missing penis, thus reassuring the male that as she is not really castrated, his sexual identity is also safe: 'in his flannel trousers Id like to have tattered them down off him before all the people and give what that one calls flagellate till he was black and blue do him all the good in the world' (*U*, p. 629), Molly announces, and in this way evidently offers relief from the threat of sexual difference. By transferring punitive patriarchal power to a female lover, Retuccia argues, Joyce uses women characters to enact his own escape from patriarchy: 'That [Molly] wants a penis and does not want one – or metaphorically has one and does not have one – makes her the fetishized phallic mother Joyce needed in order to do battle successfully with the authority he wished to overturn'.[32]

While here interpreting 'Penelope' in a similar way, I am also concerned to complicate the notion of the 'law of the father' with which these readings work. Restuccia uses this phrase to denote Stephen's experiences at the hands of priests and teachers, and especially his endurance of physical violence, but the terms of Joyce's masochistic contract are also affected by the particular problems which beset Irish patriarchy – the phallic woman brings consolation for more than the 'universal' fear of castration. In Chapter 18, Joyce transforms the weak mother who desires to love, but cannot, into a strong but selfish mother, who may choose to withhold her gifts. The male victim and the patriarchal oppressor blend into one another, and so the sadistic woman is also an avenger on women's behalf. The self-assertive woman is then not just erotically fascinating, but also politically correct – in Joyce, the strong, punishing woman was originally the feminist. The passive, native woman and the aggressive, nationalist woman were first opposed, thanks to a mechanism of psychic defence; in 'Penelope', however, they are both elements in a new strategy for masculine survival, and they now triumphantly merge. And because the weak woman is associated with the allegorical national mother, and the strong woman with political nationalism, feminism itself remains linked with the politics of the nation. A revised relationship with the mother thus makes possible a revised relationship with the motherland. Molly may then provide us with the ultimate sense of 'Nostos' in *Ulysses*: in this, however, 'Penelope' represents an imaginary solution to real contradictions, rather than any kind of 'return' to a maternal origin.

But in order to appreciate how Joyce maintains this link with public politics in Molly's monologue, we must re-examine those divisions between public and private, male and female, nationality and universality, which we reviewed in recent feminist criticism of Joyce. Such accounts of *Ulysses*, as we have seen, assume that the political counterpart of Joyce's modernist writing would be a tolerant, compassionate society, in which narrow, selfish creeds like nationalism could have no place. Critics often relate this to 'femininity', proposing that if those modes of relationship now existing in the private sphere – which effectively exclude aggression and narcissistic identifications with any particular territory – could be translated into public life, we might eliminate 'Force, hatred, history, all that' (*U*, p. 273). One would expect this interpretation to be based on Joyce's depiction of how women relate to each other (or to men or children) but yet we normally turn to a supposedly androgynous Leopold Bloom, rather than to any of Joyce's female characters, to illustrate it. Feminist celebrations of Molly, then, are frequently no more 'countersigns to Bloom's passport to eternity' (*SL*, p. 285), carrying with them the specific implications that he bears for local politics. But such readings ignore the fact that, in crucial ways, Leopold and Molly contrast with and strategically complement each other. I will argue that Molly facilitates the political phenomenon of 'Bloom' by draining away into the private world of their household all those aggressive and vengeful instincts of which he alone seems free in everyday Dublin life. In this way, Joyce redistributes the gender roles within one of the key family units depicted in *Ulysses*. If we overlook this element of the text's sexual politics, we risk misrepresenting its public political vision.

Like the distinction between Bloom and his fellow citizens in Chapter 12, this role-reversal is first suggested through styles of language. In general, comic exploitation of women's words in *Ulysses* is based on the juxtaposition of their voices with traditionally 'feminine' stereotypes. Their discourse is as graphically forceful as anything we hear from the men – 'Most aggravating that young brat is. If he doesn't conduct himself I'll wring his ear for him a yard long' (*U*, p. 212) – but, in addition, it is registered as amusingly incongruous. Gerty's 'sweet girlish shyness' (*U*, p. 286), for example, is at odds with her her private thoughts: 'Little monkeys common as ditchwater. Someone ought to take them and give them a good hiding for themselves to keep them in their places, the both of them' (*U*, p. 294). Dedalus's sisters, unlike himself, have evidently inherited Simon's skill in invective, and are prepared to use it against 'Our father who art not in heaven' (*U*, p. 186), as Boody describes Mr Dedalus. These girls display none of their mother's pious resignation, being instead – so Simon informs Dilly on the street – 'An insolent pack of bitches' (*U*, p. 195). But significantly, these women are 'unfeminine' to the extent that they sound Irish. For in this society, as in many colonial situations, genteel speech is not just a matter of class, but of culture – the most regionally inflected accents would thus be the least 'ladylike'. In this context, Joyce acknowledges that Molly's Hiberno-English is surprising for one brought up so far away from Ireland, and tells us that, as a young girl, she feared that it might discourage her British soldier boyfriend: 'I was afraid he mightnt like my accent first he so English all father left me' (*U*, p. 627). Language is literally her only patrimony, and as Restuccia has shown, Joyce lends such 'masculine' properties to women for good strategic reasons. In this sense, it is precisely in her speech that Molly does not, *pace* Henke, escape 'the male-biased rhetoric of cultural inscription'.

Molly Bloom does indeed comment caustically, but with strange familiarity, on the public sphere which her husband inhabits: 'theyre a nice lot of them well theyre not going to get my husband again into their clutches if I can help it making fun of him then behind his back I know well when he goes on with his idiotics' (*U*, p. 636). Throughout the episode she disparages many of her husband's companions with a cynical wit which parallels their own: 'that other beauty Burke . . . youd vomit a better face' (*U*, p. 629). So, if 'Penelope' represents Joyce's revision of Odysseus's slaying the suitors, here Molly stands up for Bloom, who is so reluctant to defend himself: 'Tom Kernan that drunken little barrelly man that bit his tongue off falling down the mens WC drunk in some place or other and Martin Cunningham and the two Dedaluses and Fanny MCoys husband white head of cabbage skinny thing with a turn in her eye'. These features of Molly's language lead Mark Schechner to observe:

> The critic of Irish manhood, she is also its rhetorical counterpart, for the bulk of her censorious monologue is like nothing else in the book so much as the anonymous narrative of 'Cyclops' . . . . Most of 'Penelope' has a tone, a style and a content that elsewhere in *Ulysses* are reserved for the meanest of male figures – the Irish pubster. Both are censorious, vulgar and arrogant and both take attitudes of critical superiority to the chaotic sprawl of sex and childrearing in Dublin. On Bloom and Joyce's behalf, then, Molly is the figure who confronts and defeats Ireland on its own terms,

aggressive wit and unselfconscious assumption of moral superiority.[33]

Her physical separation from this world, and her criticisms of it, do not disguise the fact that her language, and many of her opinions, would not be out of place there. In her own relationship with Leopold, for example, Molly is reluctant to lose an argument, and impatient with compromise – 'that was why we had the standup row over politics he began it not me . . . I was fuming with myself after for giving in' (*U*, p. 612) – and her descriptions of her infidelity are far removed from the euphemism and compromise for which Leopold's critics have commended him. 'its all his own fault if I am an adulteress' (*U*, p. 641), Molly claims, threatening to: 'let him know if thats what he wanted that his wife is fucked yes and damn well fucked up to my neck nearly not by him 5 or 6 times handrunning there the mark of his spunk on the sheet I wouldnt bother to even iron it out '(*U*, p. 641). Moreover, her attitude towards her husband is by no means free of the very sexual jealousy that he has apparently transcended – 'if its not that its some little bitch or other he got in with somewhere or picked up on the sly . . . not that I care two straws now who he does it with or knew before that way though Id like to find out' (*U*, p. 609) – and like the citizen and unlike Bloom she will have no strangers or rivals in her home: 'that slut that Mary . . . I gave it to him anyhow either she or me leaves the house' (*U*, p. 609). We cannot turn to Molly's monologue for easy readings in the politics of love. Leopold's deconstruction of masculinity is in inverse proportion to what is, by conventional standards, the 'defeminization' of the women, especially Molly, which Joyce portrays. The 'feminization' of the public sphere (Leopold) is countered by the 'masculinization' of the private sphere (Molly) – loudly proclaimed in the mild 'liberal' idiom given to Bloom and the sexually aggressive idiom given to Molly. We may resolutely side with *eros* rather than *thanatos* in the realm of culture, but when culture and power are as intricately intertwined as they are in *Ulysses*, such partisanship is more self-congratulatory than illuminating.

The last words of *Finnegans Wake*, like Molly's '*yes*' in *Ulysses*, apparently testify to a mature, joyful celebration of human experience, attuned to natural cycles of growth and decay. The River Liffey plunges into the sea, only to be reborn in the Wicklow hills: 'One body offers its death, the other its birth, but they are merged in a two-bodied image'.[34] ALP accepts the fact of her own mortality, and thus the 'riverrun' (*FW*, p. 3) of human culture – itself as irrepressible as a force of nature – begins again. 'If there is a "propriety of woman"', Hélène Cixous writes 'it is paradoxically her capacity to depropriate unselfishly, body without end, without appendage, without principal "parts". . . . Her writing can only keep going, without ever inscribing or discerning contours'.[35] But ALP departs from this carnivalesque paradigm in the poignancy of her death. We must turn very quickly from the last page of *Finnegans Wake* to the first – or be instructed that there is no real break between them – to repress her grief successfully. Whatever the next Viconian round may bring, for this particular subjectivity, material dissolution means extinction. In these pages, Joyce depicts a female figure who is not outside history, not seasonal nor cyclical nor eternal. Indeed far from embodying transcendence, the central female character is here the most time-bound of all.

If ALP represents a 'depropriating' feminine self, she suffers for her generosity: 'But I read in Tobecontinued's tale that while blubles blow there'll still be sealskers. There'll be others but non so for me . . . . O bitter ending!' (*FW*, p. 626–7). In spite of this, such critics as Richard Ellmann insist that although ALP has seen through her husband, 'she is full of submission, if not precisely to him, at least to the male principle'.[36] But we should not underestimate ALP's final demystification. She is not merely disappointed with HCE's inadequacy – his fallibility, and the pathos attached to it, have been central themes from the outset. Throughout *Finnegans Wake*, the virtues of a fluid, life-affirming 'femininity' have been contrasted with the petty products of men's ambitions, but whose interests has this supposed deconstruction of masculinity actually served? If ALP now submits to male power, she does so in the angry realisation that patriarchy has, after all, survived the ascendancy of the 'feminine'. For while HCE has tended towards rigidity and violence, ALP has corrected his excesses. She may be responsible for the subversive documents which implicate him in some dreadful crime, but by Wakean logic, those same texts provide his most convincing defence. As the bearer of the female principle, ALP has not torn down the edifice of 'male' culture – indeed, she has protected and conserved it. A good mother knows that her charges are self-destructive little creatures, who need looking after: the infantilization involved in reducing social to psychic reality does not just diminish the father, but makes him appealingly vulnerable. So while men remain the master-builders, women become salvagers and rescuers; instead of a univocal history of progress, they are the purveyors of an essential and sustaining gossip, and carriers of a tradition of resignation and survival.

ALP, as nurturing mother, also partakes of that ideal of national motherhood that we traced – in a very different style – in relation to Molly Bloom. There we saw how the fantasy of maternal power helps to provide a secure subject-position for the male. In a significant progression, this cultural fiction is now exposed by the symbol of 'feminity' herself. But ALP is also a revised version of that native temptress who goes over the colonist: 'I was the pet of everyone then. A princeable girl. And you were the pantymanny's Vulking Corsergoth. The invision of Indelond. And, by Thorr, you looked it! My lips went livid for from the joy of fear'. She, unlike the traditional Mother Ireland, has welcomed diversity and change. Her rejection of nationalist xenophobia is positively treated – the marriage of HCE and ALP has allowed a new hybrid Irish history to unfold. But it is then notable that, in bitter retrospection, ALP supports her individualistic, proto-feminist complaint by alluding to what she now understands as the parallel betrayal of the national territory. Her monologue is introduced with an allusion to de Valera's acceptance of the partition – 'But she's still her deckhuman amber too' [document number two] (*FW*, p. 619) – and continues:

> Like almost now. How? How you said how you'd give me the keys of me heart. And we'd be married till delth to uspart. And though dev do espart. O mine! Only, no, now it's me who's got to give. As duv herself div. In this linn. (*FW*, p. 626)

She thus effectively reverses the woman-as-nation allegory, in drawing – from the point of view of women – a parallel between their repression, and the repression of national community. For ALP is no 'poor old women' (*U*, p. 12), crying for her four green fields. Rather, her last words undercut any such symbolic deployment of womanhood. But none the less, ALP and Ireland – woman and nation – are both victims. The forces which have oppressed them have not openly asserted superior might, or masculine authority: ALP's lament demonstrates the limitations of those distinctively modern ideologies of liberation which, in promising release from the constrictions of any particular sexual or cultural identity, merely provide instead new disguises for exploitation.

Finnegans Wake is thus a work in which the idea of an emanicipatory modernity is ultimately rebuked. What I have been arguing here is that it is precisely this element of critique *within* the work that has been ignored by its feminist commentators. When ALP-as-river joins the sea, something specific is lost in an oceanic chaos. As with her, so with Ireland. Both have entered the devil's era of modernity, liberated into difference, lost to identity. This is not a simple transition. Joyce both celebrates and mourns it; his readers have so far tended only to join in the celebration.

NOTES

PREFACE

1 E.J. Hobsbawm, *Nations and Nationalism Since 1780* (Cambridge: Cambridge University Press, 1990), p. 14.

2 A number of critics have argued that in the second half of *Ulysses*, and in *Finnegans Wake*, Joyce produces a recognizably postmodernist literature, in which a potentially critical practice of style has been abandoned, apparently reflecting a sheerly heterogeneous social reality (see, for example, Patrick McGee, *Paperspace: Style as Ideology in Joyce's* Ulysses (Lincoln: University of Nebraska Press, 1988), on Joyce as 'a symbolic bridge between the modern and the postmodern', p. 2). My reading of *Ulysses*, however, will seek to uncover critical elements in Joyce's representation of modernity, and in reading *Finnegans Wake* I will attempt to account for its *difference* from postmodern fiction. Therefore I have considered it appropriate to describe Joyce as modernist throughout.

INTRODUCTION: MODERNISM AND NATIONALISM

1 Letter to Harriet Shaw Weaver, *Letters of James Joyce*, Vol. I, ed. Stuart Gilbert (London: Faber & Faber, 1957), p. 276.

2 Michael Long, 'The Politics of English Modernism: Eliot, Pound and Joyce', *Visions and Blueprints: Avant-garde Culture and Radical Politics in Early Twentieth-century Culture*, ed. Edward Timms and Peter Collier (Manchester: Manchester University Press, 1988), p. 111.

3 Ezra Pound, 'James Joyce: At Last the Novel Appears' (1917), *Pound/Joyce: The Letters of Ezra Pound to James Joyce, with Pound's Essays on Joyce*, ed. Forrest Read (London: Faber & Faber, 1967), p. 91.

4 Long, 'The Politics of English Modernism', p. 110–11.

5 Richard Ellmann, *James Joyce*, revised edn (Oxford: Oxford University Press, 1982), p. 609.

6 David Harvey, *The Condition of Postmodernity* (Oxford: Blackwell, 1989),

p. 24, pp. 275–6.

7 Pound, 'The Non-Existence of Ireland' (1915), *Pound/Joyce*, p. 32.

8 Pound, 'Dubliners and Mr James Joyce' (1914), *Pound/Joyce*, p. 28–9.

9 Ibid., p. 29.

10 Ibid., p. 91.

11 Wyndham Lewis, *Time and Western Man* (London: Chatto & Windus, 1927), p. 96.

12 Karl Marx, 'The Communist Manifesto', *Selected Writings*, ed. David McLellan (Oxford: Oxford University Press, 1977), p. 224.

13 Lewis, *Time and Western Man*, p. 98.

14 Cairns Craig, *Yeats, Eliot, Pound and the Politics of Poetry* (London: Croom Helm, 1982), p. 270.

15 See T.S. Eliot, '*Ulysses*, Order and Myth', *Dial*, LXXV (November 1923), p. 483.

16 Pound, *Pound/Joyce*, p. 90.

17 Ibid., p. 267.

18 Ibid., p. 256.

19 Ibid.

20 T.S. Eliot, 'A Foreign Mind' (1919), quoted by Cairns Craig, *Yeats, Eliot, Pound and the Politics of Poetry* (London: Croom Helm, 1982), p. 112.

21 Michael Long, 'Eliot, Pound, Joyce: Unreal City?', *Unreal City: Urban Experience in Modern European Literature and Art*, ed. Edward Timms and David Kelley (Manchester: Manchester University Press, 1985), p. 150.

22 Raymond Williams, 'Beyond Cambridge English', *Writing in Society* (London: Verso, 1983), p. 222.

23 Derek Attridge and Daniel Ferrer, 'Introduction: Highly Continental Evenements', *Post-structuralist Joyce*, ed. D. Attridge and D. Ferrer (Cambridge: Cambridge University Press, 1984), p. 1.

24 Derek Attridge, 'Preface', *The Cambridge Companion to James Joyce*, ed. D. Attridge (Cambridge: Cambridge University Press, 1990), p. x.

25 Attridge and Ferrer, *Post-structuralist Joyce*, p. 2, p. 9. My emphasis.

26 Franco Moretti, 'The Long Goodbye: *Ulysses* and the End of Liberal Capitalism', *Signs Taken for Wonders*, revised edn (London: Verso, 1983), p. 190.

27 Terry Eagleton, 'Nationalism, Colonialism and Literature: Nationalism, Irony and Commitment', Field Day Pamphlet No. 13 (Derry: Field Day, 1988), p. 15.

28 Moretti, *Signs Taken for Wonders*, p. 189–90.

29 Suzette Henke, *James Joyce and the Politics of Desire* (London: Routledge, 1990), p. 128.

30 Phillippe Sollers, 'Joyce and Co.', *In the Wake of the Wake*, ed. David Hayman and Elliot Anderson (Madison: University of Wisconsin

Press, 1978), p. 108.

31 Hélène Cixous, 'Sorties', *The Newly Born Woman*, Hélène Cixous and Catherine Clement, trans. Betsy Wing (Minneapolis: University of Minnesota Press, 1985), pp. 87–8; quoted by Henke, *James Joyce and the Politics of Desire*, p. 209.

32 Henke, *James Joyce and the Politics of Desire*, p. 212.

33 Hugh Kenner, *A Colder Eye: The Modern Irish Writers* (London: Allen Lane, 1983), p. 3–4, p. 227.

34 Ellmann, *James Joyce*, p. 218.

35 See Elie Kedourie, *Nationalism* (London: Hutchinson, 1961), for an account of nationalism's philosophical basis in German idealism; and Ernest Gellner, *Nations and Nationalism* (Oxford: Blackwell, 1983), for a history of its origins as a cohesive ideology peculiar to vernacular, literate and secular modern societies. Kedourie opens his study with the declaration: 'Nationalism is a doctrine invented in Europe at the beginning of the nineteenth century' (p. 9). Gellner is more sceptical about the power of ideas in history, but characterizes nationalism as suffering from 'pervasive false consciousness'. As a doctrine which pretends to defend the 'folk' and 'community', and instead facilitates the spread of mass society, Gellner tells us that 'Its self-image and its true nature are inversely related, with an ironic neatness seldom equalled even by other successful ideologies' (p. 124).

36 Lewis, *Time and Western Man*, p. 94–5.

37 Ibid., p. 100.

38 Ibid., p. 99.

39 Ibid., p. 100.

40 Ibid., p. 102.

41 Ibid., p. 95.

42 Ibid., p. 93, p. 94.

43 Pound, *Pound/Joyce*, p. 33.

44 See Terence Brown, 'Yeats, Joyce and Irish Critical Debate', *Ireland's Literature* (Mullingar: Lilliput Press, 1988).

45 James Connolly, 'Labour and the Proposed Partition of Ireland' (1914), *Selected Writings*, ed. Peter Berresford Ellis (London: Pluto Press, 1988), p. 275.

46 P.S. O'Hegarty, quoted by R.F. Foster, '"We Are All Revisionists Now"', *Irish Review*, No. 1 (1986), p. 15.

47 See, for examples, Foster, '"We Are All Revisionists Now"'; Ronan Fanning, 'The Meaning of Revisionism', *Irish Review*, No. 4 (1988), pp. 15–19; Michael Laffan, 'Insular Attitudes: The Revisionists and their Critics', *Revising the Rising*, ed. Máirín Ní Dhonnchadha and Theo Dorgan (Derry: Field Day, 1991), pp. 106–21.

48 See Terence Brown's account of this period in *Ireland: A Social and*

Cultural History 1922–79 (London: Fontana, 1981).

49 Richard Kearney, 'Myth and Motherland', *Ireland's Field Day* (London: Hutchinson, 1985), pp. 69–70.

50 See Chapter 1, pp. 44–6.

51 An interpretation inaugurated in the English-speaking world by Colin MacCabe's *James Joyce and the Revolution of the Word* (London: Macmillan, 1978).

52 Richard Kearney, *Transitions: Narratives in Modern Irish Culture* (Manchester: Manchester University Press, 1988), p. 7.

53 See David Lloyd, *Nationalism and Minor Literature: James Clarence Mangan and the Emergence of Irish Cultural Nationalism* (Berkeley: University of California Press, 1988), for a critique of Irish cultural nationalism in these terms.

54 See Sollers, 'Joyce and Co.', pp. 108–9.

55 Seamus Deane, 'Heroic Styles: The Tradition of an Idea', *Ireland's Field Day*, p. 56.

56 Ibid., p. 58.

57 Seamus Deane, 'Joyce the Irishman', *The Cambridge Companion to James Joyce*, p. 35.

58 Seamus Deane, 'History as Fiction/Fiction as History', *Joyce in Rome*, ed. Giorgio Melchiori (Rome: Bulzoni, 1984), p. 132.

59 Marshall Berman, *All That is Solid Melts into Air: The Experience of Modernity* (London: Verso, 1983), p. 14.

60 In his review of *All That is Solid Melts into Air*, Perry Anderson thus argues, *pace* Berman, that the ambition of political radicals should be 'neither to prolong nor to fulfil modernity, but to abolish it'. Perry Anderson, 'Modernity and Revolution', *New Left Review*, No. 144 (1984), p. 113.

61 See Aijaz Ahmad, *In Theory: Classes, Nations, Literatures* (London: Verso, 1992), p. 219.

62 As David Lloyd points out, Irish revisionist history, for example, often criticizes 'the anti-modernist and Manichean tendencies of nationalism only to valorize British imperialism as an essentially modernising force', see D. Lloyd, *Anomalous States: Irish Writing and the Post-Colonial Moment* (Dublin: Lilliput, 1993), p. 124.

63 G.J. Watson, 'The Politics of *Ulysses*', *Joyce's* Ulysses: *the Larger Perspective*, ed. Robert D. Newman and Weldon Thornton (London, AUP, 1987), pp. 58, 41, 56.

64 Francis Shaw S.J. ,'The Canon of Irish History: A Challenge', *Studies* Vol. LXI, No. 242 (1972), p. 142.

65 Roy Foster, *Modern Ireland 1600–1972* (Harmondsworth: Allen Lane, 1988), p. ix.

66 Ibid.

67 Lewis, *Time and Western Man*, p. 95.

68 Dominic Manganiello, *Joyce's Politics* (London: Routledge & Kegan Paul, 1980), p. 16, p. 147. My emphasis. Conor Cruise O'Brien's *States of Ireland* (London: Hutchinson, 1972) was the first major revisionist study of Irish nationalism.

69 Manganiello, *Joyce's Politics*, p. 163. My emphasis.

70 Theresa O'Connor, 'Demythologizing Nationalism: Joyce's Dialogized Grail Myth', *Joyce in Context*, ed. Vincent J. Cheng and Timothy Martin (Cambridge: Cambridge University Press, 1992), p. 100.

71 Conor Cruise O'Brien's '*The Irish Mind*: A Bad Case of Cultural Nationalism', *Passion and Cunning and Other Essays* (London: Weidenfeld & Nicolson, 1988), for example, offers a revisionist response to contemporary Irish cultural criticism. For recent critiques of the political biases of historical revisionism see, for example, Luke Gibbons, 'Challenging the Canon: Revisionism and Cultural Criticism', *The Field Day Anthology of Irish Writing*, Vol. III, ed. Seamus Deane (Derry: Field Day, 1991), pp. 561–79; and Seamus Deane, 'Wherever Green is Read', *Revising the Rising*, ed. Máirín Ní Dhonnchadha and Theo Dorgan, pp. 91–105.

72 Manganiello, *Joyce's Politics*, p. 138; Richard Ellmann, *The Consciousness of Joyce* (London: Faber & Faber, 1977), p. 89.

73 Richard Davis, *Arthur Griffith and Non-violent Sinn Fein* (Dublin: Anvil Books, 1974), pp. 106, 107.

74 Arthur Griffith, Preface to John Mitchel, *Jail Journal* (Dublin: M.H. Gill, 1913).

75 Gibbons, 'Challenging the Canon', p. 595.

1 JOYCE AND THE IRISH LITERARY REVIVAL

1 For Yeats's description of this encounter, see Richard Ellmann, *James Joyce*, revised edn (Oxford: Oxford University Press, 1982), p. 102.

2 W.B. Yeats, 'Nationality and Literature' (1893), *Uncollected Prose*, ed. John P. Frayne (London: Macmillan, 1970), pp. 269, 271.

3 Quoted by Ulick O'Connor, *Celtic Dawn: A Portrait of the Irish Literary Renaissance* (London: Hamish Hamilton, 1984), p. 128–9.

4 See Standish O'Grady, *History of Ireland Volume I: Heroic Period* (1878) (Dublin: E. Ponsonby, 1970) and *Early Bardic Literature: Ireland* (1879) (Dublin: E. Ponsonby, 1970), and 'The Great Enchantment', *Ideals in Ireland* (London: At the Unicorn VII Cecil Court, 1901), ed. Augusta Gregory, pp. 77–83.

5 AE (George Russell), 'Nationality and Imperialism', in *Ideals in Ireland*, pp. 15–16.

6 M.M. Bakhtin, 'Epic and Novel', *The Dialogic Imagination*, ed. Michael Holquist (Austin: University of Texas Press, 1981), p. 13.

7 See John Hutchinson, *The Dynamics of Cultural Nationalism: The Gaelic Revival and the Creation of the Irish Nation State* (London: Allen & Unwin, 1987), especially Chapter 4.

8 Quoted by O'Connor, *Celtic Dawn*, p. 171.

9 W.B. Yeats, *Autobiographies* (London: Macmillan, 1955), p. 263.

10 W.B. Yeats, 'A General Introduction to my Work' (1937), *Essays and Introductions* (London: Macmillan, 1961), p. 515.

11 Bakhtin, 'Epic and Novel', p. 13.

12 Bakhtin, 'Epic and Novel', p. 12.

13 Bakhtin, 'Discourse in the Novel', *The Dialogic Imagination*, p. 370.

14 Bakhtin, 'From the Prehistory of Novelistic Discourse', *The Dialogic Imagination*, p. 68.

15 See Benedict Anderson, *Imagined Communities: Reflections on the Origin and Spread of Nationalism* (London: Verso, 1983), especially Chapter 2, and Walter Benjamin, 'The Storyteller', *Illuminations*, ed. Hannah Arendt (Glasgow: Fontana, 1973).

16 Anderson, *Imagined Communities*, p. 40.

17 Ibid., p. 19.

18 Homi K. Bhabha, 'DissemiNation: Time, Narrative, and the Margins of the Modern Nation', *Nation and Narration*, ed. Homi K. Bhabha (London: Routledge, 1990), p. 294. Simon During summarizes this case, in the same volume: 'Modernity reproduces itself in nation states, there are few signs of it happening otherwise. To reject nationalism absolutely or to refuse to discriminate between nationalisms is to accede to a way of thought by which intellectuals – especially post-colonial intellectuals – cut themselves off from effective political action' ('Literature – Nationalism's Other? The Case for Revision', *Nation and Narration*, p. 139).

19 John Wilson Foster, *Fictions of the Irish Literary Revival: A Changeling Art* (Syracuse: University of Syracuse Press, 1987), pp. 181–2.

20 Thomas Kinsella, 'The Irish Writer', Thomas Kinsella and W.B. Yeats, *Davis, Mangan, Ferguson?: Tradition and the Irish Writer* (Dublin: Dolmen Press, 1970), p. 65.

21 Ellmann, *James Joyce*, p. 102.

22 See Max Horkheimer and Theodor Adorno, 'Odysseus or Myth and Enlightenment', *Dialectic of Enlightenment*, trans. John Cumming (London: Allen Lane, 1973); Benjamin, 'The Storyteller', p. 102.

23 Marshall Berman, *All That is Solid Melts into Air: The Experience of Modernity* (London: Verso, 1983), p. 15.

24 Benjamin, 'The Storyteller', p. 102.

25 Ellmann, *James Joyce*, p. 253.

26 Anthony Burgess, quoted by Mark Patrick Hederman, 'The Dead Revisited', *The Crane Bag Book of Irish Studies*, ed. Mark Patrick

Hederman and Richard Kearney (Dublin: Woolfhound Press, 1982), p. 183.

27 For an account of this tendency in a survey of criticism of 'The Dead', see Hederman, 'The Dead Revisited', pp. 178–86. John V. Kelleher, for example, finds the ancient Irish story of *Togail Bruidhne Da Derga* (The Destruction of Da Derga's Hostel) lurking in the plot of 'The Dead', 'Irish History and Mythology in James Joyce's "The Dead"', *The Review of Politics* 27 (1976), pp. 414–33.

28 W.B. Yeats, 'Stories of Red Hanrahan' (1897), in *Mythologies* (London: Macmillan, 1989), p. 260.

29 Quoted by William H. O'Donnell, *A Guide to the Prose Fiction of W.B. Yeats* (Epping: Bowker, 1983), p. 43.

30 Ellmann, *James Joyce*, p. 251.

31 Foster, *Fictions of the Irish Literary Revival*, pp. 169, 174.

32 See Ellmann, *James Joyce*, p. 163.

33 Benjamin, 'The Storyteller' p. 101.

34 Ibid., p. 102.

35 Bakhtin, 'Epic and Novel', p. 36.

36 Anderson, *Imagined Communities*, p. 19.

37 Arthur Clery, 'Is Ireland a Country or a County?' (1915), *Dublin Essays* (Dublin: Maunsel, 1919), p. 33.

38 This distinction is borrowed from Patrick McGee, *Paperspace: Style as Ideology in James Joyce's* Ulysses (Lincoln: University of Nebraska Press, 1988), p. 9.

39 David Lloyd, *Nationalism and Minor Literature: James Clarence Mangan and the Emergence of Irish Cultural Nationalism* (Berkeley: University of California Press, 1988), p. 162.

40 Foreword to Maud Ellmann, 'Disremembering Dedalus: *A Portrait of the Artist as a Young Man*', *Untying the Text: A Post-Structuralist Reader*, ed. Robert Young (London: Routledge & Kegan Paul, 1981), p. 189.

41 Maud Ellmann, 'Disremembering Dedalus', p. 194.

42 R.B. Kershner discusses Stephen's paradoxical devotion to scientific positivism in his essay, 'Genius, Degeneration and the Panopticon', *A Portrait of the Artist as a Young Man*, ed. R.B. Kershner (Boston: Bedford Books, 1993).

43 Tom Kettle, 'The Future of Private Property' (1912), quoted by J.B. Lyons, *The Enigma of Tom Kettle* (Dublin: Glendale Press, 1983), p. 17.

44 See Ellmann, *James Joyce*, p. 505.

45 Bakhtin, 'Discourse in the Novel', p. 348.

46 Elie Kedourie, *Nationalism* (London: Hutchinson, 1961), pp. 32, 54.

47 Quoted by Ellmann, *James Joyce*, p. 239.

48 I am not aware whether any record exists of Pearse's presence at the lecture. Richard Ellmann makes no mention of Pearse, and ascribes some of the sentiments expressed by Hughes to Arthur

Clery, and to other university students. See Ellmann, *James Joyce*, p. 93.

49 See Bakhtin, 'Discourse in the Novel', p. 333.

50 See, for example, Trevor L. Williams, 'Dominant Ideologies: The Production of Stephen Dedalus ', *James Joyce: The Augmented Ninth*, ed. by Bernard Benstock (Syracuse: University of Syracuse Press, 1988), pp. 312–22.

51 H.G. Wells, review of *Portrait of the Artist*, *James Joyce: The Critical Heritage* Vol. 1, ed. Robert H. Deming (London: Routledge & Kegan Paul, 1970), pp. 87, 88.

52 See Manganiello, *Joyce's Politics* (London: Routledge & Kegan Paul, 1980), pp. 38–9, 33, 41 and *passim*.

53 See Manganiello, *Joyce's Politics*, p. 138.

54 David Cairns and Shaun Richards, *Writing Ireland: Colonialism, Nationalism and Culture* (Manchester: Manchester University Press, 1988), p. 84.

55 F.S.L. Lyons, *Culture and Anarchy in Ireland 1890–1939* (Oxford: Oxford University Press, 1982), p. 71.

56 Manganiello, *Joyce's Politics*, p. 25.

57 See Edward Said, 'Nationalism, Colonialism and Literature: Yeats and Decolonisation', Field Day Pamplet No. 15 (Derry: Field Day, 1988), p. 16. Said defines nativism as encompassing 'compelling but often demagogic assertions about a native past, history or actuality that seem to stand free not only of the colonizer but of worldly time itself' (p. 15). As his chief example of this, in the Irish context, is the poetry of Yeats, it is obvious that I am using the word in a slightly different sense: I wish to denote by it a movement which emphasises the priority and unity of the indigenous culture, over that of the settler community, as well as the priority of the colonised culture over that of the imperialist power.

58 Yeats, *Autobiographies*, pp. 493–4.

59 George Bernard Shaw, quoted by Lyons, *Culture and Anarchy in Ireland*, p. 69

60 Roy Foster, '"We are all Revisionists Now"', *Irish Review*, No. 1 (1986), p. 1.

61 For a study of stereotypes of the Irish in Victorian English culture, see L.P. Curtis Jnr., *Anglo-Saxons and Celts: A Study of Anti-Irish Prejudice in Victorian England* (Connecticut: University of Bridgeport, 1968) and *Apes and Angels: The Irishman in Victorian Caricature* (Newton Abbot: David & Charles, 1971).

62 D.P. Moran, *The Philosophy of Irish Ireland* (Dublin: James Duffy & Co., 1905), p. 79.

63 Ibid., pp. 67, 102.

64 Ibid., p. 94.

65 As Manganiello (*Joyce's Politics*) writes, 'the purely destructive force of them [*The Leader*'s policies] Joyce ascribed to the Irish Cyclops', p. 25. See also Joan Fitzgerald, 'The Citizen in *Ulysses*: A Note', *Joyce in Rome*, pp. 116–19, who notes allusions in 'Cyclops' to Moran and to Michael Cusack.
66 Moran, *The Philosophy of Irish Ireland*, p. 2.
67 Ibid., p. 21–2.
68 See David Lloyd, 'Writing in the Shit: Beckett, Nationalism and the Colonial Subject', *Anomalous States: Irish Writing and the Post-Colonial Moment* (Dublin: Lilliput Press, 1993), p. 45.
69 Oliver MacDonagh, *States of Mind: A Study of Anglo-Irish conflict 1780-1980* (London: Allen & Unwin, 1983), p. 23.
70 Moran, *The Philosophy of Irish Ireland*, pp. 36–7.
71 Daniel Corkery, *Synge and Anglo-Irish Literature* (Cork: Cork University Press, 1931), p. 19
72 Lloyd, 'Writing in the Shit: Beckett, Nationalism and the Colonial Subject', p. 43.
73 See Raymond Williams, *Culture and Society 1780–1950* (Harmondsworth: Penguin, 1985), pp. 178–80.

2 *ULYSSES* NARRATIVE AND HISTORY

1 Matthew Hodgart, *James Joyce: A Student's Guide* (London: Routledge & Kegan Paul, 1974), p. 19.
2 Don Gifford and Robert J. Seidman, *Notes for Joyce: An Annotation of James Joyce's* Ulysses (New York: Dutton, 1974), p. 262.
3 Colin MacCabe, *James Joyce and the Revolution of the Word* (London: Macmillan, 1978), p. 159.
4 See Seamus Deane, 'Joyce and Nationalism', in *Celtic Revivals: Essays in Modern Irish Literature* (London: Faber & Faber, 1985).
5 MacCabe, *James Joyce and the Revolution of the World* p. 167–70.
6 Declan Kiberd, 'Anglo-Irish Attitudes', *Ireland's Field Day* (London: Hutchinson, 1985), p. 98.
7 Colin MacCabe, 'The Voice of Esau: Stephen in the Library', *James Joyce: New Perspectives*, ed. Colin MacCabe (Brighton: Harvester, 1982), p. 118.
8 Terry Eagleton, *The Ideology of the Aesthetic* (Oxford: Blackwell, 1990), p. 375.
9 Fredric Jameson, 'Postmodernism and Consumer Society', *The Anti-Aesthetic: Essays on Postmodern Culture*, ed. Hal Foster (Port Townsend: Bay Press, 1983), p. 114.
10 See, for example, Derek Attridge, *Peculiar Language: Literature as Difference from the Renaissance to James Joyce* (London: Methuen, 1988) p. 160–71; Patrick McGee, *Paperspace: Style as Ideology in James Joyce's*

Ulysses (Lincoln: University of Nebraska Press, 1988), pp. 74–9. See also papers collected under the title 'Sirens without Music' by Attridge, Maud Ellmann, Daniel Ferrer, Andre Topia, Jean-Michel Rabaté and Robert Young in *James Joyce: The Centennial Symposium*, ed. M. Beja *et al.* (Urbana: University of Illinois Press, 1986), delivered to the James Joyce Symposium in Dublin, June 1982.

11 MacCabe, *James Joyce*, p. 87.

12 Ibid., p. 79, 158. We will here momentarily accept the validity of an opposition between 'writing'–in the sense in which MacCabe uses the term - and nationalism, although in historical terms such a distinction is meaningless. Such commentators as Ernest Gellner and Benedict Anderson point out the role of vernacular writing in the creation of national consciousness. Nationalism belongs exclusively to the historical period of print.

13 Ibid., p. 87.

14 Richard Brown, *James Joyce and Sexuality* (Cambridge: Cambridge University Press, 1985), p. 61.

15 Attridge, *Peculiar Language*, p. 167.

16 Thomas Docherty, *Reading (Absent) Character* (Oxford: Clarendon, 1986), p. 269.

17 MacCabe, *James Joyce*, p. 86.

18 McGee, *Paperspace*, p. 77.

19 Ibid., p. 78.

20 MacCabe, *James Joyce*, p. 158.

21 Ibid., p. 159.

22 Ibid., p. 89.

23 Ibid., p. 88.

24 Patrick Pearse, 'Robert Emmet and the Ireland of Today', *Collected Works of P.H. Pearse: Political Writings & Speeches* (Dublin: Maunsel & Roberts, 1922), p. 70.

25 T.S. Eliot, 'Tradition and the Individual Talent', *Selected Prose*, ed. Frank Kermode (London: Faber & Faber, 1975), p. 38.

26 E.L. Epstein, 'Nestor', in *James Joyce's Ulysses: Critical Essays*, ed. Clive Hart and David Hayman (Berkeley: University of California Press, 1974), p. 23.

27 Epstein, 'Nestor', pp. 21, 24.

28 Ibid., p. 28, 23–4.

29 Frantz Fanon, *The Wretched of the Earth*, trans. Constance Farrington (Harmondsworth: Penguin, 1967), p. 169.

30 On the anticipation of metropolitan modernism in colonial conditions, see Terry Eagleton, 'The End of English', *Textual Practice*, Vol.1, No.1 (1987), pp. 1–9.

31 See, for example, R.M. Adams, *Surface and Symbol: The Consistency of Joyce's* Ulysses (New York: Oxford University Press, 1962), pp. 20–4.

32 Fredrich Nietzsche, quoted by Joseph A. Buttigieg, 'The Struggle against Meta(Phantasma)-physics: Nietzsche, Joyce and "the excess of history"', *Why Nietzsche Now?*, ed. Daniel O'Hara (Bloomington: University of Indiana Press, 1985), p. 188–9.

33 Walter Benjamin, 'Theses on the Philosophy of History', *Illuminations*, ed. Hannah Arendt (Glasgow: Fontana, 1973), p. 264–5.

34 MacCabe, 'The Voice of Esau', p. 115.

35 Ibid., p. 123. The last phrase is in part a translation of the Latin sentence which occurs in the episode: *In societate humana hoc est maxime necessarium ut sit amicitia inter multos* (p. 169).

36 As Goethe writes : 'A lovely, pure, noble and most moral nature, without the strength of nerve which forms a hero, sinks beneath a burden which it cannot bear and must not cast away . . . the effects of a great action laid on a soul unfit for the performance of it', from *Wilhelm Meister's Apprenticeship* (1789), quoted by Don Gifford, *Ulysses Annotated: Notes for James Joyce's* Ulysses, with Robert J. Seidman, second edn (London: University of California Press, 1988), p. 193.

37 See Matthew Arnold, 'Shelley', quoted by Gifford, *Ulysses Annotated*, p. 193.

38 See Matthew Arnold, *On The Study of Celtic Literature* (1867) (London: Macmillan, 1893). See also John V. Kelleher, 'Matthew Arnold and the Celtic Revival', in *Perspectives in Criticism No. 20: Harvard Studies in Comparative Literature*, ed. H. Levin (Cambridge, Mass.: Harvard University Press, 1950), for an account of the dissemination of Arnold's ideas in the revivalist milieu. Understandably, the Irish writers make little acknowledgement of any influence from this source.

39 Mark Schechner, *Joyce in Nighttown: A Psychoanalytical Inquiry into* Ulysses (Berkeley: University of California Press, 1974), pp. 22–3.

40 J.C.C. Mays, 'Some Comments on the Dublin of *Ulysses*', *Ulysses: Cinquante ans après*, ed. Louis Bonnerot *et al.* (Paris: Didier, 1974), p. 86.

41 Franco Moretti, 'The Spell of Indecision', *Signs Taken for Wonders*, revised edn (London: Verso 1983) p. 247.

42 Daniel Moshenberg, 'The Capital Couple: Speculating on *Ulysses*', *James Joyce Quarterly*, Vol. 25, No. 3, p. 333.

43 As Mary Lowe-Evans remarks, this is a reference to Soyer's Dublin soup kitchen which operated during the Famine of the 1840s. As she describes : 'At the sound of a bell, one hundred of the destitute entered and, using chained soupspoons, consumed what was euphemistically called "The Poor Man's Regenerator". As soon as the bowls and spoons had been swabbed and the bowls refilled, another hundred starving Irish men, women and children were ushered in. . . . After making a chemical analysis of the soup, the

English medical journal *The Lancet* pronounced it worthless: "This soup quackery (for it is no less) seems to be taken by the rich as a salve for their consciences"', M. Lowe-Evans, *Crimes Against Fecundity: Joyce and Population Control* (Syracuse: University of Syracuse Press, 1989), p. 19. Here, as so often with Bloom's historical references, it is difficult to say whether one should congratulate him on his historical memory, or remark on its neutral vagueness.

44 Gifford, *Ulysses Annotated* p. 132.

45 Ibid., p. 133.

3 'TALKING ABOUT INJUSTICE': PARODY, SATIRE AND INVECTIVE IN *ULYSSES*

1 *U*, p. 273.

2 Raymond Williams, *The Country and the City* (London: Hogarth Press, 1973), p. 245.

3 Hugh Kenner, *Dublin's Joyce* (London: Chatto & Windus, 1955), p. 2.

4 Hugh Kenner, *Ulysses* (London: Allen & Unwin, 1982), p. 100.

5 Fredric Jameson, '*Ulysses* in History', *James Joyce and Modern Literature*, ed. W.J. MacCormack and Alistair Stead (London: Routledge & Kegan Paul, 1982), p. 133.

6 Shari Benstock, 'The Dynamics of Narrative Performance: Stephen Dedalus as Storyteller', *English Literary History*, Vol. 49 (1982), pp. 710–11.

7 David Hayman, 'Cyclops' in *James Joyce's Ulysses: Critical Essays*, ed. Clive Hart and David Hayman (Berkeley: University of California Press, 1974), p. 274; Kenner, *Ulysses*, p. 95.

8 Kenner, *Ulysses*, p. 100.

9 Philip Herring, 'Joyce's Politics', *New Light on Joyce from the Dublin Symposium*, ed. Fritz Senn (Bloomington: University of Indiana Press, 1972), p. 13.

10 R.M. Adams, *Surface and Symbol: The Consistency of Joyce*'s Ulysses (New York: Oxford University Press, 1967), p. 253.

11 Vivian Mercier, 'James Joyce and the Irish Tradition of Parody', *The Irish Comic Tradition* (Oxford: Clarendon, 1962). Mercier does not assert that a relation of *influence* obtains between the Gaelic tradition and Joyce's work, but merely that analogies exist between them which give rise to the *appearance* of a distinctively Irish tradition which embraces them both.

12 Kenner, *Ulysses*, p. 139.

13 Delmore Schwartz (1953), quoted by Jeffrey Segal, 'Between Marxism and Modernism, or How to be a Revolutionist and Still Love *Ulysses*', *James Joyce Quarterly*, Vol. 25, No. 4 (1988), p. 421.

14 Lionel Trilling, 'James Joyce in his Letters', *Joyce: A Collection of Critical Essays*, ed. William M. Chace (Englewood Cliffs, NJ: Prentice-Hall, 1974), p. 158.
15 Matthew Hodgart, *James Joyce: A Student's Guide* (London: Routledge & Kegan Paul, 1974), p. 101.
16 Colin MacCabe, *James Joyce and the Revolution of the Word* (London: Macmillan, 1978), pp. 93, 101.
17 Patrick McGee, *Paperspace: Style as Ideology in Joyce's* Ulysses (Lincoln: University of Nebraska Press, 1988), p. 80.
18 Hayman, 'Cyclops', p. 267.
19 Herring, 'Joyce's Politics', p. 3.
20 Hayman, 'Cyclops', p. 260.
21 Richard Ellmann, *The Consciousness of Joyce* (London: Faber & Faber, 1977), p. 82.
22 Hayman, 'Cyclops', pp. 247–8.
23 Ibid., p. 248.
24 Norman Vance, *Irish Literature: A Social History* (Oxford: Blackwell, 1990), p. 201.
25 Hodgart, *James Joyce*, p. 102.
26 See Cormac O'Grada, *Ireland Before and After the Famine* (Manchester: Manchester University Press, 1988), pp. 81–2.
27 M.M. Bakhtin, 'Discourse in the Novel', *The Dialogic Imagination*, ed. Michael Holquist (Austin: University of Texas Press, 1981), p. 348.
28 Quoted by Richard Ellmann, *James Joyce*, revised edn (Oxford: Oxford University Press, 1982), p. 332.
29 See Max Horkheimer and Theodor W. Adorno on the association between capitalism and modern anti-Semitism: 'Commerce was not their vocation but their fate . . . . From the time when, in their capacity as merchants, they helped to spread Roman civilisation throughout Gentile Europe, they were representatives – along with their patriarchal religion – of municipal, bourgeois and, finally, industrial conditions. They carried capitalist ways of life to various countries and drew upon themselves the hatred of all who had to suffer under capitalism', M. Horkheimer and T. Adorno, *Dialectic of Enlightenment* trans. John Cumming (London: Allen Lane, 1973), p. 175.
30 See Kenner, *Ulysses*, p. 98; Hayman, 'Cyclops', p. 257.
31 C.H. Peake, *James Joyce: The Citizen and the Artist* (Stanford: Stanford University Press, 1977), pp. 235–6.
32 Conor Cruise O'Brien, *Writers and Politics* (Harmondsworth: Penguin, 1965), p. 140.
33 Hodgart, *James Joyce*, p. 105.
34 Seamus Deane, 'Civilians and Barbarians', *Ireland's Field Day* (London: Hutchinson, 1985), p. 37.

35 Quoted by Kenner, *Ulysses*, p. 93.

36 Michael Long, 'The Politics of English Modernism: Eliot, Pound and Joyce', *Visions and Blueprints: Avante-garde Culture and Radical Politics in Early Twentieth-Century Culture*, ed. Edward Timms and Peter Collier (Manchester: Manchester University Press, 1988), p. 111.

37 My emphasis. For an account of the politics of translation in Irish cultural nationalism see David Lloyd, 'Great Gaps in Irish Song', *Nationalism and Minor Literature: James Clarence Mangan and the Emergence of Irish Cultural Nationalism* (Berkeley: University of California Press, 1988).

38 Quoted by Susan Dick *et al.*, 'Introduction', *Omnium Gatherum: Essays for Richard Ellmann*, ed. Susan Dick *et al.* (Gerrards Cross: Colin Smythe, 1989), p. xvi.

39 Kenner, *Ulysses*, p. 95.

40 Augusta Gregory, *Cuchulain of Muirthemne* (Gerrards Cross: Colin Smythe, 1970), p. 5.

41 Ibid., p. 169.

42 Thomas Kinsella (trans.), *The Tain* (Portlaoise: Dolmen Press, 1972), pp. 140, 155.

43 Umberto Eco, *The Middle Ages of James Joyce* (London: Hutchinson Radius, 1989), p. 9.

44 See John Garvin, 'The Anglo-Irish idiom in the work of major Irish writers' in *The English Language in Ireland*, ed. Diarmuid O'Muirithe (Dublin: Mercier Press, 1977), pp. 100–114, especially Garvin's account of Visser's work on dialect in Joyce.

45 See A.J. Bliss, 'The Emergence of Modern English Dialects in Ireland', *The English Language in Ireland*, p. 18.

46 Hodgart, *James Joyce*, p. 103.

47 Fredric Jameson, '*Ulysses* in History', *James Joyce and Modern Literature*, ed. W.J. MacCormack and A. Stead (London: Routledge & Kegan Paul, 1982), p. 130.

48 Marilyn French, *The Book as World: James Joyce's* Ulysses (London: Abacus, 1982), p. 47.

49 Richard Kearney, *Transitions: Narratives in Modern Irish Culture* (Manchester: Manchester University Press, 1988), p. 32.

4 JOYCE'S REPRESENTATION OF POLITICAL VIOLENCE

1 Karl Radek, 'James Joyce or Socialist Realism?' (1934), in *James Joyce: The Critical Heritage*, ed. Robert H. Deming (London: Routledge & Kegan Paul, 1970), Vol. 2, p. 625.

2 F.S.L. Lyons, 'James Joyce's Dublin', *Twentieth Century Studies*, No. 4 (1970), p. 11.

3 See Richard Ellmann, *James Joyce*, revised edn (Oxford: Oxford University Press, 1982), p. 399.

4 Although even on this count, Joyce is inaccurate: Griffith was opposed simply to participation in Westminister, rather than to Parliamentarianism *per se*.

5 Malcolm Brown, *The Politics of Irish Literature* (London: Allen & Unwin, 1972), p. 224.

6 Ibid., p. 223.

7 See Norman Sherry, *Conrad's Western World* (Cambridge: Cambridge University Press, 1971), p. 261, pp. 283–84.

8 Brown, *The Politics of Irish Literature* p. 224.

9 Tom Paulin, 'The British Presence in *Ulysses*', *Ireland and the English Crisis* (Newcastle upon Tyne: Bloodaxe, 1984), p. 94.

10 Dominic Manganiello, *Joyce's Politics* (London: Routledge & Kegan Paul, 1980), p. 71.

11 F. Engels, 'About the Irish Question' (1888), K. Marx and F. Engels, *On Colonialism* (London: Lawrence & Wishart, 1968), p. 264.

12 Manganiello, *Joyce's Politics* p. 74–5.

13 See Richard Brown, *James Joyce and Sexuality*, and Mary Lowe-Evans, *Crimes Against Fecundity: Joyce and Population Control* (Syracuse: Syracuse University Press, 1989). Jane Ford compares Joyce's treatment of 'the political chorus' in *Ulysses* to Conrad's representation of the anarchists in *The Secret Agent*, to which she believes Joyce's novel is directly indebted: she even suggests that Bloom, who buys pornography and contraceptives by mail order from a London address, may be a customer of Adolf Verloc. Conrad and Joyce share, she claims, their opposition to violence and deep political scepticism. However, Joyce's message, she claims, is that Bloom is 'a reversal of Verloc': here again, we note the special favour with which Joyce's lovable 'anti-hero' is treated. See Jane Ford, 'James Joyce and the Conrad Connection: The Anxiety of Influence', *Conradiana*, Vol. XVII, No. 1 (1985), p. 10.

14 See Tony Tanner, *Adultery in the Novel: Contract and Transgression* (Baltimore: Johns Hopkins University Press, 1979), p. 13–14. As Richard Brown argues, 'Joyce is most keen to present his central characters with a variety of shades of sexual taste as if to suggest that such varieties are intrinsic to human psychology' (Brown, *James Joyce and Sexuality*, p. 61).

15 Manganiello, *Joyce's Politics*, p. 4.

16 Matthew Hodgart, *James Joyce: A Student's Guide* (London: Routledge & Kegan Paul, 1974), p. 23.

17 Philip Herring, 'Joyce's Politics', *New Light on Joyce from the Dublin Symposium*, ed. Fritz Senn (Bloomington: University of Indiana Press, 1972), p. 6.

18 Karl Marx, 'The Eighteenth Brumaire of Louis Bonaparte', *Selected Writings*,ed. David McLellan (Oxford: Oxford University Press, 1977) p. 303.

19 J.C.C. Mays, 'Some comments on the Dublin of *Ulysses*', Ulysses: *Cinquante ans après*, ed. Louis Bonnerot *et al.* (Paris: Didier, 1974), p. 90.

20 Patrick McGee, *Paperspace: Style as Ideology in Joyce's* Ulysses (Lincoln: University of Nebraska Press, 1988), p. 117.

21 M.M. Bakhtin, *Rabelais and his World*, trans. Helene Iswolsky (Cambridge, Mass.: MIT Press, 1968), p. 317–18.

22 See Kristin Ross, *The Emergence of Social Space: Rimbaud and the Paris Commune* (Minneapolis: University of Minnesota Press, 1988); Wyndham Lewis, *Time and Western Man* (London: Chatto & Windus, 1927), p. 93.

23 Edgar Holt, *Protest in Arms: The Irish Troubles 1916–1923* (London: Putnam, 1960), p. 100–1.

24 Cheryl Herr, *Joyce's Anatomy of Culture* (Urbana: University of Illinois Press, 1986), p. 167.

25 Quoted by Herr, *Joyce's Anatomy of Culture*, p. 204.

26 Ibid., p. 166.

27 See Paulin, 'The British Presence in *Ulysses*', p. 99. Paulin suggests that 'Circe' is a parodic equivalent of Robert Emmet's failed rebellion, which is commonly referred to as a 'scuffle on a Dublin street'.

28 Jacques Derrida, 'Two words for Joyce', *Post-structuralist Joyce*, ed. D. Attridge and D. Ferrer (Cambridge: Cambridge University Press, 1984) p. 145–6.

29 Stephen Heath, 'Ambiviolences', *Post-Structuralist Joyce*, p. 57.

30 George Watson, 'The Politics of *Ulysses*', *Joyce's* Ulysses: *The Larger Perspective*, ed. R. D. Newman and W. Thornton (London: AUP, 1987), pp. 48, 53.

31 Lewis, *Time and Western Man*, p. 93.

32 W.B.Yeats, 'The Statues', *Collected Poems* (London, 1961), p. 375.

5 'POOR LITTLE BRITTLE MAGIC NATION': *FINNEGANS WAKE* AS A POST-COLONIAL NOVEL

1 *FW*, p. 565.

2 Timothy Brennan, *Salman Rushdie and the Third World* (London: Macmillan, 1989), pp. 4, 26.

3 Philippe Sollers, 'Joyce and Co.', *In the Wake of the Wake*, ed. David Hayman and Elliot Anderson (Madison: University of Wisconsin Press, 1978), pp. 109, 108.

4 William York Tindall, *A Reader's Guide to Finnegans Wake* (London: Thames & Hudson, 1969), p. 3.

5 Samuel Beckett, 'Dante . . . Bruno. Vico . . Joyce', *Our Exagmination Round His Factification for Incamination of Work in Progress* (Paris: Shakespeare & Company, 1929), p. 13.

6 J. Colm O'Sullivan, *Joyce's Use of Colors:* Finnegans Wake *and the Earlier Works* (Ann Arbor: University Research Press, 1987), pp. 76, 66.

7 Richard Ellmann, *The Consciousness of Joyce* (London: Faber & Faber, 1977), p. 89.

8 See John Garvin, *James Joyce's Disunited Kingdom and the Irish Dimension* (Dublin: Gill & Macmillan, 1976) and Dominic Manganiello, *Joyce's Politics* (London: Routledge & Kegan Paul, 1980) pp. 144–89. Hugh Kenner goes so far as to suggest that the corpse being waked in the text is that of a participant in the conflict. See H. Kenner, *A Colder Eye: The Modern Irish Writers* (London: Allen Lane, 1983), p. 290.

9 Garvin, *James Joyce's Disunited Kingdom*, p. 191.

10 Manganiello, *Joyce's Politics*, p. 177.

11 See Garvin, *James Joyce's Disunited Kingdom*, pp. 147–8.

12 Flann O'Brien, *The Poor Mouth: A Bad Story About the Hard Life* (London: Paladin, 1973), p. 77.

13 David Pierce, 'The politics of *Finnegans Wake*', *Textual Practice*, Vol. 2, No. 3 (1988), p. 369.

14 Roland McHugh argues convincingly that no proper names in particular can be coherently employed to denote the individual 'characters' of *Finnegans Wake*, which are 'fluid composites, involving a blur of historical, mythical and fictitious characters', and are best represented by the sigla forms which Joyce used in his notebooks: see R. McHugh, *The Sigla of* Finnegans Wake (London: Edward Arnold, 1976), p. 10. I adopt the conventional proper names here solely for reasons of technical convenience.

15 Harriet Shaw Weaver, quoted by Cyrus R.K. Patell, *Joyce's Use of History in Finnegans Wake*, The LeBaron Russell Briggs Prize Honors Essay in English 1983 (Cambridge, Mass.: Harvard University Press, 1984), p. 1.

16 Seamus Deane, 'Joyce the Irishman', *The Cambridge Companion to James Joyce*, ed. D. Attridge (Cambridge: Cambridge University Press, 1990), p 50.

17 Joseph Valente, 'The Politics of Joyce's Polyphony', *New Alliances in Joyce Studies*, ed. Bonnie Kime Scott (Newark: University of Delaware Press, 1988), p. 66.

18 J. Colm O'Sullivan, *Joyce's Use of Colors*, pp. 62, 76. 'Blarney'-words are generally much in evidence when discussing Joyce's treatment of history in the *Wake*: taking their cue from the ballad 'Finnegan's

Wake', critics seem particularly drawn to 'shenanigans' and 'shillelaghs'.

19 Kimberly Devlin, 'Self and Other in *Finnegans Wake*', *James Joyce Quarterly* , Vol. 21, No. 1 (1983), p. 34–5, p. 37.

20 Sollers, 'Joyce and Co.', p. 108.

21 Fredric Jameson, 'On Magic Realism in Film', *Critical Inquiry*, Vol. 12, No. 2 (1986), p. 311. See also Simon During, 'Postmodernism or Post-colonialism Today', *Textual Practice*, Vol. 1, No. 1 (1987), pp. 32–47.

22 Brennan, *Salman Rushdie and the Third World*, p. 113.

23 Ibid., pp. 141–2.

24 O'Sullivan, *Joyce's Use of Colors*, p. 76.

25 Colin MacCabe, '*Finnegans Wake* at Fifty', *Critical Quarterly*, Vol. 31, No. 4 (1989), p. 4.

26 MacCabe, '*Finnegans Wake* at Fifty', p. 4

27 Johann Gottlieb Fichte, *Addresses to the German Nation* (1808), trans. R.F. Jones and G.H. Turnbull (Chicago: Open Court Publishing, 1922), p. 55.

28 See Joyce, 'Ireland, Island of Saints and Sages', *CW*, p. 161.

29 Frank Budgen, *James Joyce and the Making of* Ulysses *and Other Writings* (Oxford: Oxford University Press, 1972), p. 175.

30 See Beryl Schlossman on the relationship between Irish illumination and Joyce's writing in *Joyce's Catholic Comedy of Language* (Madison: University of Wisconsin Press, 1985), pp. 183–92.

31 Margot Norris, *The Decentered Universe of* Finnegans Wake*: A Structuralist Analysis* (Baltimore: Johns Hopkins University Press, 1974), pp. 58–9.

32 Sigmund Freud, *The Interpretation of Dreams*, trans. James Strachey and ed. Angela Richards (Harmondsworth: Penguin, 1976), pp. 422, 429.

33 Dorothy Waler Singer, *Giordano Bruno: His Life and Thought with an Annotated Translation of his Work 'On the Infinite Universe and Worlds'* (New York: Henry Schuman, 1950), p. 84.

34 Valente, 'The Politics of Joyce's Polyphony', p. 67.

35 See Roland McHugh, *Annotations to Finnegans Wake* (London: Routledge & Kegan Paul, 1980), p. 15. All my remarks on specific passages of *Finnegans Wake* are indebted to the notes which McHugh supplies in this volume.

36 See Giambattista Vico, *The New Science*, third edn (1744), trans. and ed. Thomas Goddard Bergin and Max Harold Fisch (Ithaca, NY: Cornell University Press, 1968).

37 Northrop Frye, 'Cycle and Apocalypse in *Finnegans Wake*', in *Vico and Joyce*, ed. Donald Philip Verene (Albany: State University of New York Press, 1987), p. 18.

38 'Saor Stat' is the Irish translation of the term 'Free State'.

39 Marx writes in a footnote in *Capital*: 'Would not such a history [of human technology] be easier [than one of natural theology] to compile, since, as Vico says, human history differs from natural theology in this, that we have made the former, but not the latter?'. Quoted by Martin Jay, 'Vico and Marx', *Fin-de-Siècle Socialism and Other Essays* (London: Routledge, 1988), p. 67.

40 Beckett, 'Dante . . . Bruno. Vico . . Joyce', p. 19. *Finnegans Wake*'s unintelligibility leads one commentary to remark that in this sense, the book actually inverts *The New Science*. See H.S. Harris, 'What is Mr. Ear-Vivo Supposed to be 'Earing?', *Vico and Joyce*, ed. D.P. Verene (Albany: State University of New York Press, 1987), p. 70.

41 Beckett, 'Dante . . . Bruno . . . Vico . . . Joyce', pp. 6–7.

42 Edward Said, *Beginnings: Intention and Method* (Baltimore: Johns Hopkins University Press, 1978), p. 352.

43 Said, *Beginnings*, p. 380.

44 G. Vico, *The New Science*, p. 412.

45 Ibid., pp. 78, 149.

46 Fichte, *Addresses to the German Nation*, p. 55.

47 W.B. Yeats, 'Introduction to *Words upon the Window Pane*', *Explorations* (London: Macmillan, 1962), p. 354.

48 Joseph Campbell and Henry Morton Robinson, *A Skeleton Key to Finnegans Wake* (New York: Harcourt Brace Jovanovich, 1944), p. 217.

49 James Joyce quoted by Eugene Jolas, 'My friend James Joyce', *Partisan Review*, Vol. VII, No. II (1941), p. 93.

50 Maria Jolas, 'James Joyce as Revolutionary', *New Republic*, No. CVII (1942), p. 613. See also Diarmuid Maguire, 'The Politics of *Finnegans Wake*', *Joyce in Rome*, ed. G. Melchiori (Rome: Bulzoni, 1984), p. 127.

51 Campbell and Robinson, *A Skeleton Key to Finnegans Wake*, p. 191.

52 Devlin, 'Self and Other' p. 35.

53 Beckett, 'Dante . . . Bruno. Vico . . Joyce', p. 4.

54 Campbell and Robinson, *A Skeleton Key to Finnegans Wake*, p. 218.

55 Norris, *The Decentered Universe*, p. 44.

56 Campbell and Robinson, *A Skeleton Key to Finnegans Wake*, p. 349.

57 W.B. Yeats, unsurprisingly, favoured the anti-democratic reading of Vico which was popular in fascist Italy during the time Joyce was composing *Finnegans Wake*. As he writes, 'Students of contemporary Italy, where Vico's thought is current through its influence on Croce and Gentile, think it created or in part created the present government surrounded by such able assistants as Vico foresaw', *Explorations*, p. 354. Beckett specifically attacks Croce's interpretation of *The New Science* in 'Dante . . . Bruno. Vico . . Joyce'.

58 Brennan, *Salman Rushdie and the Third World* p. 113.

59 See J.M. Bernstein, *The Philosophy of the Novel: Lukács, Marxism and the Dialectics of Form* (Brighton: Harvester, 1984), Chapter VII.
60 Deane, 'Joyce and Nationalism', *The Cambridge Companion to James Joyce* p. 107.
61 O'Sullivan, *Joyce's Use of Colors*, p. 75.
62 See Homi K. Bhabha, 'Difference, Discrimination, and the Discourse of Colonialism', *The Politics of Theory*, ed. Francis Barker *et al.* (Colchester: University of Essex, 1983), p. 200.
63 Bhabha's formulation of a unitary 'colonial discourse' is also open to the charge of neglecting the material forces of domination in the colonial situation. As Abdul R. JanMohamed writes, 'I do not wish to rule out, a priori, the possibility that at some rarefied theoretical level the varied material and discursive antagonisms between conquerors and natives can be reduced to the workings of a single "subject"; but such a unity, let alone its value, must be demonstrated, not assumed', 'The Economy of Manichean Allegory: The Function of Racial Difference in Colonialist Literature', *'Race', Writing and Difference*, ed. Henry Louis Gates, Jr. (Chicago: University of Chicago Press, 1986), p. 78–9.
64 See Albert Memmi, *The Coloniser and the Colonised* (London: Souvenir Press, 1974).
65 Fredric Jameson, 'Third-World Literature in the Era of Multinational Capital', *Social Text* 15 (1986), p. 81.
66 Jameson, 'Third-World Literature', p. 79–80.
67 Jameson's assumption of an exclusively 'First-World' standpoint in this essay has been extensively criticized. See Brennan, *Salman Rushdie and the Third World* p. 37.
68 Jameson, 'Third-World Literature', p. 65.

6 JOYCE, WOMEN AND NATIONALISM

1 *'Ich bin der [sic] Fleisch der stets bejaht.'* This is Joyce's inversion of Goethe's description of Mephistopheles in *Faust*, 'I am the spirit that always denies'. See *SL*, p. 285.
2 Quoted by Richard Ellmann, *James Joyce*, revised edn (Oxford: Oxford University Press, 1982), p. 712.
3 Hugh Kenner, *Ulysses* (London: Allen & Unwin, 1982), p. 148.
4 Robert Boyle, 'Penelope', in *Ulysses: Critical Essays*, ed. Clive Hart and David Hayman (Berkeley: University of California Press, 1974), p. 407.
5 Quoted by Ellmann, *James Joyce*, p. 528.
6 Suzette Henke, *James Joyce and the Politics of Desire* (London: Routledge, 1990), p. 127.
7 Ibid. p. 127.

8 In *Gynesis: Configurations of Women and Modernity* (Ithaca: Cornell University Press, 1985), Alice Jardine gives the name 'gynesis' to this modern 'putting into discourse of "woman". . . the valorisation of the feminine, woman, and her obligatory, that is, historical connotations, as somehow intrinsic to new and necessary modes of thinking, writing, speaking' (p. 25), and discusses the implications of this for feminism. For similar arguments about Joyce, see, for example, Bonnie Kime Scott, *James Joyce* (Brighton: Harvester, 1987), p. 129. Most feminist Joyceans ultimately conclude that this question concerning authority and the 'feminine' is 'undecidable'; however, for a decisively sceptical account of the application of French feminist theory to Joyce, see Colleen R. Lamos, 'Cheating on the Father: Joyce and Gender Justice in *Ulysses*', *Joyce in Context*, ed. Vincent Cheng and Timothy Martin (Cambridge: Cambridge University Press, 1992), pp. 91–9.

9 Henke, *James Joyce and the Politics of Desire*, p. 205.

10 See, for example, Gayatri Spivak's caustic response to Kristeva on Joyce. Expressing dissatisfaction with 'the presupposition of the necessarily revolutionary potential of the avant-garde, literary or political', she remarks: 'There is something even faintly comical about Joyce rising above sexual identities and bequeathing the proper mind-set to the women's movement'. See 'French Feminism in an International Frame', *In Other Worlds: Essays in Cultural Politics* (London: Routledge, 1988), p. 144.

11 Margaret Ward, for example, emphasises that in the crucial early decades of this century, Irish feminists' rejection of the legitimacy of the British state significantly complicated and altered their agenda. See Ward's account of the careers of a number of women activists in early twentieth-century Ireland, many of whom were both feminists and nationalists, in *Unmanageable Revolutionaries: Women and Irish Nationalism* (London: Pluto Press, 1983). For a broader discussion of the insensitivity of 'mainstream' Western feminists to issues of colonialism, race and nationalism, see *Third World Women and the Politics of Feminism*, ed. Chandra Talpade Mohanty, Ann Russo and Lourdes Torres (Bloomington: Indiana University Press, 1991).

12 Patrick McGee, *Paperspace: Style as Ideology in Joyce's Ulysses* (Lincoln: University of Nebraska Press, 1988), p. 191.

13 Bonnie Kime Scott, *Joyce and Feminism* (Brighton: Harvester, 1984), p. 206.

14 Scott, *Joyce and Feminism*, p. 174.

15 Suzette Henke, 'Re-visioning Joyce's masculine signature', *Joyce in Context*, p. 139.

16 James Fairhall, *James Joyce and the Question of History* (Cambridge: Cambridge University Press, 1993), p. 117.

17 Julia Kristeva, 'Women's Time', *The Kristeva Reader*, ed. Toril Moi (Oxford: Blackwell, 1986), p. 205.

18 In this context, it is worth recalling that the image of the pre-Oedipal mother, which some feminist theorists invoke, is itself an infantile fantasy. As Drucilla Cornell reminds us: 'When Lacan speaks of "Woman" in her relation to language, *jouissance*, etc., he is using "Woman" to stand for the infantile experience of the mother, not for actual women (or women's experience of themselves). The all-powerful archaic mother is a product of the infant's fantasy, not a real person . . . . The identification of the "essence" of "Woman" with an idealized mother is a classical example of the privileging of the "masculine" view of woman over her own'. Drucilla Cornell, 'Feminism, Negativity, Subjectivity', *Feminism as Critique*, ed. Seyla Benhabib and Drucilla Cornell (Minneapolis: University of Minnesota Press, 1987), p. 147.

19 Colleen Lamos, 'Cheating on the Father: Joyce and Gender Justice in *Ulysses*', p. 92. Lamos is here summarizing, rather than agreeing with, the orthodox view.

20 Margaret Whitford, *Luce Irigaray: Philosophy in the Feminine* (London: Routledge, 1991), p. 94.

21 Suzette Henke, 'Re-visioning Joyce's masculine signature', p. 139.

22 Eavan Boland, 'A Kind of Scar: The Woman Poet in a National Tradition', LIP pamphlet (Dublin: Attic Press, 1989), p. 4.

23 See Florence L. Walz, '*Dubliners*: Women in Irish Society', *Women in Joyce*, ed. Suzette A. Henke and Elaine Unkeless (Brighton: Harvester, 1982), p. 36.

24 See Gayatri Spivak's critique of Western feminism's ethnocentrist concern with the production of 'female individualists' in 'Three Women's Texts and a Critique of Imperialism', *The Feminist Reader* , ed. Catherine Belsey and Jane Moore (London: Macmillan, 1989), where she claims that 'A basically isolationist admiration for the literature of the female subject in Europe and Anglo-America establishes the high feminist norm' (p. 176).

25 A number of critics have pointed out that Joyce significantly underplays the political radicalism of the Dubliners on which he models his fictional characters. See, for example, James Fairhall's portrait of Hanna Sheehy-Skeffington in *James Joyce and the Question of History* (Cambridge: Cambridge University Press, 1993), pp. 158–60.

26 See Seamus Deane's remarks on this parallelism in his 'Introduction', *A Portrait of the Artist as a Young Man*, ed. Seamus Deane (Harmondsworth: Penguin, 1992), pp. xxii-iii.

27 Quoted by Arthur Power, *Conversations with James Joyce* (London: Millington, 1974), p. 35; quoted by Ellmann, *James Joyce*, p. 529.

28 A number of commentators have drawn parallels between Joyce's representation of the Irish family and sociological investigations of its 'pathological', mother-centred structure, emphasizing in particular the excessively close bonds between mother and son. This, so the argument goes, produces effeminate, inadequate men who can never form a fully adult relationship with other women, thus forcing their own wives into inappropriate emotional relationships with their offspring, and perpetuating the cycle. (Similar conclusions have been drawn from studies of the 'matriarchal' African-American family in the United States.) See, for example, Florence Walz's essay, '*Dubliners*: Women in Irish Society', which draws on a famous study by Conrad Arensberg and Solon Kimball, *Family and Community in Ireland* (Cambridge, Mass.: Harvard University Press, 1968). While often illuminating, such investigations tend to emphasize emotional deprivation at the expense of the material factors which cause it, and are sometimes guilty of a marked ethnographic racism.

29 See Maud Ellmann, *The Hunger Artists: Starving, Writing, and Imprisonment* (Cambridge, Mass.: Harvard University Press, 1993), p. 43. On Freud's conception of 'femininity' as a kind of transferrable emotional disability, see Theresa Brennan, *The Interpretation of the Flesh: Freud and Femininity* (London: Routledge, 1992).

30 See Jacqueline Rose, *The Haunting of Sylvia Plath* (London: Virago, 1991), p. 33.

31 See Julia Kristeva, *The Powers of Horror: An Essay On Abjection*, trans. L.S. Roudiez (New York: Columbia University Press, 1982), p. 1.

32 See Frances Restuccia, *Joyce and the Law of the Father* (New Haven: Yale University Press, 1989).

33 Mark Schechner, *Joyce in Nighttown: A Psychoanalytical Inquiry into Ulysses* (Berkeley: University of California Press, 1974), p. 171.

34 M.M. Bakhtin, *Rabelais and His World*, trans. Helene Iswolsky (Cambridge Mass.: MIT Press, 1968) p. 322.

35 Hélène Cixous, 'The Laugh of the Medusa', *New French Feminisms*, ed. Elaine Marks and Isabelle de Courtivron (Brighton: Harvester, 1981), p. 259.

36 Richard Ellmann, *James Joyce*, pp. 712–13.

BIBLIOGRAPHY

WORKS BY JAMES JOYCE

Dubliners, the corrected text with an explanatory note by Robert Scholes (London: Jonathan Cape, 1967)

Exiles, with the author's notes and an Introduction by Padraic Colum (London: Jonathan Cape, 1952)

Finnegans Wake, third edn (London: Faber & Faber, 1964)

A Portrait of the Artist as a Young Man, the definitive text, corrected from the Dublin Holograph by Chester G. Anderson and ed. Richard Ellmann (London: Jonathan Cape, 1968)

Stephen Hero, ed. with an Introduction by Theodore Spencer, revised edn with additional material and Foreword by John J. Slocum and Herbert Cahoon (London: Jonathan Cape, 1956)

Ulysses, the corrected text, ed. Hans Walter Gabler, *et al.* (London: Bodley Head, 1986)

The Critical Writings of James Joyce, ed. Ellsworth Mason and Richard Ellmann (London: Faber & Faber, 1959)

Letters of James Joyce, Vols II and III, ed. Richard Ellmann (London: Faber & Faber, 1966)

Letters of James Joyce, ed. Stuart Gilbert (London: Faber & Faber, 1957)

Poems and Shorter Writings, including *Epiphanies, Giacomo Joyce* and 'A Portrait of the Artist', ed. Richard Ellmann, A. Walton Litz and John Whittier Ferguson (London: Faber & Faber, 1991)

Selected Letters of James Joyce, ed. Richard Ellmann (London: Faber & Faber, 1975)

WORKS BY OTHER AUTHORS

Adams, R.M., *Surface and Symbol: The Consistency of Joyce's* Ulysses (New York: Oxford University Press, 1962)

Ahmad, Aijaz, *In Theory: Classes, Nations, Literatures* (London: Verso, 1992)

Anderson, Benedict, *Imagined Communities: Reflections on the Origin and Spread of Nationalism* (London: Verso, 1983)

Anderson, Perry, 'Modernity and Revolution', *New Left Review* No. 144 (1984), pp. 96–113

Arensberg, Conrad and Kimball, Solon, *Family and Community in Ireland* (Cambridge, Mass.: Harvard University Press, 1968)

Arnold, Matthew, *On the Study of Celtic Literature* (1867) (London: Macmillan, 1893)

Attridge, Derek, *Peculiar Language: Literature as Difference from the Renaissance to James Joyce* (London: Methuen, 1988)

—— (ed). *The Cambridge Companion to James Joyce* (Cambridge: Cambridge: Cambridge University Press, 1990)

—— and Ferrer, Daniel (eds), *Post-Structuralist Joyce* (Cambridge: Cambridge University Press, 1984)

Bakhtin, M.M., *The Dialogic Imagination*, ed. Michael Holquist (Austin: University of Texas Press, 1981)

——, *Rabelais and His World*, trans. Helene Iswolsky (Cambridge, Mass.: MIT Press, 1968)

Beckett, Samuel, *et al.*, *Our Exagmination Round His Factification for Incamination of Work in Progress* (Paris: Shakespeare & Company, 1929)

Beja, M., *et al.* (ed.), *James Joyce: The Centennial Symposium* (Urbana: University of Illinois Press, 1986)

Benjamin, Walter, *Illuminations*, ed. Hannah Arendt (Glasgow: Fontana, 1973)

Benstock, Shari, 'The Dynamics of Narrative Performance: Stephen Dedalus as Storyteller', *English Literary History*, Vol. 49 (1982), pp. 707–38

Berman, Marshall, *All That is Solid Melts into Air: The Experience of Modernity* (London: Verso, 1983)

Bernstein, J.M., *The Philosophy of the Novel: Lukács, Marxism and the Dialectics of Form* (Brighton: Harvester, 1984)

Bhabha, Homi K. 'Difference, Discrimination, and the Discourse of Colonialism'. *The Politics of Theory*, ed. Francis Barker *et al.* (Colchester: University of Essex, 1983), pp. 194–211

——, 'DissemiNation: Time, Narrative, and the Margins of the Modern Nation', *Nation and Narration*, ed. by Homi K. Bhabha (London: Routledge, 1990), pp. 291–322

——, *Nation and Narration*, ed. Homi K. Bhabha (London: Routledge, 1990)

Bliss, Alan J., 'The Emergence of Modern English Dialects in Ireland', *The English Language in Ireland*, ed. by Diarmuid O'Muirithe (Dublin: Mercier Press, 1977), pp. 7–19

Boland, Eavan, 'A Kind of Scar: The Woman Poet in a National Tradition', LIP Pamphlet (Dublin: Attic Press, 1989)

Boyle, Robert, 'Penelope', *James Joyce's* Ulysses: *Critical Essays*, ed. Clive Hart and David Hayman (Berkeley: University of California Press, 1974), pp. 407–433

Brennan, Theresa, *The Interpretation of the Flesh: Freud and Femininity* (London: Routledge, 1992)

Brennan, Timothy, *Salman Rushdie and the Third World: Myths of the Nation* (London: Macmillan, 1989)

Brown, Malcolm, *The Politics of Irish Literature: From Thomas Davis to W.B. Yeats* (London: Allen & Unwin, 1972)

Brown, Richard, *James Joyce and Sexuality* (Cambridge: Cambridge University Press, 1985)

Brown, Terence, *Ireland: A Social and Cultural History 1922–79* (London: Fontana, 1981)

——, *Ireland's Literature* (Mullingar: Lilliput Press, 1988)

Budgen, Frank, *James Joyce and the Making of Ulysses and Other Writings* (Oxford: Oxford University Press, 1972)

Buttigieg, Joseph A., 'The Struggle against Meta(Phantasma)-physics: Nietzsche, Joyce and "the excess of history"', *Why Nietzsche Now?*, ed.Daniel O'Hara (Bloomington: University of Indiana Press, 1985), pp. 187–207

Cairns, David and Richards, Shaun, *Writing Ireland: Colonialism, Nationalism and*

Culture (Manchester: Manchester University Press, 1988)

Campbell, Joseph and Robinson, Henry Morton, *A Skeleton Key to Finnegans Wake* (New York: Harcourt Brace Jovanovich, 1944)

Cheng, Vincent J. and Martin, Timothy (eds), *Joyce in Context* (Cambridge: Cambridge Univeristy Press, 1992)

Cixous, Hélène, 'The Laugh of the Medusa', *New French Feminisms*, ed. Elaine Marks and Isabelle de Courtivron (Brighton: Harvester, 1981), pp. 245–64

—— and Clement, Catherine, *The Newly Born Woman*, trans. Betsy Wing (Minneapolis: University of Minnesota Press, 1985)

Clery, Arthur, *Dublin Essays* (Dublin: Maunsel, 1919)

Connolly, James, *Selected Writings*, ed. Peter Berresford Ellis (London: Pluto Press, 1980)

Corkery, Daniel, *Synge and Anglo-Irish Literature* (Cork: Cork University Press, 1931)

Cornell, Drucilla, 'Feminism, Negativity, Subjectivity'. *Feminism as Critique*, ed. Seyla Benhabib and Drucilla Cornell (Minneapolis: University of Minnesota Press, 1987), pp. 143–62

Craig, Cairns, *Yeats, Eliot and the Politics of Poetry* (London: Croom Helm, 1982)

Curtis, L.P. Jnr., *Anglo-Saxons and Celts: A Study of Anti-Irish Prejudice in Victorian England* (Connecticut: University of Bridgeport, 1968)

——, *Apes and Angels: The Irishman in Victorian Caricature* (Newton Abbot: David & Charles, 1971)

Davis, Richard, *Arthur Griffith and Non-violent Sinn Fein* (Dublin: Anvil Books, 1974)

Deane, Seamus, 'History as Fiction/Fiction as History'. *Joyce in Rome*, ed. Giorgio Melchiori (Rome: Bulzani, 1984), pp. 130–41

——, *Celtic Revivals: Essays in Modern Irish Literature* (London: Faber & Faber, 1985)

——, 'Heroic Styles: The Tradition of an Idea', *Ireland's Field Day* (London: Hutchinson, 1985), pp. 45–58

——, 'Civilians and Barbarians', *Ireland's Field Day* (London: Hutchinson, 1985), pp. 31–42

——, 'Joyce the Irishman', *The Cambridge Companion to James Joyce*, ed. Derek Attridge (Cambridge: Cambridge University Press, 1990), pp. 31–54

——, 'Wherever Green is Read', *Revising the Rising*, ed. Máirín Ní Dhonnchadha and Theo Dorgan (Derry: Field Day, 1991), pp. 91–105

—— (ed.) *The Field Day Anthology of Irish Writing*, Vol. III (Derry: Field Day, 1991)

—— (ed.) James Joyce, *A Portrait of the Artist as a Young Man* (Harmondsworth: Penguin, 1992)

Deming, Robert H. (ed.), *James Joyce: The Critical Heritage*, Vols 1 and 2 (London: Routledge & Kegan Paul, 1970)

Derrida, Jacques, 'Two words for Joyce', *Post-Structuralist Joyce*, ed. Derek Attridge and Daniel Ferrer (Cambridge: Cambridge University Press, 1984), pp. 145–60

Devlin, Kimberley, 'Self and Other in *Finnegans Wake*: A Framework for Analyzing Versions of Shem and Shaun', *James Joyce Quarterly*, Vol. 21, No. 2 (1983), pp. 31–50

Ní Dhonnchadha, Máirín and Dorgan, Theo (eds), *Revising the Rising* (Derry: Field Day, 1991)

Dick, Susan, *et al.* (ed.), *Omnium Gatherum: Essays for Richard Ellmann* (Gerrards Cross: Colin Smythe, 1989)

Docherty, Thomas, *Reading (Absent) Character* (Oxford: Clarendon Press, 1986)

During, Simon, 'Postmodernism or post-colonialism today', *Textual Practice*, Vol. 1, No. 1 (1987), pp. 32–47

——, 'Literature – Nationalism's Other? The Case for Revision', *Nation and Narration*, ed. Homi K. Bhabha (London: Routledge, 1990), pp. 138–53
Eagleton, Terry, 'The End of English', *Textual Practice*, Vol. 1, No. 1 (1987), pp. 1–9
——, 'Nationalism, Colonialism and Literature: Nationalism, Irony and Commitment', Field Day Pamplet, No. 13 (Derry: Field Day, 1988)
——, *The Ideology of the Aesthetic* (Oxford: Blackwell, 1990)
Eco, Umberto, *The Middle Ages of James Joyce* (London: Hutchinson Radius, 1989)
Eliot, T.S., '*Ulysses*, order and myth', *Dial*, No. LXXV (Nov. 1923)
——. *Selected Prose*, ed. Frank Kermode (London: Faber & Faber, 1975)
Ellmann, Maud, 'Disremembering Dedalus: *A Portrait of the Artist as a Young Man*', *Untying the Text: A Post-Structuralist Reader*, ed. Robert Young (London: Routledge & Kegan Paul, 1981), pp. 189–206
——, *The Hunger Artists: Starving, Writing, and Imprisonment* (Cambridge, Mass.: Harvard University Press, 1993)
Ellmann, Richard, *The Consciousness of Joyce* (London: Faber & Faber, 1977)
——, *James Joyce*, revised edn (Oxford: Oxford University Press, 1982)
Epstein, E.L., 'Nestor', *James Joyce's* Ulysses: *Critical Essays*, ed. Clive Hart and David Hayman (Berkeley: University of California Press, 1974), pp. 17–28
Fairhall, James, *James Joyce and the Question of History* (Cambridge: Cambridge University Press, 1993)
Fanning, Ronan, 'The Meaning of Revisionism', *Irish Review*, No. 4 (1988), pp. 15–19
Fanon, Franz, *The Wretched of the Earth* trans. Constance Farrington (Harmondsworth: Penguin, 1967)
Fichte, Johann Gottlieb, *Addresses to the German Nation* (1808), trans. R.F. Jones and G.H. Turnbull (Chicago: Open Court Publishing, 1922)
Field Day Theatre Company, *Ireland's Field Day* (London: Hutchinson, 1985)
Fitzgerald, Joan, 'The Citizen in *Ulysses*. A Note', *Joyce in Rome*, ed. Giorgio Melchiori (Rome: Bulzani, 1984), pp. 116–19
Ford, Jane, 'James Joyce and the Conrad Connection: The Anxiety of Influence', *Conradiana*, Vol. XVII, No.1 (1985), pp. 2–18
Foster, John Wilson, *Fictions of the Irish Literary Revival: A Changeling Art* (Syracuse: University of Syracuse Press, 1987)
Foster, R.F., '"We are all revisionists now"', *Irish Review*, No. 1 (1986), pp. 1–5
——, *Modern Ireland 1600–1972* (Harmondsworth: Allen Lane, 1988)
French, Marilyn, *The Book as World: James Joyce's Ulysses* (London: Abacus, 1982)
Freud, Sigmund, *The Interpretation of Dreams*, trans. and ed. James Strachey, Pelican Freud Library, Vol. 4 (ed. Angela Richards) (Harmondsworth: Penguin, 1976)
Frye, Northrop, 'Cycle and Apocalypse in *Finnegans Wake*', *Vico and Joyce*, ed. Donald Philip Verene (Albany: State University of New York Press, 1987), pp. 3–19
Garvin, John, *James Joyce's Disunited Kingdom and the Irish Dimension* (Dublin: Gill & Macmillan, 1976)
——, 'The Anglo-Irish Idiom in the Work of Major Irish Writers', *The English Language in Ireland*, ed. Diarmuid O'Muirithe (Dublin: Mercier Press, 1977), pp. 100–14
Gellner, Ernest, *Nations and Nationalism* (Oxford: Blackwell, 1983)
Gibbons, Luke, 'Challenging the Canon: Revisionism and Cultural Criticism', *The Field Day Anthology of Irish Writing*, ed. by Seamus Deane. Vol III (Derry: Field Day, 1991), pp. 561–8

Gifford, Don and Seidman, Robert J., *Notes for Joyce: An Annotation of James Joyce's* Ulysses (New York: Dutton, 1974)

——, Ulysses *Annotated: Notes for James Joyce's* Ulysses second edn, with Robert J. Seidman (London: University of California Press, 1988)

Gramsci, Antonio, *Selections from the Prison Notebooks* trans. Q. Hoare and G. Nowell Smith (London: Lawrence and Wishart, 1971)

Gregory, Augusta, *Cuchulain of Muirthemne* (Gerrards Cross: Colin Smythe, 1970)

—— (ed.), *Ideals in Ireland* (London: At the Unicorn VII Cecil Court, 1901)

Griffith, Arthur, Preface to John Mitchel, *Jail Journal* (Dublin: M.H. Gill, 1913), pp. ix–xvi

Harris, H.S., 'What is Mr. Ear-Vico Supposed to be 'Earing?', *Vico and Joyce*, ed. Donald Philip Verene (Albany: State University of New York Press, 1987), pp. 68–82

Hart, Clive and Hayman, David (eds), *James Joyce's Ulysses: Critical Essays* (Berkeley: University of California Press, 1974)

Harvey, David, *The Condition of Postmodernity* (Oxford: Blackwell, 1989)

Hayman, David, 'Cyclops'. *James Joyce's Ulysses: Critical Essays*, ed. Clive Hart and David Hayman (Berkeley: University of California Press, 1974), pp. 254–76

—— and Anderson, Elliott (eds), *In the Wake of the Wake* (Madison: University of Wisconsin Press, 1978)

Heath, Stephen, 'Ambiviolences', *Post-Structuralist Joyce*, ed. Derek Attridge and Daniel Ferrer (Cambridge: Cambridge University Press, 1984), pp. 31–68

Hederman, Mark Patrick, 'The Dead Revisited', *The Crane Bag Book of Irish Studies*, ed. Mark Patrick Hederman and Richard Kearney (Dublin: Woolfhound Press, 1982), pp. 178–86

Henke, Suzette A., *James Joyce and the Politics of Desire* (London: Routledge, 1990)

——, 'Re-visioning Joyce's Masculine Signature', *Joyce in Context*, ed. Vincent Cheng and Timothy Martin (Cambridge: Cambridge University Press, 1992), pp. 138–50

—— and Unkeless, Elaine (eds), *Women in Joyce* (Brighton: Harvester, 1982)

Herr, Cheryl, *Joyce's Anatomy of Culture* (Urbana: University of Illinois Press, 1986)

Herring, Philip, 'Joyce's Politics', *New Light on Joyce from the Dublin Symposium*, ed. Fritz Senn (Bloomington: University of Indiana Press, 1972), pp. 3–14

Hobsbawm, Eric J., *Nations and Nationalism Since 1780* (Cambridge: Cambridge University Press, 1990)

Hodgart, Matthew, *James Joyce: A Student's Guide* (London: Routledge & Kegan Paul, 1974)

Holt, Egar, *Protest in Arms: The Irish Troubles 1916–1923* (London: Putnam, 1960)

Horkheimer, Max and Adorno, Theodor W., *Dialectic of Enlightenment* trans. John Cumming (London: Allen Lane, 1973)

Hutchinson, John, *The Dynamics of Cultural Nationalism: The Gaelic Revival and the Creation of the Irish Nation State* (London: Allen & Unwin, 1987)

Jameson, Fredric, '*Ulysses* in History', *James Joyce and Modern Literature*, ed. W.J. MacCormack and Alistair Stead (London: Routledge & Kegan Paul, 1982), pp. 126–41

—— 'Postmodernism and Consumer Society', *The Anti-Aesthetic: Essays on Postmodern Culture*, ed. Hal Foster (Port Townsend: Bay Press, 1983), pp. 111–25

——, 'On Magic Realism in Film', *Critical Inquiry*, Vol. 12, No. 2 (1986), pp. 301–25

——, 'Third World Literature in the Era of Multinational Capital', *Social Text*, Vol. 15 (1986), pp. 65–88

JanMohamed, Abdul R., 'The Economy of Manichean Allegory: The Function of Racial Difference in Colonialist Literature', *'Race', Writing and Difference*, ed. Henry Louis Gates, Jr. (Chicago: University of Chicago Press, 1986), pp. 78–106

Jardine, Alice, *Gynesis: Configurations of Women and Modernity* (Ithaca: Cornell University Press, 1985)

Jay, Martin, 'The Jews and the Frankfurt School', *New German Critique*, No. 19 (1986), pp. 137–49

——, *Fin-de-Siècle Socialism and Other Essays* (London: Routledge, 1988)

Jolas, Eugene, 'My friend James Joyce', *Partisan Review*, Vol. VII, No. 11 (1941)

Jolas, Maria, 'James Joyce as Revolutionary', *New Republic*, No. CVII (1942)

Kearney, Richard, 'Myth and Motherland', *Ireland's Field Day* (London: Hutchinson, 1985), pp. 61–80

——, *Transitions: Narratives in Modern Irish Culture* (Manchester: Manchester University Press, 1988)

——, and Mark Patrick Hederman (eds), *The Crane Bag Book of Irish Studies* (Dublin: Woolfhound Press, 1982)

Kedourie, Elie, *Nationalism* (London: Hutchinson, 1961)

Kelleher, John V., 'Matthew Arnold and the Celtic Revival', *Perspectives in Criticism No. 20: Harvard Studies in Comparative Literature*, ed. Harry Levin (Cambridge, Mass.: Harvard University Press, 1950), pp. 197–221

——, 'Irish History and Mythology in James Joyce's "The Dead"', *Review of Politics* 27 (1976), pp. 414–33

Kenner, Hugh, *Dublin's Joyce* (London: Chatto & Windus, 1955)

——, *Joyce's Voices* (London: Faber & Faber, 1978)

——, *Ulysses* (London: Allen & Unwin, 1982)

——, *A Colder Eye: The Modern Irish Writers* (London: Allen Lane, 1983)

Kershner, R.B., 'Genius, Degeneration and the Panopticon', *A Portrait of the Artist as a Young Man*, ed. R.B. Kershner (Boston: Bedford Books, 1993)

Kiberd, Declan, 'Inventing Irelands', *The Crane Bag*, Vol. 8, No. 1 (1984), pp. 11–23

——, 'Anglo-Irish Attitudes', *Ireland's Field Day*, pp. 83–105

Kinsella, Thomas (trans.), *The Tain* (Portlaoise: Dolmen Press, 1972)

——, 'The Irish writer', *Davis, Mangan, Ferguson?: Tradition and the Irish Writer*, Thomas Kinsella and W.B. Yeats (Dublin: Dolmen Press, 1970)

Kristeva, Julia, *The Powers of Horror: An Essay On Abjection*, trans. L.S. Roudiez (New York: Columbia University Press, 1982)

——, 'Women's Time', *The Kristeva Reader*, ed. Toril Moi (Oxford: Blackwell, 1986)

Laffan, Michael, 'Insular Attitudes: The Revisionists and their Critics'. *Revising the Rising*, ed. Máirín Ní Dhonnchadha and Theo Dorgan (Derry: Field Day, 1991), pp. 106–21

Lamos, Colleen R., 'Cheating on the Father: Joyce and Gender Justice in *Ulysses*', *Joyce in Context*, ed. Vincent Cheng and Timothy Martin (Cambridge: Cambridge University Press, 1992), pp. 91–9

Lewis, Wyndham, *Time and Western Man* (London: Chatto & Windus, 1927)

Lloyd, David, *Nationalism and Minor Literature: James Clarence Mangan and the Emergence of Irish Cultural Nationalism* (Berkeley: University of California Press, 1988)

——, *Anomalous States: Irish Writing and the Post-Colonial Moment* (Dublin: Lilliput

Press, 1993)

Long, Michael, 'Eliot, Pound, Joyce: Unreal City?', *Unreal City: Urban Experience in Modern European Literature and Art*, ed. Edward Timms and David Kelley (Manchester: Manchester University Press, 1985), pp. 144–57

——, 'The Politics of English Modernism: Eliot, Pound and Joyce', *Visions and Blueprints: Avant-garde Culture and Radical Politics in Early Twentieth Century Culture*, ed. Edward Timms and Peter Collier (Manchester: Manchester University Press, 1988), pp. 98–112

Lowe-Evans, Mary, *Crimes Against Fecundity: Joyce and Population Control* (Syracuse: Syracuse University Press, 1989)

Lyons, F.S.L., 'James Joyce's Dublin', *Twentieth Century Studies* No. 4 (1970), pp. 6–35

——, *Ireland Since the Famine* (London: Fontana, 1971)

——, *Culture and Anarchy in Ireland 1890–1939* (Oxford: Oxford University Press, 1982)

Lyons, J.B., *The Enigma of Thomas Kettle* (Dublin: Glendale Press, 1983)

MacCabe, Colin, *James Joyce and the Revolution of the Word* (London: Macmillan, 1978)

——, 'The Voice of Esau: Stephen in the Library', *James Joyce: New Perspectives*, ed. Colin MacCabe (Brighton: Harvester, 1982), pp. 111–28

——, '*Finnegans Wake* at Fifty', *Critical Quarterly*, Vol. 31, No. 4 (1989), pp. 3–5

—— (ed.), *James Joyce: New Perspectives* (Brighton: Harvester, 1982)

MacDonagh, Oliver, *States of Mind: A Study of Anglo-Irish Conflict 1780–1980* (London: Allen & Unwin, 1983)

McHugh, Roland, *The Sigla of Finnegans Wake* (London: Edward Arnold, 1976)

——, *Annotations to Finnegans Wake* (London: Routledge & Kegan Paul, 1980)

McGee, Patrick, *Paperspace: Style as Ideology in Joyce's* Ulysses (Lincoln: University of Nebraska Press, 1988)

Maguire, Diarmuid, 'The Politics of *Finnegans Wake*', *Joyce in Rome*, ed. Giorgio Melchiori (Rome: Bulzoni, 1984), pp. 120–28

Manganiello, Dominic, *Joyce's Politics* (London: Routledge & Kegan Paul, 1980)

Marx, Karl, *Selected Writings*, ed. David McLellan (Oxford: Oxford University Press, 1977)

—— and Engels, Friedrich, *On Colonialism* (London: Lawrence and Wishart, 1968)

Mays, J.C.C., 'Some Comments on the Dublin of *Ulysses*', *Ulysses: Cinquante ans après*, ed. Louis Bonnerot, *et al.* (Paris: Didier, 1974), pp. 83–98

Melchiori, Giorgio (ed.), *Joyce in Rome* (Rome: Bulzoni, 1984)

Memmi, Albert, *The Coloniser and the Colonised* (London: Souvenir Press, 1974)

Mercier, Vivian, *The Irish Comic Tradition* (Oxford: Clarendon Press, 1962)

Mohanty, Chandra Talpade, Russo, Ann and Torres, Lourdes (ed.), *Third World Women and the Politics of Feminism* (Bloomington: Indiana University Press, 1991)

Moore, George, *Hail and Farewell*(1911), ed. Richard Cave (Gerrards Cross: Colin Smythe, 1976)

Moran, D.P., *The Philosophy of Irish Ireland* (Dublin: James Duffy & Co., 1905)

Moretti, Franco, *Signs Taken for Wonders*, revised edn (London: Verso, 1983)

Moshenberg, Daniel, 'The Capital Couple: Speculating on *Ulysses*', *James Joyce Quarterly*, Vol. 25, No.3, pp. 333–47

Norris, Margot, *The Decentered Universe of Finnegans Wake: A Structuralist Analysis* (Baltimore: Johns Hopkins Universtiy Press, 1974)

O'Brien, Conor Cruise, *Writers and Politics* (Harmondsworth: Penguin, 1965)

——, *States of Ireland* (London: Hutchinson, 1972)

——, '*The Irish Mind*: A Bad Case of Cultural Nationalism', *Passion and Cunning and*

Other Essays (London: Weidenfeld & Nicolson, 1988)

O'Brien, Flann, *The Poor Mouth: A Bad Story About the Hard Life* (London: Paladin, 1973)

O'Connor, Theresa, 'Demythologizing Nationalism: Joyce's Dialogized Grail Myth', *Joyce in Context*, ed. Vincent Cheng and Timothy Martin (Cambridge: Cambridge University Press, 1992), pp. 100–21

O'Connor, Ulick, *Celtic Dawn: A Portrait of the Irish Literary Renaissance* (London: Hamish Hamilton, 1984)

O'Donnell, William H., *A Guide to the Prose Fiction of W.B. Yeats* (Epping: Bowker, 1983)

O'Grada, Cormac, *Ireland Before and After the Famine* (Manchester: Manchester University Press, 1988)

O'Grady, Standish, *History of Ireland Volume I: The Heroic Period* (1878) (Dublin: E. Ponsonby, 1970)

——, *Early Bardic Literature: Ireland* (1879) (Dublin: E. Ponsonby, 1970)

——, 'The Great Enchantment'. *Ideals in Ireland*, ed. Augusta Gregory (London: At the Unicorn VII Cecil Court, 1901), pp. 77–83

O'Muirithe, Diarmuid (ed.), *The English Language in Ireland* (Dublin: Mercier Press, 1977)

O'Sullivan, J. Colm, *Joyce's Use of Colors: Finnegans Wake and the Earlier Works* (Ann Arbor: University Research Press, 1987)

Patell, Cyrus R.K., *Joyce's Use of History in Finnegans Wake* The LeBaron Russell Briggs Prize Essay in English 1983 (Cambridge, Mass.: Harvard University Press, 1984)

Paulin, Tom, *Ireland and the English Crisis* (Newcastle upon Tyne: Bloodaxe, 1984)

Peake, C.H., *James Joyce: The Citizen and the Artist* (Stanford: Stanford University Press, 1977)

Pearse, Patrick, *Collected Works of P.H. Pearse: Political Writings & Speeches* (Dublin: Maunsel & Roberts, 1922)

Pierce, David, 'The Politics of *Finnegans Wake*', *Textual Practice*. Vol. 2, No. 3 (1988), pp. 367–80

Pound, Ezra, *Pound/Joyce: The Letters of Ezra Pound to James Joyce, with Pound's Essays on Joyce*, ed. Forrest Read (London: Faber & Faber, 1967)

Power, Arthur, *Conversations with James Joyce* (London: Millington, 1974)

Radek, Karl, 'James Joyce or Socialist Realism?' *James Joyce: The Critical Heritage*, Vol. 2. ed. Robert H. Deming (London: Routledge & Kegan Paul, 1970), pp. 624–6

Renan, Ernest, *The Poetry of the Celtic Races and Other studies*, trans. W.G. Hutchinson (London: Walter Scott, 1897)

Restuccia, Frances, *James Joyce and the Law of the Father* (New Haven: Yale University Press, 1989)

Riquelme, John Paul, *Teller and Tale in Joyce's Fiction: Oscillating Perspectives* (Baltimore: Johns Hopkins University Press, 1983)

Rose, Jacqueline, *The Haunting of Sylvia Plath* (London: Virago, 1991)

Ross, Kristin, *The Emergence of Social Space: Rimbaud and the Paris Commune* (Minneapolis: University of Minnesota Press, 1988)

Rushdie, Salman, *Midnight's Children* (London: Cape, 1981)

——, *Shame* (London: Cape, 1983)

Russell, George ('AE'), 'Nationality and Imperialism'. *Ideals in Ireland*, ed. Augusta Gregory (London: At the Unicorn VII Cecil Court, 1901), pp. 15–24

Said, Edward, *Beginnings: Intention and Method* (Baltimore: Johns Hopkins University Press, 1978)

——, *Orientalism* (Harmondsworth: Penguin, 1985)
——, 'Nationalism, Colonialism and Literature: Yeats and Decolonisation', Field Day Pamplet, No. 15 (Derry: Field Day, 1988)
Singer, Dorothy Waley, *Giordano Bruno: His Life and Thought with an Annotated Translation of his Work 'On the Infinite Universe and Worlds'* (New York: Henry Schuman, 1950)
Schlossman, Beryl, *Joyce's Catholic Comedy of Language* (Madison: University of Wisconsin Press, 1985)
Scott, Bonnie Kime, *Joyce and Feminism* (Brighton: Harvester, 1984)
——, *James Joyce* (Brighton: Harvester, 1987)
—— (ed.), *New Alliances in Joyce Studies* (Newark: University of Delaware Press. 1988)
Schechner, Mark, *Joyce in Nighttown: A Psychoanalytical Inquiry into Ulysses* (Berkeley: University of California Press, 1974)
Segal, Jeffrey, 'Between Marxism and Modernism, or How to be a Revolutionist and Still Love *Ulysses*', *James Joyce Quarterly*, Vol. 25, No. 4 (1988), pp. 421–44
Sherry, Norman, *Conrad's Western World* (Cambridge: Cambridge University Press, 1971)
Shaw, Francis S.J., 'The Canon of Irish History: A Challenge'. *Studies*, Vol. LXI, No. 242 (1972), pp. 113–52
Sollers, Philippe, 'Joyce and Co.' *In the Wake of the Wake*, ed. David Hayman and Elliott Anderson (Madison: University of Wisconsin Press, 1978), pp. 107–21
Spivak, Gayatri, 'French Feminism in an International Frame', *In Other Worlds: Essays in Cultural Politics* (London: Routledge, 1988)
——, 'Three Women's Texts and a Critique of Imperialism'. *The Feminist Reader*, ed. Catherine Belsey and Jane Moore (London: Macmillan, 1989), pp. 175–95
Tanner, Tony, *Adultery in the Novel: Contract and Transgression* (Baltimore: Johns Hopkins University Press, 1979)
Tindall, William York, *A Reader's Guide to Finnegans Wake* (London: Thames & Hudson, 1969)
Trilling, Lionel, 'James Joyce in his Letters', *Joyce: A Collection of Critical Essays*, ed. William M. Chace (Englewood Cliffs, NJ: Prentice Hall, 1974), pp. 143–65
Valente, Joseph, 'The Politics of Joyce's Polyphony', *New Alliances in Joyce Studies*, ed. Bonnie Kime Scott (Newark: University of Delaware Press, 1988), pp. 56–69
Vance, Norman, *Irish Literature: A Social History* (Oxford: Blackwell, 1990)
Verene, Donald Philip (ed.), *Vico and Joyce* (Albany: State University of New York Press, 1987)
Vico, Giambattista, *The New Science* (third edn, 1744), trans. and ed. Thomas Goddard Bergin and Max Harold Fisch (Ithaca, NY: Cornell University Press, 1968)
Walz, Florence L., '*Dubliners*: Women in Irish Society', *Women in Joyce*, ed. Suzette Henke and Elaine Unkeless (Brighton: Harvester, 1982), pp. 31–65
Ward, Margaret, *Unmanageable Revolutionaries: Women and Irish Nationalism* (London: Pluto Press, 1983)
Watson, G.J., 'The Politics of *Ulysses*', *Joyce's* Ulysses: *The Larger Perspective*, ed. Robert D. Newman and Weldon Thornton (London: AUP, 1987), pp. 39–58
Wells, H.G., review of *A Portrait of the Artist as a Young Man*. *James Joyce: The Critical Heritage*, Vol 1, ed. Robert H. Deming (London: Routledge & Kegan Paul, 1970), pp. 86–8
Whitford, Margaret, *Luce Irigaray: Philosophy in the Feminine* (London: Routledge, 1991)

Williams, Raymond, *The Country and the City* (London: Hogarth Press, 1973)
——, *Writing in Society* (London: Verso, 1983)
——, *Culture and Society 1780–1950* (Harmondsworth: Penguin, 1985)
Williams, Trevor L. 'Dominant Ideologies: The Production of Stephen Dedalus', *James Joyce: The Augmented Ninth*, ed. Bernard Benstock (Syracuse: University of Syracuse Press, 1988), pp. 312–22
Yeats, William Butler, *Autobiographies* (London: Macmillan, 1955)
——, *Collected Poems* (London: Macmillan, 1961)
——, *Essays and Introductions* (London: Macmillan, 1961)
——, *Explorations* (London: Macmillan, 1962)
——, *Uncollected Prose*, ed. John P. Frayne (London: Macmillan, 1970)
——, 'The Stories of Red Hanrahan' (1897), *Mythologies* (London: Macmillan, 1989)
—— and Kinsella, Thomas, *Davis, Mangan, Ferguson?: Tradition and the Irish Writer* (Dublin: Dolmen Press, 1970)

INDEX

Note The following abbreviations are used in the index: *D* for *Dubliners; FW* for *Finnegan's Wake*; JJ for *James Joyce; P* for *A Portrait of the Artist as a Young Man; U* for *Ulysses.*